The Poetry of Walt Whitman

The Poetry of

Walt Whitman

EDITED BY NICK SELBY

First published 2004 by
PALGRAVE MACMILLAN
Houndmills, Basingstoke, Hampshire RG21 6XS and
175 Fifth Avenue, New York, N.Y. 10010
Companies and representatives throughout the world

PALGRAVE MACMILLAN is the global academic imprint of the Palgrave
Macmillan division of St. Martin's Press, LLC and of Palgrave Macmillan Ltd.
Macmillan® is a registered trademark in the United States, United Kingdom
and other countries. Palgrave is a registered trademark in the European
Union and other countries.

ISBN 1–4039–3316–2 hardback
ISBN 1–8404–6240–X paperback

This book is printed on paper suitable for recycling and made from fully
managed and sustained forest sources.

A catalogue record for this book is available from the British Library.

A catalog record is available from the Library of Congress

Printed in China

To Maggie,

'For every atom belonging to me as good belongs to you'

Jacob, Reuben

'A child said What is the grass? fetching it to me with full hands;
How could I answer the child? I do not know what it is any more than he.'

and Miranda and Charlie

'I think I could turn and live with animals, they are so placid and self-contain'd
I stand and look at them long and long ...
They bring me tokens of myself, they evince them plainly in their possession.'

CONTENTS

Acknowledgements   xi

Introduction   1

Discusses the ways in which Walt Whitman's poetry can be seen to engage in a debate about American culture and ideology. Extracts from Emerson's essay 'The Poet' (1844) and from Whitman's 'Preface' to the first (1855) edition of Leaves of Grass are included, and demonstrate that Whitman's poetry explicitly answered Emerson's call for a truly new American poet, a bard of democracy. It is suggested that the rich history of critical debate about Whitman's work speaks of his desire to 'contain multitudes' and to remain one step ahead of his readers.

CHAPTER ONE   8

Early Reviews

Surveys the initial critical reaction to Whitman's poetry. Emerson's famous letter praising the first edition of Leaves of Grass is included alongside extracts from Whitman's own – though unsigned – review of Leaves of Grass in order to examine Whitman's role as self-publicist. These are followed by a survey of good, bad and indifferent reviews of Whitman. Charles A. Dana's review written for the New York Daily Tribune sets a tone of bemused ambivalence towards Whitman's poetry that also expresses ambivalent attitudes towards America itself. This is also seen in the reviews by Charles Eliot Norton for Putnam's Monthly, in the snobbishly English attitude of the London journal The Critic, and in the scandalised tone of the anonymous reviewer for the Criterion. The final three extracts, however, are much more sympathetic towards Whitman's efforts. These are by Edward Everett Hale, Henry David Thoreau and John Robertson. All three see freshness and vitality as being at the heart of Whitman's new poetic vision of America and democracy. Robertson's was the first book-length discussion of Whitman and as such can be seen to herald many of the subsequent critical attitudes towards Whitman and his poetry.

CHAPTER TWO   28

Whitman in the Early Twentieth Century

The first two extracts in this chapter – by John Addington Symonds and
George Santayana – were written in the years immediately following
Whitman's death. Though opposed in their actual estimations of the
worth of Whitman's poetry they do both struggle to come to terms with
their own sense of bafflement with Whitman. Symonds' essay (1893) on
Leaves of Grass sees it as a poetic puzzle that raises difficult questions
about selfhood and identity. Santayana's essay 'The Poetry of Barbarism'
(1900), though, describes Whitman's poetics as barbaric, the uncouth
expression of American populism. The other two extracts of the chapter
see Whitman's accommodation to modernism. A brief extract from Ezra
Pound's 'What I feel about Walt Whitman' (1909) is followed by a long
extract from D. H. Lawrence's influential book *Studies in Classic American
Literature* (1923).

CHAPTER THREE   55

Whitman and the 'American Renaissance'

Examines Whitman's central place in what F. O. Matthiessen describes
as an 'American Renaissance' that took place in antebellum America.
The first long extract is taken from Matthiessen's *American Renaissance*
(1941), and examines Whitman's energetic and novel language-use. This
is followed by an extract from Charles Feidelson's *Symbolism and
American Literature* (1953) that attempts to align Whitman's poetry with
New Critical models of reading. The third extract is from Randall Jarrell's
spirited and witty reading of Whitman, 'Some Lines from Whitman'
(1955). Jarrell's essay displays his fine ear for Whitman's poetic com-
plexities and delicacies, and is a model of the sort of patient and appre-
ciative critical reading practice demanded by Whitman but often lost in
critical bluster and exclamation.

CHAPTER FOUR   75

Whitman, Myth Criticism and the Growth of
American Studies

The two extracts that comprise this chapter are crucial documents in the
development of American Studies. This chapter examines the myths
of America that have been employed in order to explain Whitman's place
as the poet of America. The first extract is from R. W. B. Lewis' *The
American Adam* (1955), a book which set the terms for 'Americanist'

criticism, and which placed Whitman as central in a literary tradition in which America is mythicised as a new Eden. The second extract is from Roy Harvey Pearce's highly influential *The Continuity of American Poetry* (1961), a book that, along with Lewis', finally sees Whitman established as the central and defining American poet.

CHAPTER FIVE 93

Whitman, Cultural Materialism and 'Reconstructive' Readings

Deals with the influence of 'cultural materialism' on Whitman criticism. The three extracts in this chapter place Whitman's poetry in the context of the mid-nineteenth-century American culture of which it is a product. These critical extracts all examine *Leaves of Grass* in relation to specific aspects of antebellum American culture. The extract from M. Wynn Thomas' *The Lunar Light of Whitman's Poetry* (1987) examines the impact of the post-artisanal phase of capitalism on Whitman's poetry, and the extract from Ed Folsom's *Whitman's Native Representations* (1994) discusses Whitman in relation to baseball. In the final essay, David S. Reynolds' 'Whitman and Nineteenth-Century views of Gender and Sexuality', Whitman's poetry is examined in relationship to contemporary views of gender and sexuality.

CHAPTER SIX 116

Ideology and Desire: Whitman and Sexuality

This chapter suggests that there is a long history of critical discussion of sex, the body, sexuality and desire in relation to Whitman's poetry. The three extracts in this chapter all examine claims about Whitman's sexuality and its importance and application to the reading of his poetry. Malcolm Cowley's essay 'Whitman: The Poet and the Mask' (1948) was one of the first critical examinations of Whitman's poetry to claim that it stemmed from (repressed) homosexuality. The second extract is taken from Robert K. Martin's watershed book *The Homosexual Tradition in American Poetry* (originally published in 1979), and which sees Whitman as central to an 'underground', homosexual tradition in American poetry. Nick Selby's essay ' "Queer Shoulders to the wheel": Whitman, Ginsberg and a Bisexual Poetics' (1997) argues against such narrowly deterministic readings of Whitman and sexuality as that advanced by Martin, and offers a model of 'bisexual' poetics for reading Whitman as a product of nineteenth-century discourses of capital.

CHAPTER SEVEN   137

Ideology and Deconstruction: Whitman and
'New Americanist' Critiques

Presents some 'deconstructive' perspectives on *Leaves of Grass*. The three extracts in this chapter show the complicity of Whitman's poetry in an American ideological agenda. The extract from Karen Sanchez-Eppler's *Touching Liberty: Abolition, Feminism and the Politics of the Body* (1993) argues for a Whitman who is radically ruptured in his poetic attempts to render a democratic polity. His poetics of the body uneasily exposes, she argues, an agenda of white cultural superiority. Allen Grossman's essay (1985) measures Whitman's rhetoric against that of Abraham Lincoln and finds both to be scenes of political persuasion despite their claims for democratic freedom. And in the final extract of this critical guide, Jonathan Arac (1996) argues for a more 'internationalist' reading of Pound. Rather than reading him into narrowly formulated assumptions about America and its culture, he argues instead that Whitman's very poetic language itself is 'creolized' and that our critical endeavours with him should be to read him out of America and into a broader, trans-national, history of modernity.

NOTES   159

BIBLIOGRAPHY   168

INDEX   173

ACKNOWLEDGEMENTS

The editor and publishers wish to thank the following for permission to use copyright material:

Jonathan Arac, for material from 'Whitman and the Problems of the Vernacular' from *Breaking Bounds: Whitman and American Cultural Studies*, eds. Betsy Erkkila and Jay Grossman, pp. 44–58. Copyright © 1996 by Betsy Erkkila and Jay Grossman, by permission of Oxford University Press, Inc.

Malcolm Cowley, for material from 'Whitman: The Poet and the Mask' from *Complete Poetry and Prose of Walt Whitman*, ed. Malcolm Cowley. Copyright © 1948, renewed 1975 by Malcolm Cowley, by permission of Hill and Wang, a division of Farrar, Straus and Giroux, LLC.

Charles Feidelson, for material from *Symbolism and American Literature* by Charles Feidelson (1953), pp. 16–27, by permission of The University of Chicago Press.

Ed Folsom, for material from *Walt Whitman's Native Representations* by Ed Folsom (1994), pp. 28–54, by permission of Cambridge University Press.

Allen Grossman, for material from 'The Poetics of Union in Whitman and Lincoln: An Inquiry Toward the Relationship of Art and Policy' in *The American Renaissance Reconsidered*, eds. Walter Benn Michaels and Donald E. Pease (1984), pp. 184–98, by permission of The Johns Hopkins University Press.

Randall Jarrell, for material from *Poetry and the Age* by Randall Jarrell (1955), pp. 106–23, by permission of Faber and Faber.

R. W. B. Lewis, for material from *The American Adam: Tragedy and Tradition in the Nineteenth Century* by R. W. B. Lewis (1955), pp. 28–53, by permission of The University of Chicago Press.

Robert K. Martin, for *The Homosexual Tradition in American Poetry: An Expanded Edition* by Robert K. Martin (1998), pp. 51–89, by permission of the University of Iowa Press.

F. O. Matthiessen, for material from *American Renaissance: Art and Expression in the Age of Emerson and Whitman* by F. O. Mattheissen (1941), pp. 517–613. Copyright © 1941 by Oxford University Press, Inc, by permission of Oxford University Press, Inc.

Roy Harvey Pearce, for material from *The Continuity of American Poetry* by Roy Harvey Pearce, Princeton University Press (1961), pp. 164–74 [reissued by Wesleyan University Press (1987)], by permission of Wesleyan University Press.

Ezra Pound, for material from 'What I Feel About Walt Whitman' included in *Selected Prose 1909–1965* by Ezra Pound (1973), pp. 115–16 Copyright © 1973 by the Estate of Ezra Pound, by permission of Faber and Faber and New Directions Publishing Corp.

David Reynolds, for material from 'Whitman and Nineteenth-Century Views of Gender and Sexuality' from *Walt Whitman of Mickle Street, A Centennial Collection*, ed. Geoffrey M. Sill (1994), pp. 38–45, by permission of Geoffrey M. Sill.

Karen Sanchez-Eppler, for material from *Touching Liberty: Abolition, Feminism, and the Politics of the Body* by Karen Sanchez-Eppler (1993), pp. 50–82. Copyright © 1993 The Regents of the University of California, by permission of the University of California Press.

Nick Selby, for material from "Queer Shoulders at the Wheel": Whitman, Ginsberg and a Bi-sexual Poetics' from *The Bisexual Imaginary: Representation, Identity and Desire*, by Nick Selby, Cassell (1997), pp. 120–40, by permission of Continuum International Publishing Group Ltd.

M. Wynn Thomas, for material from *The Lunar Light of Whitman's Poetry* by M. Wynn Thomas (1987), pp. 2, 40–2, 51–3, 56–7, 66–9, 70–1. Copyright © 1987 by the President and Fellows of Harvard College, by permission of Harvard University Press.

Every effort has been made to trace the copyright holders but if any have been inadvertently overlooked the publishers will be pleased to make the necessary arrangement at the first opportunity.

Introduction

L ike America, Walt Whitman and his critical reputation is vast and seemingly everexpanding. This sort of statement, which makes a direct connection between Whitman himself and the country that produced him, has frequently been made by his readers and critics. Indeed, to open this guide to critical readings of Whitman with such a statement might seem to assert that the *only* way of reading *Leaves of Grass* is to see it as an expression of exclusively American concerns. And this may well also be the impression gained from the majority of essays in this book. However, it is also important to ask – as indeed recent Whitman critics have done – which particular concerns does Whitman's poetry express? What version of America does it promote? By tracing the critical history of Whitman's poetry from the mid-nineteenth century up to the present day, the overall aim of this guide is to show that there are perhaps as many versions of America as there are versions of Whitman. Whitman studies then, do indeed 'contain multitudes'.

Because Whitman's typically expansive poetic gesture has so often been read as an index of America's struggles in the middle years of the nineteenth century to articulate, develop and maintain a culture for itself it is sometimes difficult to stand back from his reputation and image in order to properly assess the sheer impact of his poetry. It is always instructive, however, to try to read Whitman's poetry without bringing to that reading the weight of scholarship, critical opinion and general gossip that has accumulated around the figure of Walt Whitman – the bard of democracy, America's representative Everyman, the first truly American writer, the 'good grey poet'. How fresh and challenging, deliciously subversive and magnificently self-confident these lines must have sounded to Whitman's first readers in 1855:

■ Do I contradict myself?
Very well the n ....
I contradict myself;
I am large ... I contain multitudes.[1] □

But, as we shall be continually reminded throughout this critical guide, the act of reading Whitman's poetry can never be innocent of either the cultural circumstances in which it was written, or those in which it is read. If – like America – Whitman is large and contains multitudes, then his role as America's representative poet is constructed from a bewildering set of readings and rereadings, assertions and counter-assertions.

1

One measure, then, of the power of Whitman's poetry might be seen in its ability to survive as a poetry of rare freshness and vividness, of delicacy and wonder, despite (rather than because of) the plethora of critical interpretations of it. In fact, even before it was published, *Leaves of Grass* was not, so to speak, innocent of the cultural and critical circumstances from which it arose and into which it was plunged.

When the first edition of *Leaves of Grass* was published in July 1855 it did seem to answer America's call for a literature of its own, a call that had been made repeatedly since (at least) the Declaration of Independence in 1776, and had most forcefully been voiced in the 1830s and 1840s by writers such as Herman Melville and Nathaniel Hawthorne and by Transcendental thinkers such as Henry David Thoreau and, most especially, Ralph Waldo Emerson. In his essay of 1844, 'The Poet', Emerson had issued the call for a new poetry that would be commensurate with the new American nation. Making explicit the connection between America and its poetry, between political and literary nationalities, Emerson saw poetry as the means of defining and producing America as a mythical and epic landscape. Through its poetry, Emerson argued, America would truly declare cultural independence. According to Emerson, the urgent task for America, then, is that of finding a poet fit for the United States:

■ I look in vain for the poet whom I describe. We do not, with sufficient plainness, or sufficient profoundness, address ourselves to life, nor dare we chant our own times and social circumstance. If we filled the day with bravery we should not sink from celebrating it. Time and nature yield us many gifts, but not yet the timely man, the new religion, the reconciler, whom all things await. Dante's praise is, that he dared to write his autobiography in colossal cipher, or into universality. We have yet had no genius in America, with tyrannous eye, which knew the value of our incomparable materials, and saw, in the barbarism and materialism of the times, another carnival of the same gods whose picture it so much admires in Homer; then in the middle age; then in Calvinism. Banks and tariffs, the newspaper and caucus, methodism and unitarianism, are flat and dull to dull people, but rest on the same foundations of wonder as the town of Troy and the temple of Delphi and are as swiftly passing away. Our logrolling, our stumps and their politics, our fisheries, our Negroes, and Indians, our boats, and our repudiations, the wrath of rogues, and the pusillanimity of honest men, the northern trade, the southern planting, the western clearing, Oregon and Texas are yet unsung. Yet America is a poem in our eyes; its ample geography dazzles the imagination, and it will not wait long for metres.[2] □

Whitman took it upon himself to fulfil the role of American poet that Emerson here describes. Born on Long Island on 31 May 1819, the young Whitman had worked at various jobs in New York in the 1830s and 1840s – office boy, printer, teacher, carpenter – but gradually, through his work as a newspaper editor in Brooklyn, became involved in New York's literary and bohemian set. Sometime in the 1850s, it seems, Whitman first became acquainted – whether directly or at second-hand – with Emerson's Transcendental philosophy.[3] This intellectual encounter provided Whitman with the spur that turned him from newspaper hack, and sometime author of sensationalist tracts (his only 'novel', *Franklin Evans*, a moralistic temperance tale, was published in 1842), into poet. In 1860 Whitman apparently told John Townsend Trowbridge that 'I was simmering, simmering, simmering; Emerson brought me to a boil', thus attributing the sudden burst of creative energy that resulted in the publication of *Leaves of Grass* in the summer of 1855 to his reaction to Emerson.[4] So, if Emerson in the passage earlier predicts the imminent arrival of the first truly American poet, he can also be seen to have been directly responsible for producing that poet.

And it was Whitman himself, in the 'Preface' to that first edition of *Leaves of Grass* who provided a very Emersonian rationale for the curious poetic medley that was to follow. Taking up especially Emerson's sense of the inevitable coincidence of America's poetic and actual geographies, Whitman's 'Preface' presents – like the poetry to come in the subsequent pages – a sweeping overview of America. The vast continent *is* the justification for America's devotion to democracy and to the common working people. It is also, according to Whitman (and echoing Emerson) the foundation for its poetry, the *ground* (literally and figuratively) of an American poetics:

■ The Americans of all nations at any time upon the earth have probably the fullest poetical nature. The United States themselves are essentially the greatest poem. In the history of the earth hitherto the largest and most stirring appear tame and orderly to their ampler largeness and stir. Here at last is something in the doings of man that corresponds with the broadcast doings of the day and night. Here is not merely a nation but a teeming nation of nations. Here is action untied from strings necessarily blind to particulars and details magnificently moving in vast masses. Here is the hospitality which forever indicates heroes .... Here are the roughs and beards and space and ruggedness and nonchalance that the soul loves. Here the performance disdaining the trivial unapproached in the tremendous audacity of its crowds and groupings and the push of its perspective spreads with crampless and flowing breadth and showers its prolific and splendid extravagance. One sees it must indeed own the riches of the summer and winter, and need never be bankrupt while corn grows from the ground or the orchards drop apples or the bays contain fish or men beget children upon women.

Other states indicate themselves in their deputies .... but the genius of the United States is not best or most in its executives or legislatures, nor in its ambassadors or authors or colleges or churches or parlors, nor even in its newspapers or inventors ... but always most in the common people. Their manners speech dress friendships – the freshness and candor of their physiognomy – the picturesque looseness of their carriage ... their deathless attachment to freedom – their aversion to anything indecorous or soft or mean – the practical acknowledgement of the citizens of one state by the citizens of all other states – the fierceness of their roused resentment – their curiosity and welcome of novelty – their self-esteem and wonderful sympathy – their susceptibility to a slight – the air they have of persons who never know how it felt to stand in the presence of superiors – the fluency of their speech – their delight in music, the sure symptom of manly tenderness and native elegance of soul ... their good temper and openhandedness – the terrible significance of their elections – the President's taking off his hat to them not they to him – these too are unrhymed poetry. ...

The American poets are to enclose old and new for America is the race of races. Of them a bard is to be commensurate with a people. To him the other continents arrive as contributions ... he gives them reception for their sake and his own sake. His spirit responds to his country's spirit. ... he incarnates its geography and natural life and rivers and lakes. Mississippi with annual freshets and changing chutes, Missouri and Columbia and Ohio and Saint Lawrence with the falls and beautiful masculine Hudson, do not embouchure where they spend themselves more than they embouchure into him. The blue breadth over the inland sea of Virginia and Maryland and the sea off Massachusetts and Maine and over Manhattan bay and over Champlain and Erie and over Ontario and Huron and Michigan and Superior, and over the Texan and Mexican and Floridian and Cuban seas and over the seas off California and Oregon, is not tallied by the blue breadth of the waters below more than the breadth of above and below is tallied by him. When the long Atlantic coast stretches longer and the Pacific coast stretches longer he easily stretches with them north or south. He spans between them also from east to west and reflects what is between them. □   (Walt Whitman, 'Preface', 1855)[5]

In this 'Preface', then, Whitman sets out the terms by which he felt his poetry should be read. His is explicitly a poetics of democracy and union, of self and identity, of the relationship between one's political and one's imaginative environments. And whilst all these have been seen as profoundly American themes, setting in train a host of studies of Whitman tracing aspects of his 'Americanness', they should also be seen as the raw materials from which Whitman attempted to forge a poetry of human consciousness. 'An individual', Whitman notes at the end of this 'Preface', 'is as superb as a nation when he has the qualities which make a superb nation ... The proof of a poet is that his country absorbs him as affectionately as he has absorbed it.'[6]

As we will see in this guide, the critical history of *Leaves of Grass* has witnessed a continual process by which Whitman's poetry has both absorbed and been absorbed by the ways in which it has been read. Indeed, what is made very apparent by the critical history of Whitman's poetry is that it has always been read for a particular purpose, whether overt or covert, or whether for specific cultural, ideological or aesthetic reasons. The aim of this Readers' Guide is twofold. Not only does it draw together some of the most significant, important and interesting critical analyses of Whitman, but, by doing this, it also seeks to demonstrate how Whitman has always been read with a purpose. All the critical pieces in this guide show how reading Whitman makes apparent the turbulent pressure upon national and individual identity from which America was constructing itself in the second half of the nineteenth century.

Starting this Readers' Guide by playing-off extracts from reviews of the first edition of *Leaves of Grass* (1855) against essays by Emerson and Whitman himself, Chapter 1 aims to give a flavour of the scandal and notoriety that Whitman's poetry attracted. The early reviews that are gathered together in this opening chapter demonstrate the sorts of literary expectations that, on both sides of the Atlantic, Whitman was transgressing, whilst they also set the tone and terms for subsequent analyses of his work. In Chapter 2, Whitman's gradual critical elevation in the early years of the twentieth century, from America's poetic savage into its spokesman, its 'good gray poet', is dealt with. Though ambivalent about Whitman's literary worth, both D. H. Lawrence and Ezra Pound find they cannot deny his cultural power. He is, for such modernist writers, a poet whose work strongly prefigures their own troubled negotiations with modernity. Continuing chronologically into the middle years of the twentieth century, Chapters 3 and 4 assess the crucial role played by Whitman's poetry, and critical evaluations of it, in establishing and developing the very idea of what American literature might be. These chapters examine Whitman's place in the growth of 'American Studies' in the 1940s and 1950s, and the critical extracts in these chapters are from 'classic' examinations of American literature, ones which place Whitman's work at the heart of a mythic American literary consciousness.

The final three chapters break slightly with the chronological progression of the rest of the Guide in order to discuss Whitman more thematically and in the light of (generally) recent cultural materialist, and more theoretically positioned readings of Whitman. These chapters offer some revisionary interventions into Whitman's position as American's poet par excellence through the various attention they give to his relationship to some of the shaping discourses of his time such as slavery, democratic individualism, political reform, emerging capitalism, sexuality and even baseball. From these chapters it is clear that Whitman's poetry still arouses considerable critical controversy and debate, and in ways perhaps unimaginable when it was first published. Indeed what these evaluations point to – in fact, what this Guide as a whole makes clear – is that such a massive, sprawling and apparently provisional poetic project as *Leaves of Grass* is impossible, critically, to pin down to any final and definitive reading. What this Readers' Guide offers, then, is an overview of the ways in which some of Whitman's best critics have attempted to deal with his poetry and its cultural legacy.

Finally, though, what is most apparent from the selection of critical highlights that comprise this book, is that Whitman's enthusiasms and differentiations, the power of his poetry *as* poetry, escapes the simplifications of critical and national discourses through which it has been categorised and assessed. If critical responses to Whitman founder on the frustration of their own partial reading of the poetry, as suggested by Roy Harvey Pearce's exasperated comment that 'the complete critic [of Whitman] is impossible, since the life and work teach us that nothing is inclusive and definitive – above all, a conception of man', then Whitman and his poetry seem most powerful at those moments when they slip away from the efforts of critics and readers to evaluate them. In one of the last poems he wrote, Whitman sees himself emerging from the pages of his book and into the physical embrace of his readers. But at this moment he also deftly, humorously and defiantly bids farewell and slips away:[7]

■ My songs cease, I abandon them,
From behind the screen where I hid I advance personally solely to you.

Camarado, this is no book,
Who touches this touches a man,
(Is it night? are we here together alone?)
Is it I you hold and who holds you,
I spring from the pages into your arms – decease calls me forth

[...]

Dear friend whoever you are take this kiss,
I give it especially to you, do not forget me,
I feel like one who has done work for the day to retire awhile,
I receive now again of my many translations, from my avataras
                              ascending, while others doubtless await me,
An unknown sphere more real than I dream'd, more direct, darts
                              awakening rays about me, *So long!*
Remember my words, I may again return,
I love you, I depart from materials,
I am as one disembodied, triumphant, dead □
                              (Walt Whitman, 'So Long?')[8]

The critical evaluations of Whitman's work that follow all seek to trace the weight of Whitman's touch upon our readerly sensibilities. Inevitably, whilst the critical successes and shortcomings of these essays are a measure of their own partial reading practices, they are also testament to a remarkable poet whose work still touches us, still calls us forth across a century-and-a-half.

CHAPTER ONE

Early Reviews

W hitman's role as self-publicist is both exemplified and tested by the reception of the publication of the first edition of *Leaves of Grass* in 1855. The extracts that comprise this chapter, from early reviews and assessments of Whitman's poetry, can all be seen as attempts to come to terms with a radically challenging poetic voice and persona. In these early reviews, *Leaves of Grass* is measured both against Whitman's poetic persona as 'one of the roughs', and against his contention that his poems are 'commensurate with America'.[1] Whether favourable towards Whitman or not, these first readings of him set the terms for subsequent evaluations of his poetry. Indeed, the contrasting tones of the sometimes bewildered consternation and excited adulation that we encounter towards Whitman in these early pieces sound repeatedly throughout the history of the critical reception of *Leaves of Grass*. Interestingly, too, the way in which these reviews measure Whitman's poetry against models of, on the one hand, a self-reliant poetic egotism and, on the other, America and its democratic promise, sounds a strongly Emersonian note that has also been heavily marked in critical dealings with Whitman.

In fact Emerson himself was one of Whitman's very first readers and critics. Already deeply indebted to Emerson's thought (as we saw in the Introduction to this Guide) and eagerly seeking approval from the father-figure of American letters, Whitman had sent him a copy of the first edition of *Leaves of Grass*. Whitman could hardly have wished for a more rapturous response from the man he felt to be his (and America's) literary 'Master'.[2] If Emerson's essay 'The Poet' had seemed to Whitman to call for a truly American bard, a poet of and for America, then Emerson's letter to him of 21 July 1855, seemed to acknowledge that Whitman was indeed this poet and that *Leaves of Grass* was America's long-awaited poem:

■ Dear Sir,
I am not blind to the worth of the wonderful gift of *Leaves of Grass*. I find it the most extraordinary piece of wit & wisdom that America has yet contributed. I am very happy in reading it, as great power makes us happy.

It meets the demand I am always making of what seemed the sterile and stingy Nature, as if too much handiwork or too much lymph in the temperament were making our western wits fat & mean. I give you joy of your free & brave thoughts. I have great joy in it. I find incomparable things said incomparably well, as they must be. I find the courage of treatment, which so delights us, & which large perception can only inspire. I greet you at the beginning of a great career, which yet must have had a long foreground somewhere for such a start. I rubbed my eyes a little to see if this sunbeam were no illusion; but the solid sense of the book is a sober certainty. It has the best merits, namely, of fortifying & encouraging.

I did not know until I, last night, saw the book advertised in a newspaper, that I could trust the name as real & available for a post-office. I wish to see my benefactor, & have felt much like striking my tasks, & visiting New York to pay you my respects. □   (R. W. Emerson)[3]

Clearly flattered by Emerson's greeting of him at the start of a 'great career', Whitman capitalised on Emerson's apparently glowing letter of recommendation, and quoted from it in pamphlet advertisements for later editions of *Leaves of Grass*. To Emerson's dismay, Whitman included this letter in an appendix to the second edition of *Leaves of Grass* which was published in August 1856.

Emerson was doubly aggrieved by Whitman's publication of his letter. First, he was annoyed that what he felt to be a private letter had been reproduced without permission. In fact, he declared Whitman to have been 'very wrong indeed' over this.[4] Second, Emerson was increasingly ambivalent about being so closely associated with a publication that, especially in its second edition, seemed deliberately to be courting controversy in its more explicit dealings with matters of the body and of sex. With these objections in mind, it is possible to read Emerson's letter as a far more cautious estimate of Whitman's achievement and importance than Whitman took it to be. By greeting Whitman at the start of his career, Emerson praises not so much what *Leaves of Grass* achieves, as its potential. His implication is, perhaps, that though displaying a charged and dynamic American literary spirit – one that is 'fortifying and encouraging' – it is neither very mature nor finished as a work of art. Whilst responding to Whitman's epic sweep – Whitman's portrayal of himself as a mythic American bard – the closing comments of Emerson's letter sound strangely cautious about Whitman's poetic persona. His doubt, here, over whether Whitman was real or not, a name he 'could trust', echoes his mistrust – in the essay 'The Poet' – of what he sees as the shallow amateurism of poets who 'write poems from the fancy, and at a safe distance from their own experience'.[5]

The question of the distance – or otherwise – of the poet of *Leaves of Grass* from Whitman's real self and from his cultural conditions is one, as we shall see, that has continually occupied Whitman's literary critics. It is a question that is particularly troubling to most of Whitman's earliest readers as they struggle to formulate ways of reading Whitman's poetry and to articulate responses to it other than bemused shock. And it is particularly pointed in the following anonymous review of *Leaves of Grass* that appeared in the literary journal *United States Review* shortly after the first publication of the collection. Here, the reviewer hails the appearance of a truly representative American poet, one who will be a myth-maker for the new nation, one who will spread a self-reliant and democratic spirit across the continent through the 'sweeping movement' and force of his poems.

This review is especially interesting and important in the history of the critical reception of *Leaves of Grass* on two counts. Not only does it so clearly set the tone for future laudatory appraisals of Whitman's poetry through its delineation of a mythic American literary nationalism, but it also marks, and makes complicated, the relationship between Whitman himself and the 'American bard' that he claims to be in the collection. If many of the terms by which this reviewer heaps praise upon *Leaves of Grass* sound remarkably familiar (seemingly culled from the collection's opening poem 'Song of Myself'), then this is hardly surprising given that the reviewer was, in fact, Whitman himself. So it can be seen from this review that whilst Whitman's elaborate playfulness with poetic identity, with his personal, political and poetic selves is part of a strategy to give voice to the multifarious poem that is America, it is also a marketing strategy. By putting on the garb of critic, Whitman acts here as self-publicist, aiming to increase sales of his book. The breathtaking audacity of this (which is itself typically Whitmanesque) is matched by the review's impassioned rhetoric:

■ An American bard at last! One of the roughs, large, proud, affectionate, eating, drinking, and breeding, his costume manly and free, his face sunburnt and bearded, his posture strong and erect, his voice bringing hope and prophecy to the generous races of young and old. We shall cease shamming and be what we really are. We shall start an athletic and defiant literature. We realize now how it is, and what was most lacking. The interior American republic shall also be declared free and independent ...

Self-reliant, with haughty eyes, assuming to himself all the attributes of his country, steps Walt Whitman into literature, talking like a man unaware that there was ever hitherto such a production as a book, or such a being as a writer. Every move of him has the free play of the muscle of one who never knew what it was to feel that he stood in the presence of a superior. Every word that falls from his mouth shows silent disdain and defiance of the old theories and forms. Every phrase announces new laws; not once do his lips unclose except in conformity with them. With light and rapid touch he first indicates in prose the principles of the foundation of a race of poets so deeply to spring form the American people, and become ingrained through them, that their Presidents shall not be the common referees so much as that great race of poets shall. He proceeds himself to exemplify this new school, and set models for their expression and range of subjects. He makes audacious and native use of his own body and soul. He must recreate poetry with the elements always at hand. He must imbue it with himself as he is, disorderly, fleshy, sensual, a lover of things, yet a lover of men and women above the whole of the other objects of the universe. His work is to be achieved by unusual methods. Neither classic or romantic is he, nor a materialist any more than a spiritualist. Not a whisper comes out of him of the old stock talk and rhyme of poetry – not the first recognition of gods or goddesses, or Greece or Rome. No breath of Europe, or her monarchies or priestly conventions, or her notions of gentlemen and ladies, founded on the idea of caste, seems ever to have fanned his face or been inhaled into his lungs.

The movement of his verses is the sweeping movement of great currents of living people, with a general government and state and municipal governments, courts, commerce, manufactures, arsenals, steamships, railroads, telegraphs, cities with paved streets, and aqueducts, and police, and gas – myriads of travellers arriving and departing – newspapers, music, elections, and all the features and processes of the nineteenth century, in the wholesomest race and the only stable forms of politics at present upon the earth. Along his words spread the broad impartialities of the United States. No innovations must be permitted on the stern severities of our liberty and equality. Undecked also is this poet with sentimentalism, or jingle, or nice conceits, or flowery similes. He appears in his poems surrounded by women and children, and by young men, and by common objects and qualities. He gives to each just what belongs to it, neither more nor less. That person nearest him, that person he ushers hand in hand with himself. Duly takes places in the flowing procession, and step to the sounds of the jubilant music, the essences of American things, and past and present events – the enormous diversity of temperature, and agriculture, and mines – the tribes of red aborigines – the weather-beaten vessels entering new ports, or making landings on rocky coasts – the first settlements north and south – the rapid stature and impatience of outside control – the sturdy defiance of '76, and the war and peace, and the leadership of Washington, and the formation of the constitution – the union always surrounded by blatherers and always calm and impregnable – the perpetual coming of immigrants – the wharf-hemmed cities and superior marine – the unsurveyed interior – the log-houses and clearings, and wild animals and hunters and trappers – the fisheries, and whaling, and gold-digging – the endless gestation of new States – the convening of Congress every December, the members coming up from all climates, and from the uttermost parts – the noble character of the free American workman and workwoman – the fierceness of the people when well roused – the ardor of their friendships – the large amativeness – the equality of the female with the male – the Yankee swap – the New York fireman and the target excursion – the southern plantation life – the character of the northeast and of the northwest and southwest – and the character of America and the American people everywhere. ...

The rules of polite circles are dismissed with scorn. Your stale modesties, he seems to say, are filthy to such a man as I. ... No skulker or tea-drinking poet is Walt Whitman. He will bring poems to fill the days and nights – fit for men and women with the attributes of throbbing blood and flesh. The body, he teaches, is beautiful. Sex is also beautiful. Are you to be put down, he seems to ask, to that shallow level of literature and conversation that stops a man's recognizing the delicious pleasure of his sex, or a woman hers? Nature he proclaims inherently clean. Sex will not be put aside; it is a great ordination of the universe. He works the muscle of the male and the teeming fibre of the female throughout his writings, as wholesome realities, impure only by deliberate intention and effort. To men and women he says, You can have healthy and powerful breeds of children on no less terms than these of mine. Follow me, and there shall be taller and richer crops of humanity on the earth.

Especially in the *Leaves of Grass* are the facts of eternity and immortality largely treated. Happiness is no dream, and perfection is no dream. Amelioration is my lesson, he says with calm voice, and progress is my lesson and the lesson of all things. Then his persuasion becomes a taunt, and his love bitter and compulsory. With strong and steady call he addresses men. Come, he seems to say, from the midst of all that you have been your whole life surrounding yourself with. Leave all the preaching and teaching of others, and mind only these words of mine. ... Doubtless in the scheme this man has built for himself, the writing of poems is but a proportionate part of the whole. It is plain that public and private performance, politics, love, friendship, behavior, the art of conversation, science, society, the American people, the reception of the great novelties of city and country, all have their equal call upon him, and receive equal attention. In politics he could enter with the freedom and reality he shows in poetry. His scope of life is the amplest of any yet in philosophy. He is the true spiritualist. He recognizes no annihilation, or death, or loss of identity. He is the largest lover and sympathizer that has appeared in literature. He loves the earth and sun and the animals. He does not separate the learned from the unlearned, the northerner from the southerner, the white from the black, or the native from the immigrant just landed at the wharf. Every one, he seems to say, appears excellent to me; every employment is adorned, and every male and female glorious.

... Right and left he flings his arms, drawing men and women with undeniable love to his close embrace, loving the clasp of their hands, the touch of their necks and breasts, and the sound of their voice. All else seems to burn up under his fierce affection for persons. Politics, religions, institutions, art, quickly fall aside before them. In the whole universe, he says, I see nothing more divine than human souls.

... Must not the true American poet indeed absorb all others, and present a new and far more ample and vigorous type?

Has not the time arrived for a school of live writing and tuition consistent with the principles of these poems? consistent with the free spirit of this age, and with the American truths of politics? consistent with geology, and astronomy, and phrenology, and human physiology? consistent with the sublimity of immortality and the directness of common sense?

If in this poem the United States have found their poetic voice and taken measure and form, is it any more than a beginning? Walt Whitman himself disclaims singularity in his work, and announces the coming after him of a great succession of poets, and that he but lifts his finger to the signal.

Was he not needed? Has not literature been bred in-and-in long enough? Has it not become unbearably artificial? ...

You have come in good time, Walt Whitman! In opinions, in manners, in costumes, in books, in the aims and occupancy of life, in associates, in poems, conformity, to all unnatural and tainted customs passes without remark, while perfect naturalness, health, faith, self-reliance, and all primal expressions of the manliest love and friendship, subject one to the stare and controversy of the world. ☐ (Walt Whitman, *Leaves of Grass*, 1855)[6]

It would have been very difficult for Whitman's early readers not to have identified him as the author of this review. And on this evidence, it would seem that Whitman wants to draw the attention of his readers towards the 'naturalness' of his poetry, towards his attempts to refresh a literature that he feels has 'become unbearably artificial'. His agenda is therefore cultural as well as poetic; it is an attempt to give voice to America. Whitman, however (and most probably *because* of his zealous self-promoting Americanness), was roundly criticised by the anonymous reviewer of the *New York Daily Times* in 1856. This critic noted, 'It is a lie to write a review of one's own book ... and send it out to the world as an impartial editorial utterance. ... It is a dishonesty committed against one's own nature.'[7] Despite this note of censure, the reviewer goes on to express considerable praise for *Leaves of Grass* itself and details its 'wondrous, unaccountable fascination'.

What this reviewer admires in *Leaves of Grass* is Whitman's unsophisticated, or 'uncultivated', rawness and the connection to 'natural' Americanness that this seems to endorse: '[Whitman] gives token everywhere that he is a huge uncultivated thinker. No country save this could have given birth to the man. His mind is Western – brawny, rough, and original.' Such a pattern of associating Whitman's rawness with the American landscape is typical of critical attitudes towards his poetry. As we shall see in the following extracts, this association can lead to outright condemnation of Whitman as a barbarous American, or to praise of his ability to sound a new and distinctly American poetic voice. Whatever the judgement though, it depends – of course – upon the prejudices and assumptions about America and its literary culture of each particular reviewer. In the following extract, from the very first notice of *Leaves of Grass* (published in the *New York Daily Tribune*, 23 July 1855), praise for Whitman's freshness and excitement sits uncomfortably next to worries about his coarseness and vulgarity. What is at stake here, then, is more than just a collection of poems. What is at stake is an image of America as the New World, as a reclaimed paradise:

■ ... *Leaves of Grass* are doubtless intended as an illustration of the natural poet. They are certainly original in their external form, have been shaped on no pre-existent model out of the author's own brain. Indeed, his independence often comes coarse and defiant. His language is too frequently reckless and indecent, though this appears to arise from a naïve unconsciousness rather than from an impure mind. His words might have passed between Adam and Eve in Paradise, before the want of fig-leaves brought no shame; but they are quite out of place amid the decorum of modern society, and will justly prevent his volume from free circulation in scrupulous circles. With these glaring faults, the *Leaves of Grass* are not destitute of peculiar poetic merits, which will awaken an interest in the lovers of literary curiosities. They are full of bold, stirring thoughts – with occasional passages of effective description, betraying a genuine intimacy with Nature and a keen appreciation of beauty – often presenting a rare felicity of diction, but so disfigured with eccentric fancies as to prevent a consecutive perusal without offense, though no impartial reader can fail to be impressed with the vigor and quaint beauty of isolated portions.[8] □

Written by Charles A. Dana who was, at the time, the managing editor of the *Tribune*, this review's tone of mixed and muted praise seems to express some of Dana's own sense of disappointed American idealism. Dana had been involved in the transcendental utopian community at Brook Farm in the early 1840s, and had witnessed its dissolution after its destruction by fire in 1846.[9] His reading of Whitman's expansive and idealistic poetry is tinged by his own sense that the rhetoric of innocent optimism that characterised America in the early years of the nineteenth century has been replaced by a deep sense of loss. Dana's image, then, of Adam and Eve in the garden of Eden has a peculiar resonance for his reading of *Leaves of Grass*. It is as though he sees Whitman's poetry – however vigorous – as unable to withstand a fall from innocence that was being witnessed in the culture all around it. Interestingly, this image of Whitman as a modern-day Adam in an American Eden has become a mainstay of critical readings of his poetry. It is an image, as we shall see repeatedly throughout this Readers' Guide, that has provided Whitman's readers with some critical, and mythical, coordinates for measuring the success of the poetry in evoking distinctly American themes.

If Dana's review was ambivalent over the importance (if not the impact) of Whitman's poetry to the rapidly changing cultural scene of antebellum (i.e., the period in the run-up to the American Civil War) America, the following three reviews pull no punches in their condemnation of *Leaves of Grass*. These reviewers share a profound animosity towards Whitman's roughness. By extension, they also exhibit deep disquiet at the discourses of (Adam-like) innocence, 'naturalness', and uncultivated rawness that were increasingly associated in the America of the 1850s with the desire to return to the supposedly naïve and open principles of Jacksonian democracy. More than simply plotting the snobbish attitudes of the literary élites in Boston, London and (perhaps surprisingly) New York towards a version of America as a nation forging itself out of its struggles on the western frontier, these reviews also bear witness to the way in which Whitman's poetry has always been implicated in political debate. Here the debate over Whitman's poetry is most pointedly also a debate about the origins, and direction, of a distinctly American literary sensibility.

Charles Eliot Norton's review of *Leaves of Grass* (from the September 1855 edition of *Putnam's Monthly*) acknowledges that nowhere but America could have produced such a 'curious and lawless collection of poems'. He even seems to concede that the book's affront to what he takes to be common decency, its 'contempt for public taste', is a deliberate ploy. Indeed the book is described in terms of its powerful dualities, as 'preposterous yet somehow fascinating', and Norton sees these dualities as the key to its radically dangerous American message. But this does not, in Norton's eyes, lead him to recommend Whitman's book. Clearly, then, Whitman's and Norton's visions of America were very different:

■ Our account of the last month's literature would be incomplete without some notice of a curious and lawless collection of poems, called *Leaves of Grass*, and issued in a thin quarto without the name of publisher or author. The poems, twelve in number, are neither in rhyme nor blank verse, but in a sort of excited prose broken into lines without any attempt at measure or regularity, and, as many readers will perhaps think, without any idea of sense or reason. The writer's scorn for the wonted usages of good writing extends to the vocabulary he adopts; words usually banished from polite society are here employed without reserve and with perfect indifference to their effect on the reader's mind; and not only is the book one not to be read aloud to a mixed audience, but the introduction of terms never before heard or seen, and of slang expressions, often renders an otherwise striking passage altogether laughable. ...

[T]he poems themselves ... may briefly be described as a compound of the New England transcendentalist and New York rowdy. A fireman or omnibus driver, who had intelligence enough to absorb the speculations of that school of thought which culminated at Boston some fifteen or eighteen years ago, and resources of expression to put them forth again in a form of his own, with sufficient self-conceit and contempt for public taste to affront all visual propriety of diction, might have written this gross yet elevated, this superficial yet profound, this preposterous yet somehow fascinating book. As we say, it is a mixture of Yankee transcendentalism and New York rowdyism, and, what must be surprising to both these elements, they here seem to fuse and combine with the most perfect harmony. The vast and vague conceptions of the one, lose nothing of their quality in passing through the coarse and odd intellectual medium of the other; while there is an original perception of nature, a manly brawn, and an epic directness in our new poet, which belong to no other adept of the transcendental school. ...

As seems very proper in a book of transcendental poetry, the author withholds his name from the title page, and presents his portrait, neatly engraved on steel, instead. This, no doubt, is upon the principle that the name is merely accidental; while the portrait affords an idea of the essential being from whom these utterances proceed. We must add, however, that this significant reticence does not prevail throughout the volume, for we learn on p. 29, that our poet is 'Walt Whitman, an American, one of the roughs, a kosmos'. That he was an American, we knew before, for, aside from America, there is no quarter of the universe where such a production could have had a genesis. That he was one of the roughs was also tolerably plain; but that he was a kosmos, is a piece of news we were hardly prepared for. Precisely what a kosmos is, we trust Mr. Whitman will take an early occasion to inform the impatient public. □
(Charles Eliot Norton, 'Review of Leaves of Grass', 1855)[10]

Norton's exasperated impatience with Whitman at the close of his review is echoed – surpassed even – by that of the anonymous reviewer from whom the next extract is taken.

This review was written for the London literary journal, the *Critic* (1 April 1856). Here, a tone of supercilious mockery towards Whitman is sustained throughout. No concessions are given (as in previous reviews above) to Whitman's strength of expression, or the powerful naturalness of his 'native' poetics. From the outset this review sees America as a freakish nation consisting of natural oddities, a dangerous popular culture (as exemplified by Phineas T. Barnum's showmanship), and a feminised and uncultured literature (as exemplified by the likes of women authors and polemicists such as Fanny Fern).[11] Most interestingly, the reviewer's condemnation of Whitman displays stereotypically English attitudes of the time towards America. Whitman exemplifies for this reviewer the monstrosity that is America – loud, brash and untamable. Here, the reviewer claims, is evidence that Americans are little more than savages, hardly better than beasts. Though deliciously funny – 'Walt Whitman is as unacquainted with art, as a hog is with mathematics' – the invective barely masks a bitter and dangerous sense of cultural superiority when the reviewer notes that the poems 'resemble nothing so much as the war-cry of the Red Indians'. Such imagery of beasts and savagery is especially telling because it so clearly denotes the reviewer's struggles to come to terms with a poetry undiluted by literary sentiment. The irony, of course, is that Whitman's dealings with, and descriptions of, animals and native Americans in *Leaves of Grass* are delicately poised and subtle in contrast to the vast oversimplifications of the reviewer here.

■ We had ceased, we imagined, to be surprised at anything that America could produce. We had become stoically indifferent to her Woolly Horses, her Mermaids, her Sea Serpents, her Barnums, and her Fanny Ferns; but the last monstrous importation from Brooklyn, New York, has scattered our indifference to the winds. Here is a thin quarto volume without an author's name on the title-page; but to atone for which we have a portrait engraved on steel of the notorious individual who is the poet presumptive. This portrait expresses all the features of the hard democrat, and none of the flexile delicacy of the civilised poet. The damaged hat, the rough beard, the naked throat, the shirt exposed to his waist, are each and all presented to show that the man to whom those articles belong scorns the delicate arts of civilisation. The man is the true impersonation of his book – rough, uncouth, vulgar. It was by the merest accident that we discovered the name of this erratic and newest wonder; but at page 29 we find that he is –

Walt Whitman, an American, one of the roughs, a Kosmos,
Disorderly, fleshly, and sensual.

The words 'an American' are a surplusage, 'one of the roughs' too painfully apparent; but what is intended to be conveyed by 'a Kosmos' we cannot tell, unless it means a man who thinks that the fine essence of poetry consists in writing a book which an American reviewer is compelled to declare 'is not to be read aloud to a mixed audience'.[12] We should have passed over this book, *Leaves of Grass*, with indignant contempt, had not some few Transatlantic critics attempted to 'fix' this Walt Whitman as the poet who shall give a new and independent literature to America – who shall form a race of poets as Banquo's issue formed a line of kings. Is it possible that the most prudish nation in the world will adopt a poet whose indecencies stink in the nostrils? We hope not; and yet there is a probability, and we will show why, that this Walt Whitman will not meet the stern rebuke which he so richly deserves. America has felt, oftener perhaps than we have declared, that she has no national poet – that each one of her children of song has relied too much on European inspiration, and clung too fervently to the old conventionalities. It is therefore not unlikely that she may be in the dawn of a thoroughly original literature, now there has arisen a man who scorns the Hellenic deities, who has no belief in, perhaps because he has no knowledge of, Homer and Shakespeare; who relies on his own rugged nature, and trusts to his own rugged language, being himself what he shows in his poems. Once transfix him as the genius of a new era, and the manner of the man might be forgiven or forgotten. But what claim has this Walt Whitman to be considered a poet at all? We grant freely enough that he has a strong relish for nature and freedom, just as an animal has; nay, further, that his crude mind is capable of appreciating some of nature's beauties; but it by no means follows that, because nature is excellent, therefore art is contemptible. Walt Whitman is as unacquainted with art, as a hog is with mathematics. His poems – we must call them so for convenience – twelve in number, are innocent of rhythm, and resemble nothing so much as the war-cry of the Red Indians. Indeed, Walt Whitman has had near and ample opportunities of studying the vociferations of a few amiable savages. Or rather perhaps, this Walt Whitman reminds us of Caliban throwing down his logs, and setting himself to write a poem. In fact Caliban, and not Walt Whitman, might have written this:

I too am not a bit tamed – I too am untranslatable.
I sound my *barbaric yawp* over the roofs of the world.

Is this man with the 'barbaric yawp' to push Longfellow into the shade, and he meanwhile to stand and 'make mouths' at the sun?...
...The American critics are, in the main, pleased with this man because he is self-reliant, and because he assumes all the attributes of his country. If Walt Whitman has really assumed those attributes, America should hasten to repudiate them, be they what they may. The critics are pleased also because he talks like a man unaware that there ever was such a production as a book, or ever such a being as a writer. This in the present day is a qualification exceedingly rare, and *may* be valuable, so we wish those gentlemen joy of their GREAT UNTAMED. ...
We will neither weary nor insult our readers with... extracts from this notable book. Emerson *has praised it*, and called it the 'most extraordinary piece of wit and wisdom America has yet contributed'.[13] Because Emerson has grasped substantial fame, he can afford to be generous; but Emerson's generosity must not be mistaken for justice. If this work is really a work of genius – if the principles of those poems, their free language, their amazing and audacious egotism, their animal vigour, be real poetry and the divinest evidence of the true poet – then our studies have been in vain, and vainer still the homage which we have paid to the monarchs of Saxon intellect, Shakespeare, and Milton, and Byron. This Walt Whitman holds that his claim to be a poet lies in his robust and rude health. He is, in fact, as he declares, 'the poet of the body'. Adopt this theory, and Walt Whitman is a Titan; Shelley and Keats the merest

pigmies. If we had commenced a notice of *Leaves of Grass* in anger, we could not but dismiss it in grief, for its author, we have just discovered, is conscious of his affliction. He says, at page 33,

> *I am given up by traitors;*
> *I talk wildly, I am mad.* □
> (Anonymous Review of *Leaves of Grass*, the *Critic*, 1856)[14]

Drawing heavily on Norton's earlier review, this critic seems keen to establish an emerging critical consensus about *Leaves of Grass*, and draws on English critical values of literary decorum and decency in order to do this. The closing charges against Whitman – that he is little better than a beast or, worse still, mad – reverberate throughout assessments of Whitman's work. They illustrate something that we have all but lost today: the powerful initial impact of Whitman's poetry, the uncanny sense of its being unlike any other poetry. This sense is important because it both helps to explain the obvious consternation of critics when trying to fit Whitman into their predetermined models of what poetry should do and be, and also allows us to reclaim the experience of reading Whitman as one that is purposefully radical and challenging.

In the *Critic* review and in those extracts that follow, another common point of critical consternation, or at least anxious attention, is the question (noticed by Emerson) of just how real are the experiences detailed in the poems. For Norton, the *Critic* reviewer, and the unnamed reviewer in the following piece from the *Boston Intelligencer* (3 May 1856), Whitman the poet and Walt Whitman the poetic persona are taken to be synonymous. The madness, beastliness and indecencies, as they see them, of *Leaves of Grass* are therefore an index of Whitman's overarching 'egotism', the presumed end-point of an Emersonian doctrine of self-reliance. The scorn heaped upon the book in the following review is cruel and unforgiving. In its failure to separate poet from poetic persona, the review becomes viciously personal in a quite elaborate metaphor borrowed (as though to reinforce its clear prejudices) from the literary journal *Criterion*:

■ We were attracted by the very singular title of this work, to seek the work itself, and what we thought ridiculous in the title is eclipsed in the pages of this heterogeneous mass of bombast, egotism, vulgarity and nonsense. The beastliness of the author is set forth in his own description of himself, and we can conceive no better reward than the lash for such a violation of decency as we have before us. The *Criterion* says: 'It is impossible to imagine how any man's fancy could have conceived it, unless he were possessed of the soul of a sentimental donkey that had died of disappointed love.'

This book should find no place where humanity urges any claim to respect, and the author should be kicked from all decent society as below the level of a brute. There is neither wit nor method in his disjointed babbling, and it seems to us he must be some escaped lunatic, raving in pitiable delirium. ☐ (Anonymous review, *Boston Intelligencer*, 1856)[15]

In contrast to the critical delirium here, the final three extracts of this chapter are much more willing to see Whitman's poetry as a mask of his true self, and to concede that he is adopting the role of democratic poet, of a representative American character, in his poetry. They read, that is, beneath Whitman's self-publicising swagger and bluster to discover a poetry of profound humanity and affectionate sympathies.

For Edward Everett Hale, writing in the *North American Review* (January 1856), Whitman's poetry speaks in wonder and touching innocence about the world in which it finds itself. Hale's review – the first unabashedly positive reaction to *Leaves of Grass* (excepting, of course, Whitman's own) – sees Whitman's sympathetic identification with beasts as a virtue, and not a sign of supposedly rough, uncultured Americanness. For Hale, Whitman sees the world with fresh and innocent eyes, and invites the reader to do so too. His poetic sweep is powerful, he argues, because of his unaffected abilities to translate American life, in all its vigorous realities, onto paper. Whitman, then, speaks basic truths with a childlike ease through his invented persona as 'one of the roughs'. Hale's review is vitally important in the history of Whitman criticism because it emphasises, as a positive quality, the direct and simple equation between Whitman's poetry and the 'Genius of the United States'. In other words, it sees Whitman's writing of America as a poem, as the undeniable poetic strength of *Leaves of Grass*. Discovering *Leaves of Grass* is, for Hale, like discovering a new world; though 'odd and out of the way', it is a 'truly accomplished' work of American literature:

■ Everything about the external arrangement of this book was odd and out of the way. The author printed it himself and it seems to have been left to the winds of heaven to publish it. ... It bears no publisher's name, and, if the reader goes to a bookstore for it, he may expect to be told at first ... that there is no such book, and has not been. Nevertheless, there is such a book, and it is well worth going twice to the bookstore to buy it. Walter Whitman 'one of the roughs – no sentimentalist, no stander above men and women, or apart from them, no more modest than immodest' has tried to write down here, in a sort of prose poetry, a good deal of what he has seen, felt, and guessed at in a pilgrimage of some thirty-five years. He has a horror of conventional language of any kind. His theory of expression is, that, 'to speak in literature with the perfect rectitude and *insouciance* of the movements of animals, is the flawless triumph of art'. Now a great many men have said this before. But generally it is the introduction to something more artistic than ever, – more conventional and strained. ... In this book, however, the prophecy is fairly fulfilled in the accomplishment. 'What I experience or portray shall go from my composition without a shred of my composition. You shall stand by my side and look in the mirror with me.'

So truly accomplished is this promise...that this thin quarto deserves its name. That is to say, one reads and enjoys the freshness, simplicity, and reality of what he reads, just as the tired man, lying on the hill-side in summer, enjoys the leaves of grass around him, – enjoys the shadow, – enjoys the flecks of sunshine, – not for what they 'suggest to him', but for what they are....

Claiming...a personal interest in everything that has ever happened in the world, and, by the wonderful sharpness and distinctness of his imagination, making the claim effective and reasonable, Mr. 'Walt Whitman' leaves it a matter of doubt where he has been in this world, and where not. It is very clear, that with him, as with most other effective writers, a keen, absolute memory, which takes in and holds every detail of the past...is a gift of his organization as remarkable as his vivid imagination. What he has seen once, he has seen forever. And thus there are in this curious book little thumb-nail sketches of life in the prairie, life in California, life at school, life in the nursery, – life, indeed, we know not where not, – which, as they are unfolded one after another, strike us as real, – so real that we wonder how they came on paper.

For the purpose of showing that he is above every conventionalism, Mr. Whitman puts into the book one or two lines which he would not address to a woman nor to a company of men. There is not anything, perhaps, which modern usage would stamp as more indelicate than are some passages in Homer. There is not a word in it meant to attract readers by its grossness, as there is in half the literature of the last century, which holds its place unchallenged on the tables of our drawing-rooms. For all that, it is a pity that a book where everything else is natural should go out of the way to avoid the suspicion of being prudish. ☐

(Edward Everett Hale, *North American Review*, 1856)[16]

A similar sense of Whitman's naturalness and simplicity is described by Henry David Thoreau in a letter to Harrison Blake in December 1856. Thoreau had just received a copy of the second edition of *Leaves of Grass* from Whitman. Though not without some qualifications, his response is positive, seeing the collection as especially 'brave and American'. Quite apart from the fact of Thoreau's own importance to American literature and philosophy in the nineteenth century, what is especially interesting in this critical evaluation of Whitman is the emphasis upon the poem's primitiveness as a positive virtue, a wake-up call for America. In Whitman, Thoreau sees a great, and essentially American confidence, not bragging or egotistical, but simply assured:

■ That Walt Whitman of whom I wrote you, is the most interesting fact to me at present. I have just read his second edition (which he gave me), and it has done me more good than any reading for a long time....

On the whole, it sounds to me very brave and American, after whatever deductions. I do not believe that all the sermons, so called, that have been preached in this land put together are equal to it for preaching. We ought to rejoice greatly in him. He occasionally suggests something a little more than human. You can't confound him with the other inhabitants of Brooklyn or New York. How they must shudder when they read him! He is awfully good.

To be sure I sometimes feel a little imposed on. By his heartiness and broad generalities he puts me into a liberal frame of mind prepared to see wonders, – as it were, sets me upon a hill or in the midst of a plain, – stirs me up well, and then – throws in a thousand of brick. Though rude and sometimes ineffectual, it is a great primitive poem, – an alarum or trumpet-note ringing through the American camp. ...

Since I have seen him, I find that I am not disturbed by any brag or egoism in his book. He may turn out to be the least braggart of all, having a better right to be confident.

He is a great fellow. □

(Henry David Thoreau, *Letters to Various Persons*, 1865)[17]

Here Whitman is a 'great fellow' because of his poetic forthrightness, an attribute that marks him out – for Thoreau – as a truly American writer. So, already by the second edition of *Leaves of Grass* (1856), Whitman's greatness is felt to be deeply entwined with his status as a national figure. The following extract, with which this chapter of early critical readings of Whitman closes, is from one of the first extended critical commentaries on him written during his lifetime. It develops and examines the relationship between Whitman's poetry and his position as a national 'bard'. In fact, by 1884, when John Robertson published his small book, *Walt Whitman: Poet and Democrat*, Whitman was already a literary celebrity, an American *cause célèbre*, and he enjoyed the epithet of the 'Good Grey Poet'. Not simply a plea, then, for recognition of Whitman, Robertson's pamphlet is the first attempt at a more systematic evaluation of Whitman's cultural impact and importance. Of crucial importance to Robertson's reading of Whitman is the notion – hinted at, but not expanded upon in Thoreau's letter – of Democracy, and of Whitman's representative position as an exemplary American democrat and poet. Indeed Robertson's exploration of this theme in Whitman leads him to declare the poetry to be fully as serious and important as any produced in Britain.

From the opening parallel that he draws between Milton's writing of an epic English poem, to his closing remarks dismissing those poets and critics who see Whitman as a 'magnificent barbarian in art', Robertson continually seeks to read Whitman against the grain of received (especially English) critical opinions. It is this, he notes, that makes a purely poetic evaluation of Whitman especially troublesome. Like America itself this poetry is difficult to classify: it asks us to reinvent our world, and our opinions: 'No body of poetry is so difficult to account for or classify on any theory as his. Like the democracy it celebrates, it refuses to conform to old formulas.' For Robertson, then, Whitman's mixed critical reception points up the larger ironies of a supposedly democratic culture that has consistently failed to recognise the democratic idealism of one of its poets, presuming, instead, that he is 'nothing but a coarse propounder of loose notions on sexual morality'. Fascinatingly, Robertson seems at some pains to trace this irony back into the deeply divided political and ideological circumstances of America in the post-Civil War years when he notes that the conflict at the heart of Whitman's critical reception is essentially 'one between optimism and pessimism'. For it is precisely the conflict between these opposed strains of optimism and pessimism that has come to be seen as characteristic of America during the 'Gilded Age'.

Robertson's formulation of the irony at the heart of Whitman's critical reception is fascinating in another respect. By attending to the vexed question of Whitman's treatment of sex, and sexual morality, he opens up an entirely new field of critical investigation for readers of Whitman. Or, more accurately, he makes explicit the sort of questions and prurient rumours about Whitman that had always circulated but never been fully voiced critically since the first edition of *Leaves of Grass* was published. In this respect Robertson is ahead of his time and anticipates many, more recent, readings of Whitman. So, even as early as the 1880s (i.e., still during Whitman's lifetime), it is as clear to Robertson as to later generations of Whitman's readers that the critical controversy inspired by his poetry is a vital indication of his poetic importance, and a marker of his poetics of democracy.

■ No poet is more explicit about his creed and purpose than Whitman; perhaps none has such an all-absorbing creed and purpose to proclaim; and when that is once perceived the doubt about his poetic quality is already half disposed of. If there was a truth in Carlyle's favourite citation from Milton – that 'he who would write a heroic poem must make his life a heroic poem' – it is surely still truer that he who would sing democracy must be the most robust democrat; and Whitman is the very democrat of practice as well as of faith and philosophy....

Our democratic poetry has mostly run to generalities. But Whitman is nothing more remarkable than in the exultation, the fervour, with which he sings of love between comrades. It is practically, as he sounds it, a new note in modern poetry; and were it for nothing else he might well be forgiven on the strength of his elevation of feeling in this regard, for any seeming lack of it in other connections. His faculty of brotherly love is one of his most potent inspirations. Lincoln's homely qualities live in the memory of good democrats who feel the transfiguring effect of his death; but Whitman, while never once alluding to the assassin, sings passionately of the dead president as of a beloved friend, 'the wisest, sweetest soul' of his generation. His whole nature tends to rapturous expression: in very truth he cannot but choose to express himself as he does. From his first line he is not only the vowed singer of democracy and the dear love of comrades, but the self-poised, self-centred, self-possessed democratic unit; a manifestation of the force which *is* democracy; the typical self-asserting individual.

... Whitman sings life, history, politics as he does because he is the man he is, absolutely self-confident, sanguine, candid, loving, tolerant and eupeptic;[18] yet self-esteeming, vigorously egotistic, and exclusive by fits. All life for him relates itself to his impulses; his is the naïf popular theism of the day which finds the universe made for man, and the land for the race. Again, he has, as he points out, that very sameness in caprice which marks primitively self-assertive and genuine natures, as that of Carlyle, of whom Emerson remarked that he said the same thing day after day, week after week and year after year. And like the half-cultured continent he is profuse, straggling, miscellaneous. ...

The essential thing [however] is that the singer of democracy shall be full charged with his theme; and that an idea which feeds on optimism and confidence shall be carried with a confidence that no adversity will dash. And how Whitman's confidence rays out from his first page! Other poets have sung democracy in moments of expansion, or when goaded by the sight of war and depression: he alone ecstatically points a prosperous demos to new heights of ideal life. ...

He is just as confident in his poetic mission as in his message. 'Of all nations', he declares, 'the United States, with veins full of poetical stuff, most need poets, and will doubtless have the greatest and use them the greatest. Their presidents shall not be their common referee so much as their poets shall. Of all mankind the great poet is the equable man. Not in him but off from him things are grotesque or eccentric, or frail of their sanity. ... He is the arbiter of the diverse, and he is the key. He supplies what wants supplying, and checks what wants checking. If peace is the routine, out of him speaks the spirit of peace. ... In war he is the most deadly force of the war. ... High up out of reach he stands, turning a concentrated light. ... The time straying towards infidelity and confections and persiflage he withholds by his steady faith. ... His brain is the ultimate brain. He is no arguer; he is judgement. He judges not as the judge judges, but as the sun falling round a helpless thing. As he sees the farthest he has the most faith.'[19]

Some of the sentences in this latter passage, brilliantly enforced though they are by the others, are almost enough to prove, what full knowledge of his books absolutely establishes, that Whitman has almost no humour. The circumstance is particularly noteworthy. It is universally agreed that humour consists in the perception of the incongruous; and it has seemed natural that among the most restless population in the world, they possessing the most complex civilisation, the perception should be most highly educated. But Whitman is too enormously in earnest, too intensely faithful, to laugh. ...

It forms a somewhat grotesque commentary on Whitman's enthusiastic accounts of the elements of greatness in American life, that the respectable, cultured, American population contrive to see in the man who talks thus nothing but a coarse propounder of loose notions on sexual morality. Supposing there were no direct defence whatever for Whitman's offences against the convenances ['conventional proprieties'] in 'Leaves of Grass', the idea that his educated countrymen can with almost one accord make these offences outweigh his entire gospel is not easily to be grasped. A future age will assuredly see one of the sickliest of all the moral conditions of modern life in this collapse of the American nervous system before a mere defiance of one social law by the man who, of all his race, has most ardently set great ideals before republicans, and most austerely contemned their Radical vices; who, above all, has wasted himself in most generous but most burdensome service to his kind. Any one with a clear vision of the essentials in morals will be ready to pronounce that Whitman's loving and patient work in the hospitals through the years of the war is, with his books, sufficient attestation that he is of the salt of his people; and that whether or not all his propositions in sociology be tenable, it is simply absurd to pronounce him a force of evil. ...

Now, though it may not be apparent at first, the conflict [...] between Whitman and those who gainsay him is really one between optimism and pessimism. Theism is essentially optimistic, and those who protest against Whitman's freedoms are usually theists; but it is not easy to see how they can philosophically justify at once their agreements with him and their dissent. It may be suspected that they seldom try. The ordinary optimist pronounces all things, sin apart, good in their place, but proceeds to snub certain of the unblamed tendencies and phenomena as little better than necessary evils. He cannot in fact get rid of the inheritance of pessimism which comes down with the Christian legend; he still hangs his head in sympathy with Adam and Eve. Whitman comes about as near being a consistent optimist as any man well can, being not even put out by sin; and it will be difficult to state that he is not within his rights in claiming that the motive force of the race shall be sung as heartily as the spring, or as motherhood and friendship. He can fairly challenge the professing optimist to choose whether he will or will not renounce Schopenhauer;[20] whether he will expressly repudiate the teaching that humanity is duped by the will-to-live, or give it colour by his attitude.

... Whitman has perhaps himself to thank that his public looks narrowly to the moral bearing of his poetry, and insists rigorously on making him responsible for all it contains; but if the reader will be content to take his every poem as a simple expression of emotion, one thing will speedily be established to the reader's advantage, namely, that there is poetic feeling in a greater or lesser degree in almost all. It might, indeed, be charged against Whitman that he is at times positively carried off his feet by the afflatus – that, morals apart, he at times passes the bounds of sanity, and becomes for us a possessed enurguman [a variant spelling of 'enurgumen', meaning 'one that is wrought upon by a devil; a demonaic' (OED)] rather than an inspired truth-singer. This tendency to delirium we must just set against other displays of a leaning to the *banal*, and admit that the latter is only transient. It must be confessed, however, that the most difficult thing of all in judging Whitman is to estimate his purely poetic value. No body of poetry is so difficult to account for or classify on any theory as his. Like the democracy it celebrates, it refuses to conform to old formulas. ... The lover of English poetry who comes to Whitman for the first time will probably, in two cases out of three – unless he happens to be familiar with Blake – be merely astonished and irritated, and these sensations some readers never live down. Perhaps the best course for the reader of poetic taste who is capable of appreciating Whitman's ideas is to turn at the first shock from the poetry to the prose. That he is almost sure to find stimulating and rich in suggestion, and when he has thus got into sympathy with the man he will find the poetry much more palatable. At first he will be disposed to insist that there is hardly any difference between the prose and the poetry; that the preface to 'Leaves of Grass', dropped into clauses of systematically unequal length, might eke out 'American Feuillage' with perfect propriety; that, in short, Whitman simply makes prose pass for poetry by a particular arrangement of type. Though, however, it will be found hardly possible to defend Whitman's artistic method in the long run, that particular criticism will have to be departed from. Taken all over, the verse, hopelessly unrhythmical as it so often seems, has a distinct quality of 'lilt', which is after all the generic difference between poetry and prose. It is the difference between walking and running – the nervous tension belonging to the dance – the definition of which as 'the poetry of motion' supplies the critic with a really instructive analogy. Add that it is only in his poetry he becomes dramatic or celebrates his passion pure and simple, and the distinction between his poetry and his prose is broadly established. But to allow that his verse has poetic quality is one thing; to say it is a successful poetic product is another.

Whitman, who has a decided opinion about poetic expression, would probably accept with Emerson the conception of poetry as having its form originally determined by the pulse-beat and by the inhalation and exhalation of the lungs; but to all appearance he refuses to go any further. As in his thinking he takes his stand on primary facts and individual impulse, so in his verse he returns to elementary methods. It may fairly be said to bear to contemporary English poetry some such relation as does an African war-dance to the dances of Europe. ... And the upshot is that the world is impelled to view Whitman's aversion to graceful poetic form as it does his rejection of manners, and pronounce him a fine specimen of the barbarian. ...

There is on the other hand, a danger of being too summary in writing Whitman down a magnificent barbarian in art. A mistaken notion of his culture has been inadvertently fostered in England by Mr. W. M. Rossetti and Mr. Moncure Conway; the former rather unfortunately representing him as having used Emerson's praise to advertise 'Leaves of Grass' while entirely unacquainted with Emerson's books; and the latter apparently accepting too unreservedly the poet's remark that his reading was confined mostly to Homer and the Bible. Whitman has since given sketches of his life, from which it appears that at an early age he began to read novels omnivorously; that he did much miscellaneous work in journalism; and that he picked up plenty of general culture, as a receptive American can, without being systematic in his studies. ...

... But the poetry of Whitman, ill-smelted as so much of it is, cataloquial as is so much of his transcription from life, and lacking as his song so often is in music, somehow does not seem ... marked for doom even in respect of his didacticism. And the reason would seem to be not merely that his message is the intense expression of his deepest passion, but that the passion is the very flower of the life of the race thus far, and carries in it the seeds of things to come. He cannot soon be left behind – he has gone so far before. □

(John Robertson, *Walt Whitman: Poet and Democrat*, 1884)[21]

Robertson's passionate defence of Whitman against charges of barbarism is important in that it sets the tone for much subsequent analysis of his poetry. His reading of Whitman also anticipates some of the major objections to his work that helped shaped his poetic reputation until well into the twentieth century. As we shall see in the next chapter, Whitman's early-twentieth-century readers found him a frustratingly complex and ambiguous figure, one whose poetry never quite fitted their accounts of America and its literary culture.

CHAPTER TWO

Whitman in the Early Twentieth Century

The sense of bemused critical ambivalence towards Whitman's poetry already present in early assessments of his work increased following his death (26 March 1892) and into the early years of the twentieth century. Curiously, though, it was in this period that Whitman and his literary reputation became more solidly established. Thus, by 1922, the year in which D. H. Lawrence's *Studies in Classic American Literature* was first published (and from which the final extract of this chapter comes), to have denied Whitman's status as a 'classic' of American Literature would have seemed a perverse – even belligerent – critical position to adopt. So, despite the very serious doubts that are expressed in the critical pieces that comprise this chapter about Whitman's poetic style, about his apparent 'barbarousness' of tone, about, even, his philosophical and ideological positions, each of these critics is in little doubt that Whitman is a crucially important literary figure. Whether critically liked or loathed, by the early years of the twentieth century, Whitman's impact on American poetry and, more broadly, on Anglo-American literary relations could not be denied. The four extracts that follow, then, trace a critical trajectory for Whitman that sees him move from his position as a marginal and quaintly eccentric American oddity to being seen as *the* father-figure of American poetry.

This turnaround in Whitman's critical fortunes is perhaps accounted for in two ways. First, on a cultural level, America and its literary productions could no longer be ignored, or simply dismissed as 'uncivilised', by the literary establishment in England. So rapid and expansive was America's political growth over the early years of the twentieth century that it simply was no longer possible not to account for its literature. In fact, the first ever history of American literature, John Nichol's *American Literature*, was published towards the end of Whitman's lifetime in 1885, and though wary of American literature's tendency to 'roughness', it firmly established an American literary tradition worthy of critical attention. The most significant development in the acceptance of American literature into the critical canon, however, came in 1917 with the publication of the first volume of *The Cambridge History of American Literature*, edited by John Erskine and Carl Van Doren. From this it can be seen that early evaluations of Whitman's poetry coincide with a felt need to establish the critical terms for an evaluation of American literature itself. Indeed Whitman's poetry can be seen to play a central role in producing those terms. If Whitman is read as rough-and-ready, colloquial, like Adam in the Edenic garden of the New World, as a fresh and dynamic poetic challenge to the literary conventions of the Old World, then this is precisely because such terms were also increasingly being used to characterise American literary sensibilities more generally.

Second, on the level of critical trends, it became – especially after the First World War – much more acceptable for critics to focus on the ambivalences, contradictions and ironies of a literary text. Unlike some of the earliest readers of Whitman who were offended by his seeming inability to present a grandly cohesive aesthetic and moral position, his declaration 'Do I contradict myself? / Very well then ... I contradict myself' presented a new sort of challenge for literary critics. The readings of Whitman by (especially) Ezra Pound and D. H. Lawrence in this chapter, then, make a critical virtue out of their very mixed response to him. In doing so these readings seem to want to reassess Whitman for the modern age. They accept ambivalence as a proper critical position, one, moreover, that speaks to the increasingly relativistic world view of modernity. Such readings of Whitman, also, seem to anticipate one of the basic doctrines of what came in the late 1930s to be called New Criticism, the belief that a text's ambiguities and ironies add richness to its 'texture' and are thus of deep and lasting literary value.

These different critical pressures and approaches being brought to bear on Whitman and his legacy are evident in Ezra Pound's short poem, 'A Pact', from his 1913–14 collection *Lustra*:

> ■ I make a pact with you, Walt Whitman –
> I have detested you long enough.
> I come to you as a grown child
> Who has had a pig-headed father;
> I am old enough now to make friends.
> It was you that broke the new wood,
> Now is a time for carving.
> We have one sap and one root –
> Let there be commerce between us. □[1]

Here Pound describes a changed attitude towards Whitman. This is encapsulated in the poem's double sense that whilst 'detesting' Whitman, one also rather admires him, and the radical image of American poetry that he represents. Whitman becomes here a father figure for American letters, someone from whom other American writers can claim (however uneasily) a common descent, a pioneer figure for a pioneering literary sensibility. What is especially fascinating about this poem is the sense (that we will encounter again later in Pound's essay on Whitman) of Pound, the expatriate American in the cosmopolitan and fashionable literary London of the early years of the twentieth century, inviting, as it were, Whitman across the Atlantic in order to show him off as part of his American literary background. The 'commerce' between Pound and Whitman speaks not only of America's growing commercial hold on world markets (and the consequent sense of American culture as commercial and populist), but also of a whole set of fraught and difficult literary relations between England and America that were being tested in the modern era.

In the first critical extract of this chapter, written in 1893, shortly after Whitman's death, John Addington Symonds sees Whitman's power lying in his ability to defy easy critical assessment. Noting, in common with many other Whitman critics, that Whitman is 'extremely baffling to criticism', he ascribes this to the impossibility of extracting any single 'coherent scheme of thought from [Whitman's] voluminous writings'. Yet he does go on to attempt some sort of synthesis from Whitman's writings, arguing that his poetry is generated from a consideration of 'Personality'. In one sense, then, Symonds anticipates assessments of Whitman that attach to him the status of America's first real literary 'personality' and read him – and indeed American culture more widely – as being based in a mythologisation of celebrity. In another sense, though, Symonds is at some pains to locate Whitman's poetry and poetics not in broad-sweeping national or cultural issues, but at the level of the intimately 'personal'. He states, 'Personality presents itself to him [Whitman]...under the double aspect of soul and body, and furthermore as differentiated by sex.'

In fact, Symonds is perhaps most famous in histories of Whitman for his suspicions of, and fascinated interest in, Whitman's sexual behaviour. Between 1871 and 1890, Symonds wrote to Whitman on numerous occasions asking for confirmation of his suspicion that the poems in the 'Calamus' section of *Leaves of Grass* were based on homosexual experience. Symonds' most famous letter along these lines was received by Whitman in August 1890. In his rather exasperated reply to Symonds, Whitman stated that such suggestions 'quite daze me', denied the 'morbid inferences', and claimed to have fathered 'six children [of whom] two are dead'.[2] Though we may feel that Whitman here protests too much, what is important about Symonds' interest in Whitman is that it helps to establish Whitman as a curiously enigmatic poetic figure, despite his professed openness to his audience. It is within such ambivalent terms that Whitman seems to operate as a poet of American democracy. Symonds' critical focus on 'Personality' allows him, therefore, to investigate and develop apparently contradictory modes of approaching Whitman. His appraisal of the poet, then, is strikingly modern in its acceptance of the indeterminacies of reading Whitman.

■ Whitman, indeed, is extremely baffling to criticism. I have already said in print that 'speaking about him is like speaking about the universe.' I meant this to be appreciative, in so far as the largeness and comprehensiveness of the man's nature are concerned. But the saying has, like the famous Delphian knife, a double handle. Not merely because he is large and comprehensive, but because he is intangible, elusive, at first sight self-contradictory, and in some sense formless, does Whitman resemble the universe and defy critical analysis.

The peculiar surroundings of the man during his lifetime rendered it difficult to be impartial with regard to him. Assuming from the first an attitude of indifference to public opinion, challenging conventionalities, and quietly ignoring customary prejudice, he was exposed at the beginning of his career to unmerited insults and a petty persecution. Not only did critics and cultivated persons fling stones at him; but even a Minister of State thought it his duty to deprive him of a modest office which he held. This opposition was far from abating his courage or altering the calm of his essentially masculine nature. But it excited the pugnacious instincts of those few devoted followers and disciples who had gathered round him. Whitman began to be enveloped in a dust of controversy – indecent abuse upon the one hand, extravagant laudation on the other – outrage and depreciation, retaliated by what the French call *réclame* ['advertisement'] and *claque* ['slap'] [meaning that Whitman retaliated against his critics by hard-hitting self-advertisement]. Sane criticism found it necessary to stand aloof from the ignoble fray; feeling confident that Whitman's worth would obtain due and ultimate recognition... .

... In all his writings, Whitman has kept personality steadily in view, as the leading motive of his poetic and prophetic utterance. He regards wealth, material prosperity, culture, as nothing in comparison with vigorous manhood and womanhood.... Nations, consequently, rise or fall, according to the quality of the persons who constitute them. Human beings are nothing, possess nothing, enjoy nothing, except through, and by their self, their personality. To prove this, to demonstrate what an incomparably precious thing a free and healthy personality, self-centred, self-reliant, self-effectuated, is for the owner of it, how it transcends every other possession which riches or learning can confer, becomes the first object of his teaching. Secondly he aims at showing that nations only thrive and are strong by the character, the grit, the well-developed personality, of their inhabitants. Nothing can preserve a nation in prosperity, or perpetuate its fame, except the spiritual elements it has developed, as distinguished from brute force or accumulated capital.

... But what meaning does Whitman attach to the word Personality? How does he envisage the phenomenon of self, which is the one thing certain for each separate individual who thinks and feels, and which he has therefore selected as the main motive of his prophecy?

Personality presents itself to him ... under the double aspect of soul and body, and furthermore as differentiated by sex. He appears to have believed that in this life the soul is inextricably connected with the body, so that whatever is done in the body redounds to the advantage or disadvantage of the soul. At the same time the fleshly body is destined to dissolution. It is pronounced to be 'excrementitious,' whereas the principle of selfhood is indestructible, and the soul may be transformed but never perish.

During his life, at any rate, the body constitutes a man and forms the channel of communication between his soul and outer things.

> I too had received identity by my Body:
> That I was, I knew was of my body – and what I should be,
>   I knew should be of my body.

The body has therefore a mystic value for Whitman, not merely because of its exceeding beauty and delightfulness, but also because it is verily the temple of the divinest of all things we know, the human soul.

... No wonder, then, if Whitman, feeling thus, exclaims at times that the distinction between soul and body, so far as the individual is concerned, vanishes away.

> I have said that the soul is not more than the body,
> And I have said that the body is not more than the soul;
> And nothing, not God, is greater to one than one's self is.

We may now ask what is Whitman's ideal of human personality. Where does he find the best type of self, the manliest man, the most womanly woman? The answer to this question is not far to seek, when we bear in mind what we already know about his preference for open life and nature. His hero is sure to be some 'nonchalant and natural person'; not a man of culture or a bookworm, but one who has been born with a fine physique, capable of subduing the external world to his own purpose, and delighting in his labour; a man of healthy instincts and strong passions, vividly enjoying the boon pleasures of life, and keenly responding to the beauty and the wonder of the world.... Such men Whitman calls 'athletes', and the women he demands for the backbone of a nation must equally be 'athletic'. He is convinced that in such personalities the soul reaches its maximum of magnetic attraction and persuasiveness.... 'To effuse magnetism', to attract and persuade by merely being vigorous and sound and free, is the crown and glory of a perfected personality.

In his treatment of Love, Whitman distinguishes two broad kinds of human affection; the one being the ordinary sexual relation, the other comradeship or an impassioned relation between man and man. The former he describes as 'amativeness', the latter as 'adhesiveness'.

... The section of his complete works which deals exclusively with sexual love, is entitled 'Children of Adam'. The frankness and the rankness of the pieces composing this chapter called down a storm of insults, calumnies, unpopularity on Whitman. Yet the attitude which he assumed as poet and prophet demanded this frankness, while the spirit of his treatment deprived the subject matter of its rankness.

... To recognise the dignity of sex, to teach personalities, both male and female, that they have the right to take a pride in it, and that this pride is their duty, was for a poet of Whitman's stamp a prime consideration.... Whitman naturally treated the ordinary sexual relations with a breadth and simplicity which appear to more sophisticated minds as brutal. He does not shrink from images and descriptions, from metaphors and phrases, as closely borrowed from the facts of sex as are his pictures of the outer world, or his transcripts from the occupations of mankind. Sex, being for him so serious and excellent a thing, has the right to equal freedom of speech with sunrise or sun setting, the stars in their courses, the woods and fields, the industries of the carpenter or typesetter, the courage of soldiers, the inevitable fact of death.

... Whitman thought and wrote habitually, not with people of culture, refined tastes, literary and social traditions in view, but for the needs and aspirations of what he called 'the divine average'. He aimed at depicting robust and sane humanity in his verse. He wanted to brace character, and create through his art-work a type applicable to all sorts and conditions of men, irrespective of their previous differentiation by specific temperament or class-association. For this reason, his treatment of the sexual relations will be felt by some persons not only to be crudely frank in detail, but also to lack delicacy in its general outlines. The overwhelming attractions of sex, swaying the physique of men and women, are broadly insisted upon. The intercourse established in matrimony is regarded not so much as an intellectual and moral union, but as an association for mutual assistance in the labours of life, and for the production of noble human specimens. It is an Adamic hygienic view of marriage, satisfying the instincts of the primeval man.

... The section of Whitman's works which deals with adhesiveness, or the love of comrades, is fully as important, and in some ways more difficult to deal with, than his 'Children of Adam'. He gave it the title 'Calamus,' from the root of a water-rush, adopted by him as the symbol of this love. Here the element of spirituality in passion, of romantic feeling, and of deep enduring sentiment, which was almost conspicuous by its absence from the section on sexual love, emerges into vivid prominence, and lends peculiar warmth of poetry to the artistic treatment....

... No man in the modern world has expressed so strong a conviction that 'manly attachment', 'athletic love', 'the high towering love of comrades', is a main factor in human life, a virtue upon which society will have to lay its firm foundations, and a passion equal in permanence, superior in spirituality, to the sexual affection. Whitman regards this emotion not only as the 'consolation' of the individual, but also as a new and hitherto unapprehended force for stimulating national vitality.

There is no softness or sweetness in his treatment of this theme. His tone is sustained throughout at a high pitch of virile enthusiasm, which, at the same time, vibrates with acutest feeling, thrills with an undercurrent of the tenderest sensibility. Not only the sublimest thoughts and aspirations, but also the shyest, most shame-faced, yearnings are reserved for this love. At one time he exclaims:

> O I think it is not for life that I am chanting here my chant of
> lovers – I think it must be for Death,
> For how calm, how solemn it grows, to ascend to the atmosphere of
> lovers,
> Death or life I am then indifferent – my soul declines to prefer,
> I am not sure but the high soul of lovers welcomes death most;
> Indeed, O Death, I think now these leaves mean precisely the same
> as you mean;
> Grow up taller, sweet leaves, that I may see! Grow up out of my breast!
> Spring away from the concealed heart there!
> Do not fold yourselves so, in your pink-tinged roots, timid leaves!
> Do not remain down there so ashamed, herbage of my breast!

The leaves are Whitman's emotions and the poems they engender; the root from which they spring is 'manly attachment', 'athletic love', symbolised for him in the blushing root of the pond-calamus which he plucked one day and chose to be the emblem of the love of lovers:

> O here I last saw him that tenderly loves me – and returns again,
> never to separate from me,
> And this, O this shall henceforth be the token of comrades – this
> Calamus-root shall,
> Interchange it, youths, with each other! Let none render it back!

...The language has a passionate glow, a warmth of devotion, beyond anything to which the world is used in the celebration of friendship. At the same time the false note of insincerity or sensuousness is never heard. The melody is in the Dorian mood – recalling to our minds that fellowship in arms which flourished among the Dorian tribes, and formed the chivalry of pre-historic Hellas.

... [However] Whitman never suggests that comradeship may occasion the development of physical desire. On the other hand, he does not in set terms condemn desires, or warn his disciples against their perils. There is indeed a distinctly sensuous side to his conception of adhesiveness.... .

Like Plato in the *Phaedrus*, Whitman describes an enthusiastic type of masculine emotion, leaving its private details to the moral sense and special inclination of the individual concerned.

The poet himself appears to be not wholly unconscious that there are dangers and difficulties involved in the highly-pitched emotions he is praising. The whole tenor of two carefully-toned compositions, entitled, 'Whoever you are, Holding me now in hand', and 'Trickle, Drops', suggest an underlying sense of spiritual conflict... .

The reality of Whitman's feeling, the intense delight which he derives from the personal presence and physical contact of a beloved man, find luminous expression in 'A Glimpse', 'Recorders ages hence', 'When I heard at the close of the day', 'I Saw in Louisiana a Live Oak Growing', ... [amongst others] ...

It is clear then that, in his treatment of comradeship, or the impassioned love of man for man, Whitman has struck a keynote, to the emotional intensity of which the modern world is unaccustomed. It therefore becomes of much importance to discover the poet-prophet's *Stimmung* ['mood; atmosphere'] – his radical instinct with regard to the moral quality of the feeling he encourages. Studying his works by their own light and by the light of their author's character, interpreting each part by reference to the whole and in the spirit of the whole, an impartial critic will, I think, be drawn to the conclusion that what he calls the 'adhesiveness' of comradeship is meant to have no interblending with the 'amativeness' of sexual love. Personally, it is undeniable that Whitman possessed a specially keen sense of the fine restraint and continence, the cleanliness and chastity, that are inseparable from the perfectly virile and physically complete nature of healthy manhood. Still we have the right to predicate the same ground-qualities in the early Dorians, those founders of the martial institution of Greek love; and yet it is notorious to students of Greek civilisation that the lofty sentiment of their masculine chivalry was intertwined with much that is repulsive to modern sentiment.

... But Whitman does not conceive of comradeship as a merely personal possession, delightful to the friends it links in bonds of amity. He regards it eventually as a social and political virtue. This human emotion is destined to cement society and render commonwealths inviolable.

... Whitman recognises among the sacred emotions and social virtues, destined to regenerate political life and to cement nations, an intense, jealous, throbbing, sensitive, expectant love of man for man: a love which yearns in absence, droops under the sense of neglect, revives at the return of the beloved: a love that finds honest delight in hand-touch, meeting lips, hours of privacy, close personal contact. He proclaims this love to be not only a daily fact in the present, but also a saving and ennobling aspiration. While he expressly repudiates, disowns, and brands as 'damnable' all 'morbid inferences' which may be drawn by malevolence or vicious cunning from his doctrine, he is prepared to extend the gospel of comradeship to the whole human race. He expects democracy, the new social and political medium, the new religious ideal of mankind, to develop and extend 'that fervid comradeship', by its means to counterbalance and to spiritualise what is vulgar and materialistic in the modern world. 'Democracy', he maintains, 'infers such loving comradeship, as its most inevitable twin or counterpart, without which it will be incomplete, in vain, and incapable of perpetuating itself'.[3]...

The passages which have been quoted in illustration of Whitman's views regarding man and the universe, and the paramount importance of self or personality, leaves no doubt as to how he must have treated the subject of 'Democracy'.

The inscription, placed upon the forefront of 'Leaves of Grass', contains this paragraph:

Nor cease at the theme of One's-Self. I speak the word of the
modern, the word EN-MASSE.

In another place, he says:

My comrade!
For you, to share with me two greatnesses – a third one, rising
inclusive and more resplendent
The greatness of Love and Democracy – and the greatness of
Religion.

Whitman's comrade, the athlete, the 'nonchalant and natural', the 'powerful uneducated person', whom his heart desires, enters into full enjoyment of self through love and liberty, both blending in that sublimer conception of the cosmos and our place in it, which forms the groundwork of religion.

What the word 'En-Masse' means for Whitman is expressed at large throughout his writings. It corresponds to another of his chosen phrases, 'the divine average', 'ever the most precious in the common'. An exact light is thrown upon it by the following passage:

I speak the pass-word primeval – I give the sign of Democracy;
By God! I will accept nothing which cannot have their
counterpart of on the same terms.

Thus Democracy implies the absolute quality of heritage possessed by every man and woman in the good and evil of this life. It also involves the conception that there is nothing beautiful or noble which may not be discovered in the simplest human being....

This exposition of democracy shows that Whitman regarded it not merely as a political phenomenon, but far more as a form of religious enthusiasm. That being the case, his treatment of democracy includes far-reaching speculations on the literature and art required by the sovereign people, on the creation of national character, and on the proper place of what is called culture in a noble scheme of public education.

...Speaking broadly then, Whitman's conception of the ideal bard of Democracy implies the following main qualities or properties. He must be possessed of perfect physical health, and the normal appetites and instincts. He must be in large and vital sympathy with his own nation and his own age. He must have illimitable faith and optimistic confidence. He must comprehend the heart of the people, recognise their nobility, base his trust in the future upon their sterling virtues and their spirituality. He must be a passionate lover of liberty, a believer in the equality of all men and women as regards their capacity for comprehending and enjoying what he comprehends and enjoys. He must derive his aliment and inspiration from science, nature, fact; aiming at truth and candour; preferring the genuine to the fictitious; denying the supernatural, and finding the only divine known to us in things submitted to our percipient senses. The final result of this attitude will be to make him religious in a higher and intenser degree than any creed or dogma yet has made a man to be. As regards his special function in literature, he must be gifted with imagination penetrative to the soul and life of fundamental realities, and in his expression must be as simple, as suggestive, as inevitable, as a natural object. He will aim at creating a new and independent vehicle of language, suitable to the quality of his personal perception. □ (John Addington Symonds, *Walt Whitman: A Study*, 1893)[4]

Symonds here uses two of Whitman's most favoured terms, 'amativeness', and 'adhesiveness', to distinguish between what he sees as two different aspects of Whitman's poetics: the sexual and sensuous, and the political. Where 'amativeness' relates to procreative sexual desires, 'adhesiveness' expresses an ideal of friendship, the comradely bond that sustains an American ideal of union. However, in Symonds' reading of Whitman, there is more than a hint that the 'adhesive' poems of 'Calamus', those that celebrate male-on-male comradeship as the ideal at the heart of a robust democracy, derive from a kind of homoerotic (even homosexual) utopian fantasy. This may actually tell us more about Symonds than it does about Whitman, but what is important in terms of reading Whitman is that his poetics is seen to be built on the apparently opposed forces of one's (sexual) desires as an individual set against the political 'desires' of America that result from its promotion of itself as a nation of democratic ideals.

For Symonds, then, as for many subsequent readers of Whitman, the appeal in Whitman's poetry to the 'divine average' is its strength. It is in this appeal, such readings argue, that Whitman realises his poetic mission to write the poem that is America. His recording of the average, and the everyday, of American life is the profoundly democratic lesson of his poetry. However, it is precisely this strategy that for other – less sympathetic critics – leads to a dismissing of Whitman and his poetry as a sub-literary sort of hoax, a trick played upon a gullible public. Indeed, Whitman's use of such terms as 'amativeness', and 'adhesiveness', which proves so useful to Symonds in his examination of some of the basic pressures in Whitman's poetry, is seen by less enthusiastic critics as a mark of the pseudoscientific and poetic nonsense upon which they take Whitman's work to be erected. Derived from the immensely popular 'science' of phrenology, such terms provide the dismissive critic with evidence of Whitman's lack of 'proper' education, and his reliance on 'lowbrow' popular culture. Feeling that Whitman's poetry opts for the lowest common denominator, such critics return to the rather bemused sorts of assessments of him that characterised many of the early reviews of his work. These sorts of readings are instructive, though, because of the attitudes towards America and American literature that they so clearly betray.

This can be seen in the next critical extract, by philosopher, poet and critic George Santayana. For Santayana, Whitman epitomises what he terms 'the poetry of barbarism'. Arguing that Whitman, like Browning, writes an uncultivated, emotionally charged poetry that is not constrained by 'clear thought', Santayana's is a startlingly troubled relationship to Whitman. It matches his own troubled relationship to America itself, where he was brought from Europe as a child. His model of the barbaric in literature, then, is also a means for him to find terms for his own fraught investigations of the cultural relationship between Europe and America at the turn of the century. His essay 'The Poetry of Barbarism', first published in 1900, offers a comparative reading of Browning and Whitman. At the start of the essay Santayana defines his notion of 'barbarism'. However, even at this stage, something of his ambivalent attitude towards Whitman can be felt. Though hopelessly uncultivated and anti-intellectual, the barbaric does have the virtue of provoking powerful and dynamic emotional responses:

■ The power to stimulate is the beginning of greatness, and when the barbarous poet has genius, as he well may have, he stimulates all the more powerfully on account of the crudity of his methods and the recklessness of his emotions. The defects of such art – lack of distinction, absence of beauty, incapacity permanently to please – will hardly be felt by the contemporary public, if once its attention is arrested; for no poet is so undisciplined that he will not find many readers, if he finds readers at all, less disciplined than himself.... .

[Robert Browning and Walt Whitman] are both analytic poets – poets who seek to reveal and express the elemental as opposed to the conventional; but the dissolution has progressed much farther in Whitman than in Browning, doubtless because Whitman began at a much lower stage of moral and intellectual organisation; for the good will to be radical was present in both. The elements to which Browning reduces experiences are still passions, characters, persons; Whitman carries the disintegration further and knows nothing but moods and particular images. The world of Browning is a world of history with civilisation for its setting and with the conventional passions for its motive forces. The world of Whitman is innocent of these things and contains only far simpler and more chaotic elements. In him the barbarism is much more pronounced; it is, indeed, avowed, and the 'barbaric yawp' is sent 'over the roofs of the world' in full consciousness of its inarticulate ... □ (George Santayana, 'The Poetry of Barbarism', 1956)[5]

Throughout his reading of Whitman – as in his rather mixed explanation of 'barbarism' – Santayana attempts to negotiate between downright disgust at Whitman's effrontery, and a sneaking admiration for his blasé flouting of poetic conventions. He sees very powerfully the 'beginning of greatness' in Whitman, and yet mistrusts his own feelings towards the poetry and the form of greatness it might signify. This mistrust is due to the fact that in order to fully appreciate Whitman's impact, he feels that one's 'intellect' must be 'in abeyance'. And that, Santayana fears, would be to drown a whole history of human endeavour and intellectual achievement in something rather worryingly 'primitive and general', a 'sensuality [that] is touched with mysticism'. Santayana's ambivalence towards Whitman betrays, therefore, the worries of a whole intellectual class about the appeal by modern consciousness to the apparently primitive and the sensuous. Despite his reservations – because of them, even – Santayana's essay therefore brings Whitman into the twentieth century:

■ [...]
Many poets have had the facility to seize the elementary aspects of things, but none has had it so exclusively [as Whitman]; with Whitman the surface is absolutely all and the underlying structure is without interest and almost without existence. He had had no education and his natural delight in imbibing sensations had not been trained to the uses of practical or theoretical intelligence. He basked in the sunshine of perception and wallowed in the stream of his own sensibility, as later at Camden in the shallows of his favourite brook. Even during the Civil War, when he heard the drum-taps so clearly, he could only gaze at the picturesque and terrible aspects of the struggle, and linger among the wounded day after day with a canine devotion; he could not be aroused either to clear thought or to positive action. So also in his poems; a multiplicity of images pass before him and he yields himself to each in turn with absolute passivity. The world has no inside; it is a phantasmagoria of continuous visions, vivid, impressive, but monotonous and hard to distinguish in memory, like the waves of the sea or the decorations of some barbarous temple, sublime only by the infinite aggregation of parts.

This abundance of detail without organisation, this wealth of perception without intelligence and of imagination without taste, makes the singularity of Whitman's genius. Full of sympathy and receptivity, with a wonderful gift of graphic characterisation and an occasional rare grandeur of diction, he fills us with a sense of the individuality and the universality of what he describes – it is a drop in itself yet a drop in the ocean. The absence of any principle of selection or of a sustained style enables him to render aspects of things and of emotion which would have eluded a trained writer. He is, therefore, interesting even where he is grotesque or perverse. He has accomplished, by the sacrifice of almost every other good quality, something never so well done before. He has approached common life without bringing in his mind any higher standard by which to criticise it; he has seen it, not in contrast with an ideal, but as the expression of forces more indeterminate and elementary than itself; and the vulgar, in this cosmic setting, has appeared to him sublime.

There is clearly some analogy between a mass of images without structure and the notion of an absolute democracy. Whitman, inclined by his genius and habits to see life without relief or organisation, believed that his inclination in this respect corresponded with the spirit of his age and country, and that Nature and society, at least in the United States, were constituted after the fashion of his own mind. Being the poet of the average man, he wished all men to be specimens of that average, and being the poet of a fluid Nature, he believed that Nature was or should be a formless flux. This personal bias of Whitman's was further encouraged by the actual absence of distinction in his immediate environment. Surrounded by ugly things and common people, he felt himself happy, ecstatic, overflowing with a kind of patriarchal love. He accordingly came to think that there was a spirit of the New World which he embodied, and which was in complete opposition to that of the Old, and that a literature upon novel principles was needed to express and strengthen this American spirit.

... In Whitman's works, in which this new literature is foreshadowed, there is accordingly not a single character nor a single story. His only hero is Myself, the 'single separate person', endowed with the primary impulses, with health, and with sensitiveness to the elementary aspects of Nature. The perfect man of the future, the prolific begetter of other perfect men, is to work with his hands, chanting the poems of some future Walt, some ideally democratic bard. Women are to have as nearly as possible the same character as men: the emphasis is to pass from family life and local ties to the friendship of comrades and the general brotherhood of man. Men are to be vigorous, comfortable, sentimental, and irresponsible.

This dream is, of course, unrealised and unrealisable, in America as elsewhere. Undeniably there are in America many suggestions of such a society and such a national character. But the growing complexity and fixity of institutions necessarily tends to obscure these traits of a primitive and crude democracy. What Whitman seized upon as the promise of the future was in reality the survival of the past. He sings the song of pioneers, but it is in the nature of the pioneer that the greater his success the quicker must be his transformation into something different. When Whitman made the initial and amorphous phase of society his ideal, he became the prophet of a lost cause. That cause was lost, not merely when wealth and intelligence began to take shape in the American Commonwealth, but it was lost at the very foundation of the world, when those laws of evolution were established which Whitman, like Rousseau, failed to understand... .

Whitman, it is true, loved and comprehended men; but this love and comprehension had the same limits as his love and comprehension of Nature. He observed truly and responded to his observation with genuine and pervasive emotion. A great gregariousness, an innocent tolerance of moral weakness, a genuine admiration for bodily health and strength, made him bubble over with affection for the generic human creature. Incapable of an ideal passion, he was full of the milk of human kindness. Yet, for all his acquaintance with the ways and the thoughts of the common man of his choice, he did not truly understand him. For to understand people is to go much deeper than they go themselves; to penetrate to their characters and disentangle their inmost ideals. Whitman's insight into man did not go beyond a sensuous sympathy; it consisted in a vicarious satisfaction in their pleasures, and an instinctive love of their persons. It never approached a scientific or imaginative knowledge of their hearts.

Therefore Whitman failed radically in his dearest ambition: he can never be a poet of the people. For the people, like the early races whose poetry was ideal, are natural believers in perfection. They have no doubts about the absolute desirability of wealth and learning and power, none about the worth of pure goodness and pure love. Their chosen poets, if they have any, will be always those who have known how to paint these ideals in lively even if gaudy colours. Nothing is farther from the common people than the corrupt desire of the primitive. They instinctively look toward a more exalted life, which they imagine to be full of distinction and pleasure, and the very idea of that brighter existence fills them with hope or with envy or with humble admiration.

...[Whitman's] ultimate appeal is really to something more primitive and general than any social aspirations, to something more elementary than an ideal of any kind. He speaks to those minds and to those moods in which sensuality is touched with mysticism. When the intellect is in abeyance, when we would 'turn and live with the animals, they are so placid and self-contained', when we are weary of conscience and of ambition, and would yield ourselves for a while to the dream of sense, Walt Whitman is a welcome companion. The images he arouses in us, fresh, full of light and health and of a kind of frankness and beauty, are prized all the more at such a time because they are not choice, but drawn perhaps from a hideous and sordid environment. For this circumstance makes them a better means of escape from convention and from that fatigue and despair which lurk not far beneath the surface of conventional life. In casting off with self-assurance and a sense of fresh vitality the distinctions of tradition and reason a man may feel, as he sinks back comfortably to a lower level of sense and instinct, that he is returning to Nature or escaping into the infinite. Mysticism makes us proud and happy to renounce the work of intelligence, both in thought and in life, and persuades us that we become divine by remaining imperfectly

human. Walt Whitman gives a new expression to this ancient and multiform tendency. He feels his own cosmic justification and he would lend the sanction of his inspiration to all loafers and holiday-makers. He would be the congenial patron of farmers and factory hands in their crude pleasures and pieties, as Pan was the patron of the shepherds of Arcadia: for he is sure that in spite of his hairiness and animality, the gods will acknowledge him as one of themselves and smile upon him from the serenity of Olympus. □
(George Santayana, 'The Poetry of Barbarism', 1956)[6]

Like Santayana, both Ezra Pound and D. H. Lawrence express a profoundly ambivalent attitude towards Whitman. For these writers, both associated with the modernist movement, Whitman's poetry certainly displays modernist sentiments, but Whitman's modernity is clearly troubling to them. In the final two extracts of this chapter we encounter Pound and Lawrence trying to come to terms with a poet who they acknowledge as a major figure but who they find (as with earlier critics) unabashedly populist and lacking literary decorum. Though very different in their responses to Whitman, they share a sense that Whitman and his poetic legacy can no longer be avoided, that he must somehow be accounted for. Pound does this by seeing Whitman as deeply and unashamedly American, a writer who, unlike himself, stayed in America and did not feel the need to experience Europe in order to become a true poet. Typically forthright, Pound sees Whitman *as* America in all its crudity and 'stench'. But he also manages to write him into a venerable (i.e. European, ironically) literary tradition of poets who strive to speak and thereby revivify the spoken language of their nation. 'Like Dante', Pound notes, 'he wrote in the "vulgar tongue", in a new metric. The first great man to write in the language of his people'. For Pound, then, Whitman is the father-figure of American poetry. He is unavoidable because his poetry is the *sagetrieb*, the 'tale of the tribe', that, elsewhere, Pound describes as essential to the modern poet.[7]

■ From this side of the Atlantic [i.e., Europe] I am for the first time able to read Whitman, and from the vantage of my education and – if it be permitted a man of my scant years [Pound was 23] – my world citizenship: I see him as America's poet. The only poet before the artists of the Carmen-Hovey period, or better, the only one of the conventionally recognised 'American Poets' who is worth reading.

He *is* America. His crudity is an exceeding great stench, but it *is* America. He is the hollow place in the rock that echoes with his time. He *does* 'chant the crucial stage' and he is the 'voice triumphant'. He is disgusting. He is an exceedingly nauseating pill, but he accomplishes his mission.

Entirely free from the renaissance humanist ideal of the complete man or from the Greek idealism, he is content to be what he is, and he is his time and his people. He is a genius because he has a vision of what he is and of his function. He knows that he is a beginning and not a classically finished work. I honour him for he prophesied me while I can only recognise him as a forebear of whom I ought to be proud.

In America there is much for the healing of nations, but woe unto him of the cultured palate who attempts the dose.

As for Whitman, I read him (in many parts) with acute pain, but when I write of certain things I find myself using his rhythms. The expression of certain things related to cosmic consciousness seems tainted with this maramis.[8]

I am (in common with every educated man) an heir of the ages and I demand my birth-right. Yet if Whitman represented his time in language acceptable to one accustomed to my standard of intellectual-artistic living he would belie his time and nation. And yet I am but one of his 'ages and ages' encrustations' or to be exact, an encrustation of the next age. The vital part of my message, taken from the sap and fibre of America, is the same as his.

Mentally I am a Walt Whitman who has learned to wear a collar and a dress shirt (although at times inimical to both). Personally I might be very glad to conceal my relationship to my spiritual father and brag about my more congenial ancestry – Dante, Shakespeare, Theocritus, Villon, but the descent is a bit difficult to establish. And, to be frank, Whitman is my fatherland (*Patrium quam odi et amo* ['The Country that I hate and love'] for no uncertain reasons)[9] what Dante is to Italy and I at my best can only be a strife for a renaissance in America of all the lost or temporarily mislaid beauty, truth, valour, glory of Greece, Italy, England and all the rest of it.

And yet if a man has written lines like Whitman's to the *Sunset Breeze* one has to love him. I think we have not yet paid enough attention to the deliberate artistry of the man, not in the details but in the large.

I am immortal even as he is, yet with a lesser vitality as I am the more in love with beauty (if I really do love it more than he did). Like Dante he wrote in the 'vulgar tongue', in a new metric. The first great man to write in the language of his people.

Et ego Petrarca in lingua vetera scribo ['And I Petrarch write in the old tongue' (i.e. Latin)][10], and in a tongue my people understood not.

It seems to me I should like to drive Whitman into the old world. I sledge, he drill – and to scourge American with all the old beauty. (For Beauty *is* an accusation) and with a thousand thongs from Homer to Yeats, from Theocritus to Marcel Schwob. This desire is because I am young and impatient, were I old and wise I should content myself in seeing and saying that these things will come. But now, since I am by no means sure it would be true prophecy, I [would] fain set my own hand to the labour.

It is a great thing, reading a man to know, not 'His Tricks are not as yet my Tricks, but I can easily make them mine' but 'His message is my message. We will see that we hear it.'   □

(Ezra Pound, 'What I Feel about Walt Whitman', 1909)[11]

Equally boisterous, and equally able to hear a thoroughly modern – though particularly worrying – poetic voice in Whitman is D. H. Lawrence in the essay on Whitman in his book *Studies in Classic American Literature*, from which the final extract of this chapter is taken.

This long essay concludes Lawrence's study of American literature, and the apocalyptic note it sounds is therefore appropriate to the sense he portrays, throughout his study, of American literature as one that sweeps away all that has gone before it. And though, clearly, very deeply troubled by Whitman, Lawrence's use of him as the final figure in his survey of American writing effectively elevates him higher than the other writers discussed. Whitman becomes, therefore, Lawrence's exemplary American figure. In Whitman, he implies, all the forces of America and its poetry are brought to the fore.

Though first published in 1922, Lawrence had been working on *Studies in Classic American Literature* since 1915. Despite, maybe because of, Lawrence's extravagantly idiosyncratic and wildly refreshing style as a critic, this book has itself become a classic among critical evaluations of American literature. Throughout his study Lawrence responds to the newness he hears in the old (that is nineteenth-century) American literary classics, and struggles to wrest judgement upon them away from European critical prejudices. 'It is hard to hear a new voice', he writes, 'as hard as it is to listen to an unknown language. We just don't listen. There is a new voice in the old American classics.'[12] Though he hears a vibrantly new voice in Whitman, he is deeply troubled by it. What his essay gives us, though, is a modernist roller-coaster reading of Whitman and in so doing he turns him into a poet of the modern world. As a poet born out of the conflicts of a nation struggling to define itself, Whitman affords Lawrence the opportunity to reassess the very idea of democracy in a world blown apart by recent events in the First World War. Lawrence's passionate reading of Whitman matches perfectly – if somewhat eccentrically – Whitman's own passionate poetics of democracy. It helps us read Whitman again, to see beneath the bluster and to glimpse a sad and troubled figure, a Whitman who is not simply a naïve optimist but a poet whose essential message of hope disguises a dark and terrifying fear of death. Lawrence's Whitman represents America because the excesses of his poetry strike a precarious balance between America's joy and openness and its crass avoidance of the violence and (most especially), the slavery that underpin its democratic ideal.

■ But what of Walt Whitman?
The 'good grey poet.'
Was he a ghost, with all his physicality?
The good grey poet.
Post mortem effects. Ghosts.

A certain ghoulish insistency. A certain horrible pottage of human parts. A certain stridency and portentousness. A luridness about his beatitudes.

DEMOCRACY! THESE STATES! EIDOLONS! ['An unsubstantial image, spectre, phantom' (OED)] LOVERS, ENDLESS LOVERS!

ONE IDENTITY!
ONE IDENTITY!
I AM HE THAT ACHES WITH AMOROUS LOVE.
...
I AM HE THAT ACHES WITH AMOROUS LOVE.

What do you make of that? I AM HE THAT ACHES. First generalization. First uncomfortable universalization. WITH AMOROUS LOVE! Oh, God! Better a bellyache. A bellyache is at least specific. But the ACHE OF AMOROUS LOVE!

Think of having that under your skin. All that!

I AM HE THAT ACHES WITH AMOROUS LOVE.

Walter, leave off. You are not HE. You are just a limited Walter. And your ache doesn't include all Amorous Love, by any means. If you ache you only ache with a small bit of amorous love, and there's so much more stays outside the cover of your ache, that you might be a bit milder about it.

I AM HE THAT ACHES WITH AMOROUS LOVE.
CHUFF! CHUFF! CHUFF!
CHU-CHU-CHU-CHU-CHUFF!

Reminds one of a steam-engine. A locomotive. They're the only things that seem to me to ache with amorous love. All that steam inside them. Forty million foot-pounds pressure. The ache of AMOROUS LOVE. Steam-pressure. CHUFF!

An ordinary man aches with love for Belinda, or his Native Land, or the Ocean, or the Stars, or the Oversoul: if he feels that an ache is in the fashion.

It takes a steam-engine to ache with AMOROUS LOVE. All of it.

Walt was really too superhuman. The danger of the superman is that he is mechanical.

They talk of his 'splendid animality'. Well, he'd got it on the brain, if that's the place for animality.

> I am he that aches with amorous love:
> Does the earth gravitate, does not all matter, aching attract
> all matter?
> So the body of me to all I meet or know.

What can be more mechanical? The difference between life and matter is that life, living things, living creatures, have the instinct of turning right away from *some* matter, and of turning towards only some bits of specially selected matter. As for living creatures all helplessly hurtling together into one great snowball, why, most very living creatures spend the greater part of their time getting out of the sight, smell or sound of the rest of living creatures. Even bees only cluster on their own queen. And that is sickening enough. Fancy all white humanity clustering on one another like a lump of bees.

No, Walt, you give yourself away. Matter *does* gravitate, helplessly. But men are tricky-tricksy, and they shy all sorts of ways.

Matter gravitates because it *is* helpless and mechanical.

And if you gravitate the same, if the body of you gravitates to all you meet or know, why, something must have gone seriously wrong with you. You must have broken your mainspring.
...

Your mainspring is broken, Walt Whitman. The mainspring of your own individuality. And so you run down with a great whirr, merging with everything.
...

I am everything and everything is me and so we're all One in One identity, like the Mundane Egg, which has been addled quite a while.

Whoever you are, to endless announcements –
And of these one and all I weave the song of myself.

Do you? Well then it just shows you haven't *got* any self. It's a mush, not a woven thing. A hotch-potch, not a tissue. Your self.

Oh, Walter, Walter, what have you done with it? What have you done with yourself? With your own individual self? For it sounds as if it had all leaked out of you, leaked into the universe.

Post-mortem effects. The individuality had leaked out of him.

No, no, don't lay this down to poetry. These are post-mortem effects. And Walt's great poems are really huge fat tomb-plants, great rank graveyard growths.

All that false exuberance. All those lists of things boiled in one pudding cloth! No, no!

I don't want all those things inside me, thank you.

'I reject nothing,' says Walt.

If that is so, one must be a pipe open at both ends, so everything runs through.

Post mortem effects.

'I embrace ALL,' says Whitman. 'I weave all things into myself.'

'Do you really! There can't be much left of *you* when you've done. When you've cooked the awful pudding of One Identity.

'And whoever walks a furlong without sympathy walks to his own funeral dressed in his own shroud.'

Take your hat off then, my funeral procession of one is passing.

This awful Whitman. This post-mortem poet. This poet with the private soul leaking out of him all the time. All his privacy leaking out in a sort of dribble, oozing into the universe.

Walt becomes in his own person the whole world, the whole universe, the whole eternity of time, as far as his rather sketchy knowledge of history will carry him, that is. Because to *be* a thing he had to know it. In order to assume the identity of a thing he had to know that thing....

As soon as Walt *knew* a thing, he assumed a One Identity with it. If he knew that an Eskimo sat in a kayak, immediately there was Walt being little and yellow and greasy, sitting in a kyak.

Now will you tell me exactly what a kyak is?

Who is he that demands petty definition? Let him behold me *sitting in a kyak.*

I behold no such thing. I behold a rather fat old man full of a rather senile, self-conscious sensuosity.

DEMOCRACY. EN MASSE. ONE IDENTITY.

The universe in short, adds up to one.

One.

1.

Which is Walt.

His poems, *Democracy, En Masse, One Identity,* they are long sums in addition and multiplication, of which the answer is invariably MYSELF.

He reaches the state of ALLNESS.

And what then? It's all empty. Just an empty Allness. An addled egg.

Walt wasn't an Eskimo. A little, yellow, sly, cunning, greasy little Eskimo. And when Walt blandly assumed Allness, including Eskimoness, unto himself, he was just sucking the wind out of a blown egg-shell, no more. Eskimos are not minor little Walts. They are something that I am not, I know that. Outside the egg of my Allness chuckles the greasy little Eskimo. Outside the egg of Whitman's Allness too.

But Walt wouldn't have it. He was everything and everything was in him. He drove an automobile with a very fierce headlight, along the track of a fixed idea, through the darkness of this world. And he saw everything that way. Just as a motorist does in the night.

I, who happen to be asleep under the bushes in the dark, hoping a snake won't crawl into my neck; I, seeing Walt go by in his great fierce poetic machine, think to myself: what a funny world that fellow sees!

ONE DIRECTION! toots Walt in the car, whizzing along it.

Whereas there are myriads of ways in the dark, not to mention trackless wildernesses, as anyone will know who cares to come off the road – even the Open Road.

ONE DIRECTION! whoops America, and sets off also in an automobile.

ALLNESS! shrieks Walt at a cross-road, going whizz over an unwary Red Indian.

ONE IDENTITY! chants democratic En Masse, pelting behind in motorcars, oblivious of the corpses under the wheels.

God save me, I feel like creeping down a rabbit-hole, to get away from all these automobiles rushing down the ONE IDENTITY tack to the goal of ALLNESS.

> A woman waits for me –

He might well have said: 'The femaleness waits for my maleness.' Oh, beautiful generalization and abstraction! Oh, biological function.

'Athletic mothers of these States –' Muscles and wombs. They needn't have faces at all.

...

Everything was female to him: even himself. Nature just one great function. ...

'The Female I see –'

If I'd been one of his women, I'd have given him Female, with a flea in his ear.

Always wanting to merge himself into the womb of something or other.

'The Female I see –'

Anything, so long as he could merge himself.

Just a horror. A sort of white flux.

Post mortem effects.

He found, as all men find, that you can't really merge in a woman, though you may go a long way. You can't manage the last bit. So you have to give it up, and try elsewhere if you *insist* on merging.

In *Calamus* he changes his tune. He doesn't shout and thump and exult any more. He begins to hesitate, reluctant, wistful.

The strange calamus has a pink-tinged root by the pond, and it sends up its leaves of comradeship, comrades from one root, without the intervention of the woman, the female.

So he sings of the mystery of manly love, the love of comrades. Over and over he says the same thing: the new world will be built on the love of comrades, the new great dynamic of life will be manly love. Out of this manly love will come the inspiration for the future.

Will it though? Will it?

Comradeship! Comrades! This is to be the new Democracy of Comrades. This is the new cohering principle in the world: Comradeship.

Is it? Are you sure?

It is the cohering principle of true soldiery, we are told in *Drum Taps*. It is the cohering principle of the new unison for creative activity. And it is extreme and alone, touching the confines of death. Something terrible to bear, terrible to be responsible for. Even Walt Whitman felt it. The soul's last and most poignant responsibility, the responsibility of comradeship, of manly love.

Yet you are beautiful to me, you faint-tinged roots, you
                              make me think of death.
Death is beautiful from you (what indeed is finally beautiful
                              except death and love?)
I think it is not for life I am chanting here my chant of
                              lovers, I think it must be for death,
For how calm, how solemn it grows to ascend to the
                              atmosphere of lovers,
Death or life, I am then indifferent, my soul declines to prefer

(I am not sure but the high soul of lovers welcomes death most)
> Indeed, O death, I think now these leaves mean precisely
> > the same as you mean –

This is strange, from the exultant Walt.
Death.
Death is now his chant! Death!
Merging! And Death! Which is the final merge.
The great merge into the womb. Woman.
And after that, the merge of comrades: man-for-man love.
And almost immediately with this, death, the final merge of death.
There you have the progression of merging. For the great mergers, woman at last becomes inadequate. For those who love to extremes. Woman is inadequate for the last merging. So the next step is the merging of man-for-man love. And this is on the brink of death. It slides over into death.
David and Jonathan. And the death of Jonathan.
It always slides into death.
The love of comrades.
Merging.
So that if the new Democracy is to be based on the love of comrades, it will be based on death too. It will slip so soon into death.
The last merging. The last Democracy. The last love. The love of comrades.
Fatality. And fatality.
Whitman would not have been the great poet that he is if he had not taken the last steps and looked in to death. Death, the last merging, that was the goal of his manhood.
...Whitman is a very great poet, of the end of life. A very great post-mortem poet, of the transitions of the soul as it loses its integrity. The poet of the soul's last shout and shriek, on the confines of death....
But we have all got to die first, anyhow. And disintegrate while we still live.
Only we know this much: Death is not the *goal*. And Love, and merging, are now part of the death-process. Comradeship – part of the death-process. Democracy – part of the death-process. The new Democracy – the brink of death. One identity – death itself.
We have died, and we are still disintegrating.
But IT IS FINISHED.
Consummatum est.[12] □
> (D. H. Lawrence, *Studies in Classic American Literature,* 1923)[13]

Lawrence's energised mockery of Whitman changes at this point in the essay. He acknowledges just how powerful Whitman's poetry can be, whilst becoming far more pointed in his political critique of him. What is especially interesting from this point onwards is Lawrence's understanding of the racial politics that Whitman's poetics effectively writes over. Lawrence seems especially aware of the dangers of such an all-encompassing notion of democracy as Whitman's. Whereas in the first section of this essay Lawrence humorously mocked Whitman for his inability – in any real sense – to include the Red Indian or the Eskimo in his model of American democracy, in the latter part of the essay Whitman's inability to include any one other than white males surprisingly similar to Whitman himself is deeply troubling to Lawrence.

In the second section of his essay, Lawrence returns to the issues raised by the image of 'Walt at a cross-road, going whizz over an unwary Red Indian'. And though Lawrence can see Whitman as the 'first white aboriginal' he also sees that Whitman's version of America cannot be separated from the issue of slavery. Indeed, Lawrence suggests mockingly that Whitman's rhetoric is precisely what produced slavery, blinding, as it were, America to its political realities by erecting a myth of the 'exultant message of American Democracy'. Despite this, however, Lawrence cannot shake off his fascination with Whitman, or his sense of Whitman's central importance in the development of American literature:

■ Whitman, the great poet, has meant so much to me. Whitman, the one man breaking a way ahead. Whitman, the one pioneer. And only Whitman. No English pioneers, no French. No European pioneer-poets. In Europe the would-be pioneers are mere innovators. The same in America. Ahead of Whitman, nothing. Ahead of all poets, pioneering into the wilderness of unopened life, Whitman. Beyond him, none. His wide, strange camp at the end of the great high-road. And lots of little poets camping on Whitman's camping ground now. But none going really beyond. Because Whitman's camp is at the end of the road, and on the edge of a great precipice. Over the precipice, blue distances, and the blue hollow of the future. But there is no way down. It is a dead end.

Pisgah. Pisgah sights. And Death. Whitman like a strange, modern, American Moses. Fearfully mistaken. And yet the great leader.
...
Now Whitman was a great moralist. He was a great leader. He was a great changer of the blood in the veins of men.

Surely it is especially true of American art, that it is all essentially moral. Hawthorne, Poe, Longfellow, Emerson, Melville: it is the moral issue which engages them. They all feel uneasy about the old morality. Sensuously, passionally, they all attack the old morality. But they know nothing better, mentally. Therefore they give tight mental allegiance to a morality which all their passion goes to destroy. Hence the duplicity which is the fatal flaw in them: most fatal in the most perfect American work of art, The Scarlet Letter [(1850), by Nathaniel Hawthorne (1804–64)]. Tight mental allegiance given to a morality which the passional self repudiates.

Whitman was the first to break the mental allegiance. He was the first to smash the old moral conception that the soul of man is something 'superior' and 'above' the flesh. Even Emerson still maintained this tiresome 'superiority' of the soul. Even Melville could not get over it. Whitman was the first heroic seer to seize the soul by the scruff of her neck and plant her down among the potsherds.

'There!' he said to the soul. 'Stay there!'

Stay there. Stay in the flesh. Stay in the limbs and lips and in the belly. Say in the breast and the womb. Stay there, Oh Soul, where you belong.

Stay in the dark limbs of negroes. Stay in the body of the prostitute. Stay in the sick flesh of the syphilitic. Stay in the marsh where the calamus grows. Stay there, Soul, where you belong.

The Open Road. The great home of the Soul is the open road. Not heaven, not paradise. Not 'above'. Not even 'within'. The soul is neither 'above' nor 'within'. It is a wayfarer down the open road.

... Meeting all the other wayfarers along the road. And how? How meet them, and how pass? With sympathy, says Whitman. Sympathy. He does not say love. He says sympathy. Feeling with. Feeling with them as they feel with themselves. Catching the vibration of their soul and flesh as we pass.

It is a new great doctrine. A doctrine of life. A new great morality. A morality of actual living, not of salvation. Europe has never got beyond the morality of salvation. America to this day is deathly sick with saviourism. But Whitman, the greatest and the first and the only American teacher, was no Saviour. His morality was no morality of salvation. His was a morality of the soul living her life, not saving herself. Accepting the contact with other souls along the open way, as they lived their lives. Never trying to save them. As leave try to arrest them and throw them in gaol. The soul living her life along the incarnate mystery of the open road.

This was Whitman. And the true rhythm of the American continent speaking out in him. He is the first white aboriginal.

...

It is the American heroic message. The soul is not to pile up defences round herself. She is not to withdraw and seek her heavens inwardly in mystical ecstasies. She is not cry to some God beyond, for salvation. She is to go down the open road, as the road opens, into the unknown, keeping company with those whose soul draws them near to her, accomplishing nothing save the journey, and the works incident to the journey, in the long life-travel into the unknown, the soul in her subtle sympathies accomplishing herself by the way.

This is Whitman's essential message. The heroic message of the American future. ...

Then Whitman's mistake. The mistake of his interpretation of his watchword: Sympathy. The mystery of SYMPATHY. He still compounded it with Jesus' LOVE, and with Paul's CHARITY. Whitman, like the rest of us, was at the end of the great emotional highway of LOVE. And because he couldn't help himself, he carried on his Open Road as a prolongation of the emotional highway of Love, beyond Calvary. The highway of Love ends at the foot of the Cross. There is no beyond. It was a hopeless attempt to prolong the highway of Love.

...

Now Whitman wanted his soul to save itself: *he* didn't want to save it. Therefore he did not need the great Christian receipt for saving the soul. He needed to supersede the Christian Charity, the Christian Love, within himself, in order to give his Soul her last freedom. The highroad of Love is no Open Road. It is a narrow, tight way, where the soul walks hemmed in between compulsions.

Whitman wanted to take his soul down the open road. And he failed in so far as he failed to get out of the old rut of Salvation. He forced his Soul to the edge of a cliff, and he looked down into death. And there he camped, powerless. He had carried out his Sympathy as an extension of Love and Charity. And it had brought him almost to madness and soul-death. It gave him his forced, unhealthy, post-mortem quality. ...

Whitman's essential message was the Open Road. The leaving of the soul free unto herself, the leaving of his fate to her and to the loom of the open road. Which is the bravest doctrine man has ever proposed to himself.

Alas, he didn't quite carry it out. He couldn't quite break the old maddening bond of the love-compulsion; he couldn't quite get out of the rut of the charity habit – for Love and Charity have degenerated now into habit: a bad habit.

Whitman said Sympathy. If only he had stuck to it! Because Sympathy means feeling with, not feeling for. He kept on having a passionate feeling *for* the negro slave, or the prostitute, or the syphilitic – which is merging. A sinking of Walt Whitman's soul in the souls of these others.

...

Supposing he had felt true sympathy with the negro slave? He would have felt *with* the negro slave. Sympathy – compassion – which is partaking of the passion which was in the soul of the negro slave.

What was the feeling in the negro's soul?

'Ah, I am a slave! Ah, it is bad to be a slave! I must free myself. My soul will die unless she frees herself. My soul says I must free myself.'

Whitman came along, and saw the slave, and said to himself: 'That negro slave is a man like myself. We share the same identity. And he is bleeding with wounds. Oh, oh, is it not myself who am also bleeding with wounds?'

This was not *sympathy*. It was merging and self-sacrifice.

...

Soul sympathizes with soul. And that which tries to kill my soul, my soul hates. My soul and my body are one. Soul and body wish to keep clean and whole. Only the mind is capable of great perversion. Only the mind tries to drive my soul and body into uncleanness and unwholesomeness.

What my soul loves, I love.
What my soul hates, I hate.
When my soul is stirred with compassion, I am compassionate.
When my soul turns away from them, I turn away from [it].

That is the *true* revelation of Whitman's creed: the true revelation of his Sympathy.

And my soul takes the open road. She meets the souls that are passing, she goes along with the souls that are going her way. And for one and all, she has sympathy. The sympathy of love, the sympathy of hate, the sympathy of simple proximity; all the subtle sympathizings of the incalculable soul, from the bitterest hate to passionate love.

It is not I who guide my soul to heaven. It is I who am guided by my own soul along the open road, where all men tread. Therefore, I must accept her deep motions of love, or hate, or compassion, or dislike, or indifference. And I must go where she takes me, for my feet and my lips and my body are my soul. It is I who must submit to her.

This is Whitman's message of American democracy.

The true democracy, where soul meets soul, in the open road. Democracy. American democracy where all journey down the open road, and where a soul is known at once in its going. Not by its clothes or appearance. Whitman did away with that. Not by its family name. Not even by its reputation. Whitman and Melville both discounted that. Not by a progression of piety, or by works of Charity. Not by works at all. Not by anything, but just itself. The soul passing unenhanced, passing on foot and being no more than itself. And recognized, and passed by or greeted according to the soul's dictate. If it be a great soul, it will be worshipped in the road.

The love of man and woman: a recognition of souls, and a communion of worship. The love of comrades: a recognition of souls, and a communion of worship. Democracy: a recognition of souls, all down the open road, and a great soul seen in its greatness, as it travels on foot among the rest, down the common way of the living. A glad recognition of souls, because they are the only riches.

Love, and Merging, brought Whitman to the edge of Death! Death! Death!

But the exultance of the message still remains. Purified of MERGING, purified of MYSELF, the exultant message of American Democracy, of souls in the Open Road, full of glad recognition, full of fierce readiness, full of the joy of worship, when one soul sees the greater soul.

The only riches, the great souls. □

(Lawrence, *Studies in Classic American Literature*, 1923)[14]

From the extracts in this chapter it can be seen that the critical history of Whitman's poetry is a peculiarly sharp object lesson in the *interestedness* of our critical practices. It shows how the texts we read, and the ways we read them, reflect back our own ideological assumptions. This can be seen by how Symonds' reading of Whitman demonstrates his fascination with Whitman's sexuality, and Santayana's makes apparent his own troubled relationship to America and its supposedly barbaric culture. Both Pound and Lawrence read Whitman as a prototypically 'modern' poet, one whose difficulties, ambiguities and conflicts speak to the condition of culture after the First World War. Likewise, criticism of Whitman in the 1940s and 1950s can again be seen to be reflective of the underlying cultural and ideological concerns of the day. Whitman's poetry in this period comes to be seen as one of a handful of texts central to the idea of an 'American Renaissance'. Critical evaluations of Whitman at this time, therefore, mirror back a concern to plot and explain the growth of American literary ideology, and, by extension, a distinct American culture. It is to such critical evaluations that we shall turn in the following chapter.

CHAPTER THREE

Whitman and the 'American Renaissance'

B ecause of its radical challenges to the poetic commonplace, its many
critical ambiguities and its overtly politicised agenda, Whitman's
poetry was to become the perfect focus for a generation of young
American critics who, in the 1940s, were seeking to enlarge the scope and
reputation of American Literature. Up to this point in America's literary
and critical history, its writers were considered very much as youthful
'second-cousins' – and rather provincial ones at that – to the more serious
and mature authors of England. The recognition of *Leaves of Grass* as a
literary 'classic', of lasting significance and profound complexity in its
dealings with the world, meant that this relationship between the litera-
tures of the old and new worlds had to be reassessed. In effect, American
critics looked back, pretty much for the first time, into their *own* literary
history, and saw that a century previously, American writers were already
producing works of immense importance. They saw that other American
writers – such as Emerson, Thoreau, Hawthorne and Melville – could be
considered alongside Whitman as contributing to this first flowering of a
distinctive American literary culture. Whitman's poetry, then, came to be
seen as a crucially important declaration of American cultural independ-
ence from the aesthetic canons of England and Europe. This flowering of
native American literary culture that began around the 1840s was named
by critic F. O. Matthiessen as the 'American Renaissance'. It is from his
hugely influential book *American Renaissance: Art and Expression in the Age
of Emerson and Whitman* (1941) that the first extract in this chapter is
taken. To introduce this, it is worth highlighting some of the main themes
and ideas that the notion of an 'American Renaissance' of the 1840s
brought to American critical thought of the 1940s, in order to consider the
impact such themes and ideas had on the development of the critical
history of Whitman's poetry.

The very idea of naming America's bid for cultural independence
the 'American Renaissance' is rather paradoxical. In delineating a pecu-
liarly American literary sensibility it seems strange to call upon an
aesthetic model, the Renaissance, that is largely seen as the highpoint

of cultural expression in Europe, one that plots the turning of Europe from a medieval into a modern culture. In the opening paragraph of *American Renaissance* Matthiessen is careful to clarify his use of the term 'renaissance':

■ It may not be precisely accurate to refer to our mid-nineteenth century as a *re-birth*; but that was how the writers themselves judged it. Not as a re-birth of values that had existed previously in America, but as America's way of producing a renaissance, by coming to its first maturity and affirming its rightful heritage in the whole expanse of art and culture.[1] □

The 'American Renaissance', then, is less a break with Europe's – specifically England's – literary models, than the rightful culmination of these within the American cultural scene. The tension that is expressed here, between Europe's literary tradition and America's sense of its lack of tradition, is one of the defining motifs of Whitman criticism since Matthiessen. And in Matthiessen, as we shall shortly see, and in the other two critical pieces which comprise this chapter, *Leaves of Grass* is read as a product of precisely this tension. Whitman's poetry arises, for them, out of the collision between the established values of the old world, and those, as yet culturally untested, forces of democracy and individualism that were felt to be the defining concepts of the new world in the mid-nineteenth century. As Randall Jarrell notes in the final essay of this chapter: 'How very American! If he and his country had not existed, it would have been impossible to imagine them.'

It should not be forgotten, too, that a hundred years later, Matthiessen's own tracing of an 'American Renaissance' arose from a particular set of historical and cultural tensions. Writing in 1941, on the eve of America's entry into the Second World War, he asserts that what unifies the five writers (Emerson, Thoreau, Hawthorne, Whitman and Melville) of his *American Renaissance* is 'their devotion to the possibilities of democracy'.[2] Matthiessen's idea of an 'American Renaissance', then, demonstrates to America its historical, and continuing devotion to an ideal of democracy, at exactly the moment when that liberal-humanist ideal was being challenged by the forces of totalitarianism. In arguing the case for America's cultural maturity on the grounds of the devotion of its classic writers to democracy, *American Renaissance* also speaks of America's political duties to a world where democracy is under threat. America's rise to political pre-eminence in the post-war years seems, therefore, to go hand-in-hand with its ability, in works such as Matthiessen's, to define and defend itself culturally. It is very clear, then, how *Leaves of Grass* could become a text co-opted by its critics to reflect their own cultural concerns. For critics writing in the immediate aftermath of the First World War, Whitman had spoke to modern, post-war sensibilities. Seen as central to the idea of an 'American Renaissance' in the 1940s (and later), Whitman's poetry was now read as a text that reflected the power struggles of a world concerned to uphold democracy, and of a country seeking an identity for itself within that world.

Largely because of the powerful rhetoric of Whitman's poetry, it is his language and its forcefulness that receives the most sustained critical attention from Matthiessen and other critics of this period. His poetry is read as encoding peculiarly American speech patterns, the 'distinct identity' of American English that provides Matthiessen with the starting point for his examination of Whitman's great American 'language experiment'. But it is thereby felt also to present a new poetic relation to reality, to the America that unfolds in his verses. For Charles Feidelson and Randall Jarrell, the other two critics whose essays comprise this chapter, Whitman's poetics is one that challenges us to re-engage America, to see both poem and America as an act of the nerves (Jarrell), or an act that partakes of the 'endless becoming of reality' (Feidelson). As a rugged individual who embodies Emerson's ideal of self-reliance, though, Whitman – or at least the poetic persona he adopts in *Leaves of Grass* – is assured of his all-important role in Matthiessens's 'American Renaissance'. Whitman is seen by him, therefore, as the hero of a truly American poetic epic, 'one of the roughs' who nevertheless speaks words powerful as Shakespeare's because he speaks for the common people.

■ One aspect of Whitman's work that has not yet received its due attention is outlined in *An American Primer*, notes for a lecture that he seems to have collected mainly between 1855 and 1860 ... This lecture, which, as he says, 'does not suggest the invention but describes the growth of an American English enjoying a distinct identity', remained, like most of Whitman's lectures, undelivered and unpublished at his death. But he often talked to [Horace] Traubel about it in the late eighteen-eighties, telling him that he never quite got its subject out of his mind, that he had long thought of making it into a book, and adding: 'I sometimes think the *Leaves* is only a language experiment.' ...

He understood that language was not 'an abstract construction' made by the learned, but that it had arisen out of the work and needs, the joys and struggles and desires of long generations of humanity, and that it had 'its bases broad and low, close to the ground.' Words were not arbitrary inventions, but the product of human events and customs, the progeny of folkways. Consequently he believed that the fresh opportunities for the English tongue in America were immense, offering themselves in the whole range of American facts. His poems, by cleaving to these facts, could thereby release 'new potentialities' of expression for our native character. ...

Thus Whitman seems to show the very dichotomy between the material and the ideal, the concrete and the abstract that [can be] observed in

Emerson's remarks on language. Nevertheless, when we look at their poems, it is obvious that Whitman often bridged the gap in a way that Emerson could not.

One of Whitman's demands in the *Primer* was that words should be brought into literature from factories and farms and trades, for he knew that 'around the markets, among the fish-smacks, along the wharves, you hear a thousand words, never yet printed in the repertoire of any lexicon'. What resulted was sometimes as mechanical as the long lists in 'A Song for Occupations,' but his resolve for inclusiveness also produced dozens of snap-shot impressions as accurate as

The butcher-boy puts off his killing-clothes, or sharpens his knife
　　　　　　　　　　　　　　　at the stall in the market,
I loiter enjoying his repartee and his shuffle and break-down.

Watching men in action called out of him some of his most fluid phrases, which seem to bathe and surround the objects they describe – as this, of the blacksmiths:

The *lithe sheer* of their waists plays even with their massive arms.

Or this,

The negro holds firmly the reins of his four horses, the black *swags*
　　　　　　　　　　　　　　underneath on its tied-over chain.

Or a line that is itself a description of the very process by which he enfolds such movement:

In me the caresser of life wherever moving, backward as well as
　　　　　　　　　　　　　　forward *sluing.*

At times he produced suggestive coinages of his own:

The blab of the pave, tires of carts, sluff of boot-soles, talk of the
　　　　　　　　　　　　　　promenaders.

Yet he is making various approaches to language even in that one line. 'Blab' and 'stuff' have risen from his desire to suggest actual sounds, but 'promenaders', which also sounds well, has clearly been employed for that reason alone since it does not belong to the talk of any American folk. 'Pave' instead of 'pavement' is the kind of bastard word that, to use another, Whitman liked to 'promulge'. Sometimes it is hard to tell whether such words sprang from intention or ignorance, particularly in view of the appearance of 'semitic' in place of 'seminal' ('semitic muscle', 'semitic milk') in both the 1855 preface and the first printing of 'A Woman Waits for Me'. Most frequently his hybrids take the form of the free substitution of one part of speech for another – sometimes quite effectively ('the soothe of the waves'), sometimes less so (she that 'birth'd him').

Although it has been estimated that Whitman had a vocabulary of more than thirteen thousand words, of which slightly over half were used by him only once, the number of his authentic coinages is not very large. Probably the largest group is composed of his agent-nouns, which is not surprising for a poet who was so occupied with types and classes of men and women. Unfortunately these also furnish some of the ugliest-sounding words in his pages, 'originatress', 'revoltress', 'dispensatress', which have hardly been surpassed even in the age of the realtor and the beautician. He was luckier with an occasional abstract noun like 'presidentiad,' though this is offset by a needless monstrosity like 'savantism'. The one kind of coinage where his ear was listening sensitively is in such compounds as 'the transparent green-shine' of the water around the naked swimmer in 'I Sing the Body Electric', or that evoking the apples hanging 'indolent-ripe' in 'Halcyon Days'.

His belief in the need to speak not merely for Americans but for the workers of all lands seems to have given the impetus for his odd habit of introducing random words from other languages, to the point of talking about 'the ouvrier class'! He took from the Italian chiefly the terms of the opera, also, 'viva', 'romanza', and even 'ambulanza'. From the Spanish he was pleased to borrow the orotund way of naming his countrymen 'Americanos,' while the occasional circulation of Mexican dollars in the States during the eighteen-forties may have given him his word 'Libertad'. His favourite 'camerado', an archaic English version of the Spanish 'camerada', seems most likely to have come to him from the pages of the Waverley novels, of which he had been an enthusiastic reader in his youth. But the smattering of French which he picked up on his trip to New Orleans, and which constituted the most extensive knowledge that he ever was to have of another tongue, furnished him with the majority of his borrowings. It allowed him to talk of his 'amour' and his 'élèves', of a 'soirée' or an 'accoucheur', of 'trottoirs' and 'feuillage' and 'delicatesse'; to say that his were not 'the songs of an ennuyéed person,' or to shout, 'Allons! From all formules!... Allons! The road is before us!' Frequently he was speaking no language, as when he proclaimed himself 'no dainty dolce affetuoso.' But he could go much farther than that into a foreign jargon in his desire to 'eclaircise the myths Asiatic' in his 'Passage to India', or to fulfil 'the rapt promises and luminè of seers'. He could address God, with ecstatic and monumental tastelessness, as 'thou reservoir'.

Many of these are samples of the confused American effort to talk big by using high-sounding terms with only the vaguest notion of their original meaning. ... [Whitman's] transformations retain some battered semblance of the original word, which, with the happy pride of the half-educated in the learned term, he then deployed grandly for purposes of his own. Often the attraction for him in the French words ran counter to the identification he usually desired between the word and the thing, since it sprang from intoxication with the mere sound. You can observe the same tendency in some of the jotted lists of his notebooks, 'Cantaloupe. Muskmelon. Cantabile. Cacique City', or in his shaping such a generalized description of the earth as 'O vast rondure swimming in space'. ...

The two diverging strains in his use of language were with him to the end, for he never outgrew his tendency to lapse from specific images into undifferentiated and lifeless abstractions, as in the closing phrase of this description of his grandfather: 'jovial, red, stout, with sonorous voice and characteristic physiognomy'.... In his fondness for all his *Leaves*, he seems never to have perceived what we can note in the two halves of a single line,

I concentrate toward them that are nigh, I wait on the door slab,

– the contrast between the clumsy stilted opening and the simple close. The total pattern of his speech is, therefore, difficult to chart, since it is formed both by the improviser's carelessness about words and by the kind of attention to them indicated in his telling Burroughs that he had been 'searching for twenty-five years for the word to express what the twilight note of the robin meant to him'....

In a warm appreciation of Burns in *November Boughs*, Whitman said that 'his brightest hit is his use of the Scotch patois, so full of terms flavor'd like wild fruits or berries'. Thinking not only of Burns he relished a special charm in 'the very neglect, unfinish, careless nudity', which were not to be found in more polished language and verse. But his suggested comparison between the Scotch poet and himself would bring out at once the important difference that Whitman is not using anything like a folk-speech. Indeed, his phrasing is generally remote from any customary locutions of the sort that he jotted down as notes for one unwritten poem. This was to have been based on a free rendering of local native calls, such as 'Here goes your fine fat oysters – Rock Point oysters – here they go'. When put beside such natural words and cadences, Whitman's usual diction is clearly not that of a countryman but of what he called himself, 'a jour printer'. In its curious amalgamation of homely and simple usage with half-remembered terms he read once somewhere, and with casual inventions of the moment, he often gives the impression of using a language not quite his own. In his determination to strike up for a new world, he deliberately rid himself of foreign models. But, so far as his speech is concerned, this was only very partially possible, and consequently Whitman reveals the peculiarly American combination of a childish freshness with a mechanical and desiccated repetition of book terms that had had significance for the more complex civilization in which they had had their roots and growth. The freshness has come, as it did to Huck Finn, through instinctive rejection of the authority of those terms, in Whitman's reaction against what he called Emerson's cold intellectuality: 'Suppose his books becoming absorb'd, the permanent chyle ['digestive juice'] of American general and particular character – what a well-wash'd and grammatical, but bloodless and helpless race we should turn out!'

Yet the broken chrysalis of the old restrictions still hangs about Whitman. Every page betrays that his language is deeply ingrained with the educational habits of a middle-class people who put a fierce emphasis on the importance of the written word. His speech did not spring primarily from the contact with the soil, for though his father was a descendent of

Long Island farmers, he was also a citizen of the age of reason, an acquaintance and admirer of Tom Paine. Nor did Whitman himself develop his diction as Thoreau did, by the slow absorption through every pore of the folkways of a single spot of earth. He was attracted by the wider sweep of the city, and though his language is a natural product, it is the natural product of a Brooklyn journalist of the eighteen-forties who had previously been a country schoolteacher and a carpenter's helper, and who had finally felt an irresistible impulse to be a poet. □

(F. O. Matthiessen, *American Renaissance: Art and Expression in the Age of Emerson and Whitman*, 1941)[3]

Matthiessen's reading of Whitman maintains that what keeps his poetry alive is his power to 'show the very dichotomy between the material and the ideal, the concrete and the abstract'. When most successful, Whitman's language is equal to the task of bringing together these 'two diverging strains', and, according to Matthiessen, this ability lies at the heart of Whitman's democratic impulse for it allows him to become a poetic representative for humanity: 'When his words adhere to concrete experience and yet are bathed in imagination, his statements become broadly representative of humanity.' Effectively, what this means is that Matthiessen manages to turn a poetic virtue into a political one. For him, the density and ambiguities of Whitman's poetic texture become synonymous with his status as the representative poet of American democracy. The description, then, of Whitman's 'irresistible urge to be a poet' with which the earlier passage closes, is, Matthiessen implies, part of a wider, and equally irresistible, American urge towards democracy. Matthiessen's Whitman, therefore, in his attention to the great language experiment that is America, demonstrates his 'devot[ion] to the possibilities of democracy'.

In contrast, the next critical extract, from Charles Feidelson's *Symbolism and American Literature*, attends to the symbolic patterns of Whitman's poetry. Finding most of Whitman's antebellum poetry rather too anxious to point to issues or concerns, be they personal or cultural, that he feels are extrinsic to the text, he declares Whitman's elegy for Lincoln, 'When Lilacs last in the Dooryard Bloom'd', to be his 'best poem', because of its internally consistent patterns of imagery and symbol. He then conducts a close reading of the way in which this poem's recurring symbols of lilac, star and singing bird enact a drama of the processes of poetic composition. If this poem has a mythic and symbolic structure, he argues, then this is because it is a highly wrought work of art, and should be read as such. To attempt to read its symbolism as an index – whether conscious or unconscious – of its society, or its author's state of mind, is to do a disservice to its aesthetic worth. This ideal of aesthetic autonomy, the belief or at least the hope that the importance of literary works of art is unaffected by social and cultural circumstances, is typical of the school of thought that dominated American literary criticism of the 1950s, the so-called 'New Criticism', and will be discussed at greater length in the following chapter of this Guide.

Because of his adoption of New Critical models of thought, Feidelson dismisses Matthiessen's *American Renaissance*, which he feels to be too concerned with cultural, as opposed to aesthetic matters. This is seen in the short passage that follows, from the 'Introduction' to his *Symbolism and American Literature*:

■ The first large-scale attempt to define the literary quality of American writing at its best was Matthiessen's *American Renaissance*, which is 'primarily concerned with *what* these books were as works of art,' with 'the writers' use of their own tools, their diction and rhetoric, and ... what they could make with them.' Yet even in this magnificent work, which reorients the entire subject, the sociological and political bent of studies in American literature makes itself felt indirectly. Despite Matthiessen's emphasis on literary form, his concern with the 'artist's use of language' as 'the most sensitive index to cultural history' tends to lead him away from specifically aesthetic problems. The 'one common denominator' which he finds among the five writers treated in his book is not, in the final analysis, a common approach to the art of writing but a common theme – 'their devotion to the possibilities of democracy.'[4] □

Feidelson's argument throughout his book is neatly encapsulated in this statement. The value of American literature is not, for him, because it reveals something about democracy, or American culture, but that it works, through its use of symbolism, as literature. If the determining myth for Matthiessen is democracy, then for Feidelson it is aesthetics.

Because of this, however, Whitman proves to be a peculiarly recalcitrant figure for Feidelson. Whilst he acknowledges that Whitman's work seems to derive from his attempts to ' "tally" the American scene', his analysis of the poetry struggles to disengage it from such wider cultural circumstances. In short, his critical practice simply cannot fully engage with Whitman's poetry. This is particularly disappointing because Feidelson does seem very capable of sensing some of the most important pressures operating in Whitman. Most notably, he is able to point out more clearly than perhaps any other critic before him the way in which Whitman's poetry does not merely describe, as he puts it, a 'completed act of perception', but 'constitutes the act itself'. However, Feidelson is hamstrung by a critical practice that allows him to see such a poetics of process only as an index of 'aesthetic problems', rather than a means of unlocking and examining Whitman's 'cultural history'. From the outset he sets out to challenge Whitman through his insistence on reading his poetry as solely, 'a literary performance':

■ 'No one will get at my verses', Whitman declared, 'who insists upon viewing them as a literary performance, or attempt at such performance, or as aiming mainly toward art or aestheticism'. In his conscious literary theory literature is subordinate to sociology, 'the United States themselves are essentially the greatest poem', the poet must 'tally' the American scene, and the function of poetry is the creation of heroic citizens. Yet it is obvious that a larger principle governs both his poetic and his sociological doctrine; no one will get at his verses who insists upon viewing them as a sociological performance. Whitman intimates that the link between his poems and American life is actually a new method exemplified by both:

One main contrast of the ideas behind every page of my verses, compared with establish'd poems, is their different relative attitude towards God, towards the objective universe, and still more (by reflection, confession, assumption, &c.) the quite changed attitude of the ego, the one chanting or talking, towards himself and towards his fellow-humanity. It is certainly time for America, above all, to begin this readjustment in the scope and basis point of view of verse; for everything else has changed.

The distinctive quality of Whitman's poetry depends on this change of standpoint. In his effort 'to articulate and faithfully express ... [his] own physical, moral, intellectual and aesthetic Personality, in the midst of, and tallying, the momentous spirit and facts of its immediate days', his interest is not so much in the Personality of the environment per se as in the 'changed attitude of the ego'. The new method is better defined in the poems themselves than in the critical prose. The ego appears in the poems as a traveler and an explorer, not as a static observer; its object is 'to know the universe itself as a road, as many roads, as roads for traveling souls'. The shift of image from the contemplative eye of 'establish'd poems' to the voyaging ego of Whitman's poetry records a large-scale theoretical shift from the categories of 'substance' to those of 'process'. Whitman's 'perpetual journey' is not analogous to a sight-seeing trip, though his catalogues might give that impression; the mind and the material world into which it ventures are not ultimately different in kind. Instead, what seems at first a penetration of nature by the mind is actually a process in which the known world comes into being. The 'child who went forth every day, and who now goes, and will always go forth every day', is indistinguishable from the world of his experience: 'The first object he look'd upon, that object he became, / And that object became part of him.' The true voyage is the endless becoming of reality:

Allons! To that which is endless as it was beginningless,
To undergo much, tramp of days, rests of nights,
To merge all in the travel they tend to, and the days and nights
                                        they tend to
Again to merge them in the start of superior journeys. ...

Here there is no clear distinction among the traveler, the road, and the journey, for the journey is nothing but the progressive unity of the voyager and the lands he enters; perception, which unites the seer and the seen, is identical with the real process of becoming. God, in this context, is a 'seething principle', and human society is a flow of 'shapes ever projecting other shapes'. Whitman's 'readjustment in the scope and basic point of view of verse' is actually a transmutation of all supposed entities into events.

A poem, therefore, instead of referring to a completed act of perception, constitutes the act itself, both in the author and in the reader; instead of describing reality, a poem is a realization. When Whitman writes, 'See, steamers streaming through my poems', he is admonishing both himself and his audience that no distinction can be made between themselves, the steamers, and the words. Indeed, no distinction can be made between the poet and the reader: 'It is you talking just as much as myself, I act as the tongue of you.' His new method was predicated not only on the sense of creative vision – itself a process which renders the world in process – but also, as part and parcel of that consciousness, on the sense of creative speech. The 'I' of Whitman's poems speaks the world that he sees, and sees the world that he speaks, and does this by *becoming* the reality of his vision and of his words, in which the reader also participates.

The reader is not given statements but is set in action, 'on the assumption that the process of reading is not a half-sleep, but in the highest sense, and exercise, a gymnast's struggle'. The poem necessarily works 'by curious removes, indirections', rather than direct imitation of nature, since 'the image-making faculty' runs counter to the habit of mind which views the material world as separable from ideas and speech. ... The 'language experiment' of *Leaves of Grass* – its promise of 'new potentialities of speech' – depends on the symbolic status claimed by the book as a whole and in every part. 'From the eyesight proceeds another eyesight and from the hearing proceeds another hearing and from the voice proceeds another voice eternally curious of the harmony of things with man.'

The patent symbols of Whitman's best poem, 'When Lilacs Last in the Dooryard Bloom'd', are conditioned by the thoroughgoing symbolism of his poetic attitude. As in most elegies, the person mourned is hardly more than the occasion of the work; but this poem, unlike [Milton's] *Lycidas* or [Shelley's] *Adonais*, does not transmute the central figure merely by generalizing him out of all recognition.[5] Lincoln is seldom mentioned either as a person or as a type. Instead, the focus of the poem is a presentation of the poet's mind at work in the context of Lincoln's death. If the true subject of *Lycidas* and *Adonais* is not Edward King or John Keats but the Poet, the true subject of Whitman's 'Lilacs' is not the Poet but the poetic process. And even this subject is not treated simply by generalizing a particular situation. The act of poetizing and the context in which it takes place have continuity in time and space but no particular existence. Both are 'ever-returning'; the tenses shift; the poet is in different places at once; and at the end this whole phase of creation is moving inexorably forward.

Within this framework the symbols behave like characters in a drama, the plot of which is the achievement of a poetic utterance. The spring, the constant process of rebirth, is threaded by the journey of the coffin, the constant process of death, and in the first section it presents the poet with twin symbols: the perennially blooming lilac and the drooping star. The spring also brings to the poet the 'thought of him I love', in which the duality of life and death is repeated. The thought of the dead merges with the fallen star in Section 2; the thought of love merges with the life of the lilac, from which the poet breaks a sprig in Section 3. Thus the lilac and the star enter the poem not as objects to which the poet assigns a meaning but as elements in the undifferentiated stream of thoughts and things; and the spring, the real process of becoming, which involves the real process of dissolution, is also the genesis of poetic vision. The complete pattern of the poem is established with the advent of the bird in the fourth section. For here, in the song of the thrush, the lilac and star are united (the bird sings 'death's outlet song of life'), and the potentiality of the bird and the thought of the poet, which also unites life and death, both lay claim to the third place in the 'trinity' brought about by spring; they are, as it were, the actuality and the possibility of poetic utterance, which reconciles opposite appearances.

The drama of the poem will be a movement from possible to actual poetic speech, as represented by the 'tallying' of the songs of the poet and the thrush. Although it is a movement without steps, the whole being implicit in every moment, there is a graduation of emphasis. Ostensibly, the visions of the coffin and the star (Sections 5 through 8) delay the unison of poet and bird, so that full actualization is reserved for the end of the poem. On the other hand, the verse that renders the apparition of the coffin *is* 'death's outlet song of life'. The poetic act of evoking the dark journey is treated as the showering of death with lilac:

Here, the coffin slowly passes,
I give you my sprig of lilac ...
Blossoms and branches green to coffins all I bring,
For fresh as the morning, thus would I chant a song for you,
     O sane and sacred death.

Even as the poet lingers, he has attained his end. And the star of Section 8, the counterpart of the coffin, functions in much the same way. The episode that occurred 'a month since' – when 'my soul in its trouble dissatisfied sank, as where you sad orb, / Concluded, dropt in the night and was gone' – was a failure of the poetic spring. The soul was united with the star but not with the lilac. Yet the passage is preceded by the triumphant statement, 'Now I know what you must have meant', and knowledge issues in the ability to render the episode in verse. The perception of meaning gives life to the fact of death; the star meant the death of Lincoln, but the evolution of the meaning is poetry.

The recurrence of the song of the thrush in the following section and in Section 13 is a reminder of the poetic principle which underlies the entire poem. In a sense, the words, 'I hear your notes, I hear your call', apply to all that precedes and all that is to come, for the whole poem, existing in the eternal present, is the 'loud human song' of the poet's 'brother'. But again Whitman delays the consummation. He is 'detained' from his rendezvous with the bird – although he really 'hears' and 'understands' all the time – by the sight of the 'lustrous star' and by the 'mastering odor' of the lilac. Since both the star and the lilac are inherent in the song of the bird, he actually lingers only in order to proceed. While the song rings in the background, the poet puts the questions pre-supposed by his own poeticizing. How can the life of song be one with the fact of death? – 'O what shall I hang on the chamber walls ... / To adorn the burial-house of him I love?' The questions answer themselves. The breath by which the grave becomes part of his chant is the breath of life; within the poem the image of the 'burial-house' will be overlaid with 'pictures of the growing spring'. The delay has served only to renew the initial theme: the poet's chant, like the song of the thrush, is itself the genesis of life and therefore contains both life and death.

The final achievement of poetic utterance comes in Section 14, when the poet, looking forth on the rapid motion of life, experiences death. More exactly, he walks between the 'thought' and the 'knowledge' of death, which move beside him like companions. Just as his poem exists between the 'thought' of the dead, which is paradoxically an act of life, and the actual knowledge of the bird's song, which embodies both dying star and living lilac, the poet himself is in motion from the potential to the actual. From this point to the end of the poem, the sense of movement never flags. The poet's flight into the darkness is a fusion with the stream of music from the bird:

> And the charm of the carol rapt me,
> As I held as if by their hands my comrades in the night,
> And the voice of my spirit tallied the song of the bird.

As the motion of the poet is lost in the motion of the song, the latter is identified with the 'dark mother always gliding near', and in the 'floating' carol death itself becomes the movement of waves that 'undulate round the world'. In effect, poet and bird, poem and song, life and death, are now the sheer process of the carol; as in 'Out of the Cradle Endlessly Rocking', reality is the unfolding of the Word. ...

Yet 'When Lilacs Last in the Dooryard Bloom'd' is a successful poem only because it does not fully live up to the theory which it both states and illustrates. The poem really presupposes a static situation, which Whitman undertakes to treat as though it were dynamic; in the course of the poem the death of Lincoln, of which we always remain aware, is translated into Whitman's terms of undifferentiated flow. His other long poems generally lack this stabilizing factor. Whatever the nominal subject, it is soon lost in sheer 'process'; all roads lead into the 'Song of Myself', in which the bare Ego interacts with a miscellaneous world. The result is Whitman's characteristic disorder and turgidity. When the subject is endless, any form becomes arbitrary. While the antirational conception of a poem as the realization of language gives a new freedom and a new dignity to poetry, it apparently leads to an aimlessness from which the poem can be rescued only by returning to rational categories. ...

And much worse can be expected. In the last section of 'Passage to India', Whitman's most deliberate statement of the process theory, the tone is frenetic even for him:

Sail forth – steer for the deep waters only,
Reckless O soul, exploring, I with thee, and thou with me,
For we are bound where the mariner has not yet dared to go,
And we will risk the ship, ourselves and all.

What begins in Emerson as a mild contravention of reason – a peaceful journey 'to some frontier as yet unvisited by the elder voyagers' – becomes in Whitman a freedom from all 'limits and imaginary lines',

... from all formules!
From your formules, O bat-eyed and materialistic priests.

Thus looseness of form in Whitman's verse is not merely a technical defect; it is the counterpart of an intellectual anarchism designed to overthrow conventional reality by dissolving all rational order. ...

Nowadays we are too much in the habit of blaming 'romanticism' for any irrationality in literature. Certainly the romantic spirit was enamored of a fluid reality, which could not be contained in the old channels, and the romantic often opened the dikes deliberately, just to see what would happen. The Voyager is a romantic figure, the ocean a romantic realm. Yet a distinction is in order. The antirationalism of the romantic voyage is a wilful projection of feeling; the romantic sea is the image of a world subservient to emotion. But the symbolistic voyage is a process of becoming: Whitman is less concerned with exploration of emotion than with exploration as a mode of existence. Similarly, his poems not only are *about* voyaging but also enact the voyage, so that their content (the image of the metaphysical journey) is primarily a reflection of their literary method, in which the writer and his subject become part of the stream of language. It follows that Whitman's hostility to reason has another, more complicated source than the romantic vision of a world suffused with feeling. Like Emerson, he finds the antonym of reason not in emotion but in the 'symbolical'; like Hawthorne and Melville, he contrasts 'analysis' with 'meaning', arithmetic with 'significance'. For his object is not so much to impose a new form on the world as to adopt a new stance in which the world takes on new shapes. His difficulty is that his method works too well: the shapes proliferate endlessly, and, having deprived himself of an external standpoint, he has no means of controlling them. On the other hand, the occasional violence of his antirationalism is the result of an opposite

difficulty: while he would like to be sublimely indifferent to established dis-
tinctions, reason fights back as he seeks to transcend it, and he is forced
into the position of the iconoclast. □
                    (Charles Feidelson, *Symbolism and American Literature*, 1953)[6]

For the final critic of this chapter, Randall Jarrell (whose essay
'Some Lines from Whitman' was published in 1955, just some two
years after Feidelson's book), Whitman's iconoclastic position is
undoubted. It is, in fact, his major strength and needs to be reasserted
in order to rescue Whitman from a reputation that those who 'admire
Whitman most' are 'people who are not particularly interested in
poetry'. So, in a manner that is strikingly similar to Matthiessen and
Feidelson, Jarrell strives to bring Whitman back to poetry lovers, by
emphasising his complex and involved poetic language, and demon-
strating his consummate skills as a poet. Indeed, in some quite curious
ways, all three critical pieces in this chapter share assumptions about
America's literary performance, ones shaped by prevailing New Critical
attitudes. For the literary critic of the mid-twentieth century, then,
American poetry – with Whitman as its example – was supposed to
carve out a space for itself, to demonstrate a language and procedure
that was different from literatures that had preceded it. Underneath its
complex and richly textured poetic surface was to be discovered an aes-
thetic pattern, a bulwark against flux and chaos. As we have seen, how-
ever, assessments of Whitman's abilities to achieve such standards vary.
In major ways for both Matthiessen and Feidelson, Whitman's poetry is
flawed.

For Randall Jarrell, however, there are no question marks over
Whitman's greatness. Jarrell's response is – like that of Matthiessen and
Feidelson – to Whitman's use of language. However, as a highly accom-
plished poet himself, he has a wonderful ear for Whitman's sense of
poetic cadence, and his delicacy of touch. Here is no bombastic rhetori-
cian, Jarrell argues, 'but a poet of the greatest and oddest delicacy and
originality, and sensitivity'. Unlike other Whitman critics, Jarrell has
therefore no difficulty in reconciling himself to Whitman's mistakes. On
the one hand he is able to see them as part of a necessary poetic process
by which is developed an acutely sensitive poetic expression. And on
the other, he is simply untroubled by Whitman's inconsistencies.
Unlike Matthiessen and Feidelson he does not seek to impose a coher-
ent pattern upon Whitman's poetry; he is content to discover a genuine
American poetic voice.

Jarrell sees Whitman as a poet of 'dazzling originality' because of his
ability to deal with the here and now in his poetry. The experience of
reading Whitman is one in which 'the *thereness* and *suchness* of the
world are [made] incarnate', and it is thus an experience in which the

reader must participate. Whitman's dense poetic textures, therefore, invite participation in the poetic processes of the world. It is in this sense that Jarrell is able to reconcile the positions of Matthiessen and Feidelson, for such a participatory poetics is not only an index of Whitman's own participation in his 'cultural history', but it also demands skills of close and attentive – participatory – reading. To see Whitman as a poet who goes on his nerves, then, is to see him as deeply and unmistakably an American poet. It is this recognition that gives energy and force to Jarrell's extraordinary and powerful reading of Whitman:

■ Whitman, Dickinson and Melville seem to me the best poets of the nineteenth century here in America. Melville's poetry has been grotesquely underestimated, but ... in spite of the awkwardness and amateurishness of so much of it, it will surely be thought well of.... Dickinson's poetry has been thoroughly read, and well though undifferentiatingly loved – after a few decades or centuries almost everybody will be able to see through Dickinson to her poems. But something odd has happened to the living changing part of Whitman's reputation: nowadays it is people who are not particularly interested in poetry, people who say they read a poem for what it says, not for how it says it, who admire Whitman most. Whitman is often written about, either approvingly or disapprovingly, as if he were the Thomas Wolfe [(1900–1938): American writer famed for his fictionalized auto-biographical novels, realist prose style, and mythical hard-drinking], of nineteenth-century democracy, the hero of a de Mille [Cecil B. de Mille (1881–1959): film director, famous for his large-scale epic films, often based on biblical themes] movie about Walt Whitman....

To show Whitman for what he is one does not need to praise or explain or argue, one needs simply to quote. He himself said, 'I and mine do not convince by arguments, similes, rhymes, / We convince by our presence.' Even a few of his phrases are enough to show us that Whitman was no sweeping rhetorician, but a poet of the greatest and oddest delicacy and originality, and sensitivity, so far as words are concerned. This is, after all, the poet who said, 'Blind loving wrestling touch, sheath'd hooded sharp-tooth'd touch'; who said, 'Smartly attired, countenance smiling, form upright, death under the breast-bones, hell under the skull-bones'; who said, 'Agonies are one of my change of garments'; who saw grass as the 'flag of my disposition', saw 'the sharp-peak'd farmhouse, with its scallop'd scum and slender shoots from the gutters', heard a plane's 'wild ascending lisp', and saw and heard how at the amputation 'what is removed drops horribly in a pail'. This is the poet for whom the sea was 'howler and scooper of storms', reaching out to us with 'crooked inviting fingers'; who went 'leaping chasms with a pike-pointed staff, clinging to topples of brittle and blue'; who, a runaway slave, saw how 'my gore drips, thinn'd with the ooze of my skin'; who went 'lithographing Kronos ... buying drafts of

Osiris'; who stared out at the 'little plentiful mannikins skipping around in collars and tail'd coats, / I am aware who they are, (they are positively not worms or fleas)'. For he is, at his best, beautifully witty: he says gravely, 'I find I incorporate gneiss, coals, long-threaded moss, fruits, grain, esculent roots, / And am stucco'd with quadrupeds and birds all over'; and of these quadrupeds and birds 'not one is respectable or unhappy over the whole earth'. He calls advice: 'Unscrew the locks from the doors! Unscrew the doors from their jambs!' He publishes the results of research: 'Having pried through the strata, analyz'd to a hair, counsel'd with doctors and calculated close, / I find no sweeter fat than sticks to my own bones.' Everybody remembers how he told the Muse to 'cross out please those immensely overpaid accounts, / That matter of Troy and Achilles' wrath, and Aeneas', Odysseus' wanderings', but his account of the 'illustrious emigré' here in the New World is even better: 'Bluff'd not a bit by drainpipe, gasometer, artificial fertilizers, / Smiling and pleas'd with palpable intent to stay, / She's here, install'd amid the kitchenware.' ... How can one quote enough? If the reader thinks that all this is like Thomas Wolfe he *is* Thomas Wolfe; nothing else could explain it. Poetry like this is as far as possible from the work of any ordinary rhetorician, whose phrases cascade over us like the suds of the oldest and most-advertised detergent.

The interesting thing about Whitman's worst language (for, just as few poets have ever written better, few poets have ever written worse) is how unusually absurd, how really ingeniously bad, such language is. I will quote none of the most famous examples; but even a line like *O Culpable! I acknowledge. I exposé!* is not anything that you and I could do – only a man with the most extraordinary feel for language, or none whatsoever, could have cooked up Whitman's worst messes. For instance: what other man in all the history of this planet would have said, 'I am a habitan of Vienna'? (One has an immediate vision of him as a sort of French-Canadian half-breed to whom the Viennese are offering, with trepidation, through the bars of a zoological garden, little mounds of whipped cream.) And *enclaircise* – why it's as bad as *explicate*! We are right to resent his having made up his own horrors, instead of sticking to ones that we ourselves employ. But when Whitman says, 'I dote on myself, there is a lot of me and all so luscious', we should realize that we are not the only ones who are amused. And the queerly bad and merely queer and queerly good will often change into one another without warning: 'Hefts of the moving world, at innocent gambols silently rising, freshly exuding, / Scooting obliquely high and low' – not good, but *queer*! – suddenly becomes, 'Something I cannot see puts up libidinous prongs, / Seas of bright juice suffuse heaven', and it is sunrise.

But it is not in individual lines and phrases, but in the passages of some length, that Whitman is at his best. In the following quotation Whitman has something difficult to express, something that there are many formulas, all bad, for expressing; he expresses it with complete success, in language of the most dazzling originality:

The orchestra whirls me wider than Uranus flies,
It wrenches such ardors from me I did not know I possess'd them,
It sails me, I dab with bare feet, they are lick'd by the indolent waves,
I am cut by bitter and angry hail, I lose my breath,
    Steep'd amid honey'd morphine, my windpipe throttled in fakes of
                                             death,
At length let up again to feel the puzzle of puzzles,
And that we call Being.

One hardly knows what to point at – everything works. But *wrenches* and
did not know I possess'd them; the incredible *it sails me, I dab with bare feet;*
lick'd by the indolent; Steep'd amid honey'd morphine; my windpipe throttled
in fakes of death – no wonder Crane admired Whitman! This originality, as
absolute in its way as that of Berlioz' orchestration, is often at Whitman's
command...And he has at his command a language of the calmest and
most prosaic reality, one that seems to do no more than present:

The little one sleeps in its cradle.
I lift the gauze and look a long time, and silently brush away flies
                                          with my hand.
The youngster and the red-faced girl turn aside up the bushy hill,
I peeringly view them from the top.
The suicide sprawls on the bloody floor of the bedroom.
I witness the corpse with its dabbled hair, I note where the pistol has
                                          fallen.

It is like magic: that is, something has been done to us without our
knowing how it was done; but if we look at the lines again we see the
gauze, silently, youngster, red-faced, bushy, peeringly, dabbled – not that this
is all we see. 'Present! Present!' said James; these are presented, put
down side by side to form a little 'view of life', from the cradle to the last
bloody floor of the bedroom....
Whitman says once that the 'look of the bay mare shames silliness out
of me'. This is true – sometimes it is true; but more often the silliness and
affection and cant and exaggeration are there shamelessly, the Old Adam
that was in Whitman from the beginning and the awful new one that he
created to keep it company. But as he says, 'I know perfectly well my own
egotism, / Know my omnivorous lines and must not write any less.' He
says over and over that there are in him good and bad, wise and foolish,
anything at all and its antonym, and he is telling the truth; there is in him
almost everything in the world, so that one responds to him, willingly or
unwillingly, almost as one does to the world, that world which makes the
hairs of one's flesh stand up, which seems both evil beyond any rejection
and wonderful beyond any acceptance. We cannot help seeing that there
is something absurd about any judgement we make of its whole – for there

is no 'point of view' at which we can stand to make the judgement, and the moral categories that mean most to us seem no more to apply to its whole than our spatial or temporal or causal categories seem to apply to its beginning or end. (But we need no arguments to make our judgements seem absurd – we feel their absurdity without argument.) In some like sense Whitman is a world, a waste with here and there, systems blazing at random out of the darkness. Only an innocent and rigidly methodical mind will reject it for this disorganization, particularly since there are in it, here and there, little systems as beautifully and astonishingly organized as the rings and satellites of Saturn ...

The enormous and apparent advantages of form, of omission and selection, of the highest degree of organisation, are accompanied by important disadvantages – and there are far greater works than *Leaves of Grass* to make us realise this. But if we compare Whitman with that very beautiful poet Alfred Tennyson, the most skilful of all Whitman's contemporaries, we are at once aware of how limiting Tennyson's forms have been, of how much Tennyson has had to leave out, even in those discursive poems where he is trying to put everything in. Whitman's poems *represent* his world and himself much more satisfactorily than Tennyson's do his. In the past a few poets have both formed and represented, each in the highest degree; but in modern times what controlling, organising, selecting poet has created a world with as much in it as Whitman's, a world that so plainly *is* the world? Of all modern poets he has, quantitively speaking, 'the most comprehensive soul' – and, qualitatively, a most comprehensive and comprehending one, with charities and concessions and qualifications that are rare in any time.

'Do I contradict myself? Very well then I contradict myself', wrote Whitman, as everybody remembers, and this is not naïve, or something he got from Emerson, or a complacent pose. When you organise one of the contradictory elements out of your work of art, you are getting rid not just of it, but of the contradiction of which it was a part; and it is the contradictions in works of art which make them able to represent to us – as logical and methodical generalisations cannot – our world and our selves, which are also full of contradictions. In Whitman we do not get the controlled, compressed, seemingly concordant contradictions of the great lyric poets, of a poem like, say, Hardy's 'During Wind and Rain'; Whitman's contradictions are sometimes announced openly, but are more often scattered at random throughout the poems. For instance: Whitman specialises in ways of saying that there is in some sense (a very Hegelian one, generally[7]) no evil – he says a hundred times that evil is not real; but he also specialises in making lists of the evil in the world, lists of an unarguable reality. After his minister has recounted 'the rounded catalogue divine complete', Whitman comes home and puts down what has been left out: 'the countless (nineteen-twentieths) low of evil, crude and savage ... the barren soil, the evil men, the slag and hideous rot'. He ends another such catalogue with the plain unexcusing 'All these – all meanness and agony without end I sitting look out upon, / See, hear, and am silent.' Whitman offered himself to everybody, and said brilliantly and at length what a good thing he was offering ... Having wonderful dreams, telling wonderful lies, was a temptation Whitman could never resist; but telling the truth was a temptation he could never resist, either. When you buy him you know you are buying. And only an innocent and solemn and systematic mind will condemn him for his contradictions: Whitman's catalogues of evils represent realities, and his denials of their reality represents other realities, of feeling and intuition and desire. If he is faithless to logic, to Reality As It Is – whatever that is – he is faithful to the feel of things, to reality as it seems; this is all that a poet has to be faithful to, and philosophers have been known to leave logic and Reality for it.

Whitman is more coordinate and parallel than anybody, is *the* poet of parallel present participles, of twenty verbs joined by a single subject: all this helps to give his work its feeling of raw hypnotic reality, of being that world which also streams over us joined only by *ands*, until we supply the subordinating conjunctions; and since as children we see the *ands* and not the *becauses*, this method helps to give Whitman some of the freshness of childhood. How inexhaustibly interesting the world is in Whitman! ... The *thereness* and *suchness* of the world are incarnate in Whitman as they are in few other writers.

They might have put on his tombstone WALT WHITMAN: HE HAD HIS NERVE. He is the rashest, the most inexplicable and unlikely – the most impossible, one wants to say – of poets. He somehow *is* in a class by himself, so that one compares him with other poets about as readily as one compares [Lewis Carroll's] *Alice* with other books. (Even his free verse has a completely different effect from anybody else's.) Who would think of comparing him with Tennyson or Browning or Arnold or Baudelaire? – it is Homer, or the sagas, or something far away and long ago, that comes to one's mind only to be dismissed; for sometimes Whitman *is* epic, just as [Melville's] *Moby-Dick* is, and it surprises us to be able to use truthfully this word we have misused so many times. Whitman *is* grand, and elevated, and comprehensive, and real with an astonishing reality, and many other things – the critic points at his qualities in despair and wonder, all method failing, and simply calls them by their names. And the range of these qualities is the most extraordinary thing of all. We can surely say about him, 'He was a man, take him for all in all. I shall not look upon his like again' – and wish that people had seen this and not tried to be his like: one Whitman is miracle enough, and when he comes again it will be the end of the world.

...

Let me finish by mentioning another quality of Whitman's – a quality, delightful to me, that I have said nothing of. If some day a tourist notices, among the ruins of New York City, a copy of *Leaves of Grass*, and stops and picks it up and reads some lines in it, she will be able to say to herself: 'How very American! If he and his country had not existed, it would have been impossible to imagine them.' □

(Randall Jarrell, 'Some Lines from Whitman', 1955)[8]

Jarrell's reading of Whitman is so successful because it pushes against its contemporary critical practises and does not attempt to squeeze Whitman into a preconceived pattern of significance, or make assumptions about just what American poetry can and cannot achieve. The essay's overall assertion, that we should pay nervous and dynamic attention to Whitman's poetry as it unfolds before us, is important in that it slightly redresses the critical record which, by the mid-1950s and with the centenary of the first edition of *Leaves of Grass*, was dominated by highly formalist discussions of Whitman. The following chapter discusses two of the most important formalist readings of Whitman, by R. W. B. Lewis and Roy Harvey Pearce. These are readings that might be described as exercises in 'myth criticism': they seek to place Whitman within the canon of American literature by examining the mythical underpinnings of his poetry. In so doing, they also contribute to the growing academic discipline of American Studies.

CHAPTER FOUR

Whitman, Myth Criticism and the Growth of American Studies

In the previous chapter it was suggested that the struggles of Matthiessen and Feidelson to develop a critical language fully appropriate to Whitman was due, in large part, to their inability to shake off New Critical methodologies and assumptions. The two extracts from essays by Lewis and Pearce that comprise this chapter seem better able to move on from such critical orthodoxies, and in doing so they play a key role in articulating the terms of a new (though closely related to New Criticism) critical approach, 'myth criticism', and of the emerging academic discipline of American Studies. Before moving on to these extracts, and to a discussion of their place in American Studies, it is worthwhile describing New Criticism in more detail as a measure of the hugely dominant and powerful critical model against which such readings of Whitman were pitching themselves.

During the 1930s, and especially amongst American critics, a re-evaluation of literary criticism took place, one that was to have far-reaching and lasting effects on ways of reading texts. This overhauling of critical values and practices came to be known as New Criticism, and its effects on critical practice on both sides of the Atlantic remained dominant into the 1960s and 1970s. Indeed, it was only really with the more ideologically framed and more culturally determined reading practices of the 1980s that literary criticism finally seemed able to ease itself away from the dominance of New Critical ideas and practices. New Critics espoused a set of critical doctrines that prioritised aesthetic impersonality and objectivity, and the detailed close reading of texts, and saw myth as a powerful means of unifying human experience, one which worked from a seemingly de-historicised sense of literary tradition. Such a critical environment was exactly that within which we saw the essays of the previous chapter working. However, as we shall see, Whitman's poetry is in many ways inimical to such an environment. Whereas the pressure of Whitman's poetry seems always outwards, to the cultural and ideological conditions from which it is produced, the pressure of New Critical thought is inwards, back towards the aesthetic autonomy of the literary work. Thus, because New Criticism was particularly dominant in American criticism over the 1940s and 1950s, Whitman's poetry received a very mixed reception in these years.

New Criticism can be seen to have represented the attempt of young critics to establish literary criticism as a respectable academic endeavour, one that could be thought of as being intellectually as rigorous and meticulous as research in the sciences. In this sense it still exerts a powerful influence over critical practice. Though fundamentally at odds with each other in terms of basic assumptions about the relationship of literary texts to language, culture and society, New Criticism and 'literary theory' share an attempt to systematise and theorise reading practices. Indeed, New Criticism can be thought of as a precursor to much contemporary critical practice because of the stress it puts upon seeing literary language as socially and culturally determined rather than as a means for the expression of purely personal emotions. This underlining of the social function of language may seem, initially, to contradict a basic tenet of New Criticism, namely that the literary text should be thought of as standing outside social considerations as a unified artistic whole, impervious to the stresses and tensions of mundane experience. However, New Critics felt that by emphasising the autonomy of the literary text, and by concentrating on its aesthetic unity by a process of close reading that would reveal the delicate balance of ironies and tensions underpinning its formal properties, they would discover far deeper truths about the human condition. They believed that a text was complex and ambiguous, not because the author's own particular emotional experience was complex and ambiguous, but because the unchanging nature of human experience is one of complexity and ambiguity.[1] Any critical response that tried to deduce the author's state of mind from a text was, they felt, bound to fail: it could only ever amount to a second guessing of the author's intentions. Such a mistake in critical practice, the 'Intentional Fallacy' as it was named in 1946 by Wimsatt and Beardsley, indulges romantic views of authorship rather than upholding critical and objective criteria of reading. For New Critics, then, a text becomes an aesthetic icon, something that is self-contained and isolated, detached from the world of everyday concerns. The literary text (and for New Critics it was nearly always a poem) was to be seen as a container of mythic truths about human consciousness. It was, as the title of Cleanth Brooks' highly important and influential book of New Criticism has it, a 'Well-Wrought Urn'.[2] And it was from such a position, New Critics believed, that the poem was able to comment upon – though remain unaffected by – the real world. So, although it has been noted that 'New Criticism was the ideology of an uprooted, defensive liberal intelligentsia who reinvented in literature what they could not locate in reality', its powerful influence over critical thought has been to focus attention on the text's status and function as an aesthetic object within reality.[3] Whether defensive or not, then, New Criticism's espousal of a doctrine of objectivity and impersonality has exposed some of the contradictions and pressures that operate within any critical practice, and which have, themselves, had a profound effect on ways of reading Whitman's poetry.

In one sense, the adoption and deployment New Critical attitudes represented a radical attack upon what were felt to be outmoded – even Victorian – standards of critical judgement. These new critical standards were, as Catherine Belsey has pointed out, 'one of the most important assaults on the orthodoxy of expressive realism' that dominated literary criticism in the early years of the century.[4] Such an assault upon orthodoxy rested in a hard-edged seriousness, a desire for scientific objectivity in dealing with texts, and a deep mistrust of any subjective value judgements. Here it was felt that, finally, literary criticism could be adequate to the experience of modernity. New Criticism would deliver new ways of reading texts, and in so doing it could offer new understandings of the world. These assumptions sit rather uneasily with Whitman's poetry with its seeming reliance upon particularly expressive, and romantic, notions of selfhood, poetry and American literary nationality. Such a sense of unease with prevailing New Critical methods characterises the essays in this chapter.

In some interesting and important ways, though, it may also be possible to read Whitman's challenging poetics as precisely the reason why New Criticism reacted so warily towards him. In fact, despite the apparently revolutionary changes in critical theory and practice represented by New Criticism, these can be seen to be far less radical than they may at first seem. American New Criticism has its roots in the Southern states, and is formulated in the work of such influential critics as John Crowe Ransom, Cleanth Brooks, W. K. Wimsatt, Allen Tate and R. P. Blackmur, all of whom came from – or spent significant amounts of time in – the South. New Criticism is, therefore, unavoidably part of an intellectual expression of a traditional, and deeply conservative, southern culture that is embedded in an organic relationship to the land. Its conservatism stems from traditions that feel themselves to be alienated from, even antagonistic towards, the mainstream American culture of the north-eastern seaboard. The curious mix of conservatism and radicalism that we encounter in New Critical ideology, then, is a significant effect of the South's attempts to test the limits of a Liberal democracy which it felt had been imposed on its own culture by the economically prosperous, industrialised North.[5] It is, in this sense, a critical practice profoundly antithetical to Whitman's Yankee concerns and democratic ideals.

The fact of New Criticism's southern heritage may throw some light on its typical assertion of the aesthetic autonomy of a text – that a text's

meaning derives from formal and intrinsic properties of its textual exis-
tence rather than from the personal, political or cultural circumstances
out of which it is produced – by seeing such an assertion as deriving
from a culture desperate to assert its own autonomy. However, it
remains based in a reactionary attitude towards literature and culture.
Such an attitude precludes any consideration of concerns in the text
other than aesthetic ones; it effectively silences the political or cultural
responsibilities of the critic by settling for a doctrine of disinterested-
ness. In its theory and practice, therefore, New Criticism is, in the
words of Terry Eagleton 'a recipe for political inertia, and thus for sub-
mission to the status quo'.[6]

Such apparently contradictory impulses in New Criticism reflect
back interestingly onto Whitman's poetry. They lend a sense of critical
urgency to the extracts which comprise this chapter and which strug-
gle, in their readings of Whitman, to break free of New Critical assump-
tions. Both Lewis' *The American Adam* (1955) and Pearce's *The Continuity
of American Poetry* (1961) share the assumption that the analysis of myth
and symbol is the key to understanding Whitman and his central place
in American literature. And for both these critics Whitman's work can-
not be severed from its cultural circumstances to be read as an
autonomous aesthetic object. For Lewis especially, the tension that gen-
erates Whitman's poetry is its social circumstances. Any properly
informed reading of it, he feels, must therefore attend to its portrayal of
Whitman's poetic persona as 'the new world's representative man'. In
order to achieve this, Lewis turns to a basic myth, that of Adam in the
Garden of Eden, as a means of exploring and explaining Whitman's sig-
nificance in American literature.

For Lewis, the story of Adam and his expulsion from Eden repre-
sents *the* fundamental American myth. The figure of Adam, he believes,
provides America with a mythic personality, a hero who is the embod-
iment of those forces which underpin American culture. American cul-
ture, he argues, is founded upon the twin ideas of newness and hope.
In the colonial imagination of its early settlers the American continent
was a New World that promised a new chance for mankind. But by the
mid-nineteenth century, the historical period upon which Lewis' study
focuses, that promise had more or less evaporated. The story of Adam
in the Garden of Eden is repeated, according to Lewis, by this pattern
of innocence and hope corrupted. He notes that the literary texts of his
chosen period (which for Matthiessen, as we have seen, were devoted
to democracy) repeatedly portray rugged figures of romantic individu-
alism, which he terms 'American Adams'.

The figure of the 'American Adam', then, provides Lewis with a myth,
and a set of symbols, for reading mid-nineteenth-century American

culture as a whole. This, in turn, answers a need of mid-twentieth-century American culture. It helps to articulate some of the tensions in 1950s America between, on the one hand, the hopeful prosperity with which America emerged from the second World War, and, on the other hand, the guilt, suspicion and paranoia which this disguised. Unsurprisingly, Lewis' *The American Adam* has come to be seen as one of the first 'classics' of American Studies. As the starting point for his study of the Adamic myth in America, Lewis' reading of *Leaves of Grass* plays an absolutely vital role throughout the book. He sees the poems as the 'exemplary celebration of novelty in America', and Whitman as an 'Adamic archetype'. In Lewis, Whitman finds a critical championing of his place at the heart of American sensibilities. Here, Whitman's poem is justified as *the* poem of America.

■ The fullest portrayal of the new world's representative man as a new, American Adam was given by Walt Whitman in *Leaves of Grass* – the liberated, innocent, solitary, forward-thrusting personality that animates the whole of that long poem. *Leaves of Grass* tells us what life was made of, what it felt like, what it included, and what it lacked for the individual who began at that moment, so to speak, where the rebirth ritual of [Thoreau's] *Walden* [1854] leaves off. With the past discarded and largely forgotten, with conventions shed and the molting season concluded, what kind of personality would thereupon emerge? What would be the quality of the experience that lay in store for it?

Leaves of Grass was not only an exemplary celebration of novelty in America: it also, and perhaps more importantly, brought to its climax the many-sided discussion by which – over a generation – innocence replaced sinfulness as the first attribute of the American character. Such a replacement was indispensable to Whitman's vision of innocence, though, of course, it did not account for his poetic genius. ...

When [Emerson's] cordial letter welcoming *Leaves of Grass* in 1855 was published in the *New York Tribune*, Emerson muttered in some dismay that had he intended it for publication, he 'should have enlarged the *but* very much – enlarged the *but*'. *Leaves of Grass* 'was pitched in the very highest key of self-reliance', as a friend of the author maintained; but Emerson, who had given that phrase its contemporary resonance, believed that any attitude raised to its highest pitch tended to encroach dangerously on the truth of its opposite.

It would be no less accurate to say that Walt Whitman, instead of going too far forward, had gone too far backward: for he did go back, all the way back, to a primitive Adamic condition, to the beginning of time.

In the poetry of Walt Whitman, the hopes which had until now expressed themselves in terms of progress crystallized all at once in a complete recovery of the primal perfection. ...

[When] Whitman ... said of Coleridge that he was 'like Adam in paradise, and just as free from artificiality' ... [this] was a more apt description of himself, as he knew:

I, chanter of Adamic songs,
Through the new garden of the West,
    The great cities calling.

It is, in fact, in the poems gathered under the title *Children of Adam* (1860) that we have the most explicit evidence of his ambition to reach behind tradition to find and assert nature untroubled by art, to re-establish the natural unfallen man in the living hour. Unfallen man is, properly enough, unclothed as well; the convention of cover came with the Fall; and Whitman adds his own unnostalgic sincerity to the Romantic affection for nakedness:

As Adam, early in the morning,
Walking forth from the bower refresh'd with sleep,
Behold me where I pass, hear my voice, approach,
Touch me, touch the palm of your hand to my body as I pass
Be not afraid of my body.

For Whitman ... the quickest way of framing his novel outlook was by lowering, and secularizing, the familiar spiritual phrases ... [with] the ... intention of salvaging the human from the religious vocabulary to which (he felt) it had given rise. Many of Whitman's poetic statements are conversions of religious allusion: the new miracles were acts of the senses ...; the aroma of the body was 'finer than prayer'; his head was 'more than churches, bibles and all creeds'. If I worship one thing more than another', Whitman declaimed, in a moment of Adamic narcissism, 'it shall be the spread of my own body'. These assertions gave a peculiar stress to Whitman's seconding of the hopeful belief in men like gods: 'Divine am I, inside and out, and I make holy whatever I touch.' Whitman's poetry is at every moment an act of turbulent incarnation.

But although there is, and was meant to be, a kind of shock-value in such lines, they are not the most authentic index to his pervasive Adamism, because in them the symbols have become too explicit and so fail to work symbolically. Whitman in these instances is stating his position and contemplating it; he is betraying his own principle of indirect statement; he is telling us too much, and the more he tells us, the more we seem to detect the anxious, inflated utterance of a charlatan. We cling to our own integrity and will not be thundered at. We respond far less willingly to Whitman's frontal assaults than we do to his dramatizations; when he is enacting his role rather than insisting on it, we are open to persuasion. And he has been enacting it from the outset of *Leaves of Grass*.

This is the true nature of his achievement and the source of his claim to be the representative poet of the party of Hope. For the 'self' in the very earliest of Whitman's poems is an individual who is always moving forward. To say so is not merely to repeat that Whitman believed in progress; indeed, in some senses it is to deny it. The young Whitman, at least, was not an apostle of progress in its customary meaning of a motion from worse to better to best, an improvement over a previous historical condition, a 'rise of man'. For Whitman, there was no past or 'worse' to progress from; he moved forward because it was the only direction (he makes us think) in which he could move; because there was nothing behind him – or if there were, he had not yet noticed it. There was scarcely a poem of Whitman's before, say, 1867, which does not have the air of being the first poem ever written, the first formulation in language of the nature of persons and of things and of the relations between them; and the urgency of the language suggests that it was formulated in the very nick of time, to give the objects described their first substantial existence.

...While European romanticism continued to resent the effect of time, Whitman was announcing that time had only just begun. He was able to think so because of the facts of immediate history in America during the years when he was maturing: when a world was, in some literal way, being created before his eyes. It was this that Whitman had the opportunity to dramatize; and it was this that gave *Leaves of Grass* its special quality of a Yankee Genesis: a new account of the creation of the world – the creation, that is, of a new world; an account this time with a happy ending for Adam its hero; or better yet, with no ending at all; and with this important emendation, that now the creature has taken on the role of creator.

...Whitman achieves the freedom of the new condition by scrupulously peeling off every source of, or influence upon, the 'Me myself', the 'what I am'. As in section 4 of 'Song of Myself':

> Trippers and askers surround me
> People I meet, the effect upon me of my early life, or the ward and
> the city I live in or the nation. .....
> The sickness of one of my folks, or of myself, or the ill-doing or loss
> or lack of money, or depressions or exaltations,
> Battles, the horror of fratricidal wars, the fever of doubtful news,
> the fitful events,
> These come to me days and nights and go from me again,
> But they are not the Me myself.
> Apart from the pulling and hauling stands what I am;
> Stands amused, complacent, compassionate, idle, unitary;
> Looks down, is erect, or bends an arm on an impalpable certain
> rest,
> Looking with side-curved head curious what will come next,
> Both in and out of the game, and watching and wondering at it.

There is Emerson's individual, the 'infinitely repellent orb'. There is also the heroic product of romanticism, exposing behind the mass of what were regarded as inherited or external or imposed and hence superficial and accidental qualities the true indestructible secret core of personality. There is the man who contends that 'nothing, not God, is greater to one than one's self'.

There, in fact, is the new Adam. If we want a profile of him, we could start with the adjectives Whitman supplies: amused, complacent, compassionating, idle, unitary; especially unitary, and certainly very easily amused; too complacent, we frequently feel, but always compassionate – expressing the old divine compassion for every sparrow that falls, every criminal and prostitute and hopeless invalid, every victim of violence or misfortune. With Whitman's help we could pile up further attributes, and the exhaustive portrait of Adam would be composed of a careful gloss on each of them: hankering, gross, mystical, nude, turbulent, fleshy, sensual, eating, drinking, and breeding; no sentimentalist, no stander above men and women; no more modest than immodest; wearing his hat as he pleases indoors and out; never skulking or ducking or deprecating; adoring himself and adoring his comrades; afoot with his vision,

Moving forward then and now and forever,
Gathering and showing more always and with velocity,
Infinite and omnigenous.

And, announcing himself in language like that. For an actual illustration, we could not find anything better than the stylized daguerreotype of himself which Whitman placed as the Frontispiece of the first edition. We recognize him at once: looking with side-curved head, bending an arm on the certain rest of his hip, evidently amused, complacent, and curious: bearded, rough, probably sensual; with his hat on.

Whitman did resemble this Adamic archetype, according to his friend John Burroughs. 'There was a look about his', Burroughs remembered, 'hard to describe, and which I have seen in no other face, – a gray, brooding, elemental look, like a granite rock, something primitive and Adamic that might have belonged to the first man'. The two new adjectives are 'gray' and 'brooding'; and they belong to the profile, too, both of Whitman and of the character he dramatized. There was bound to be some measure of speculative sadness inherent in the situation. Not all the leaves Whitman uttered were joyous ones, though he wanted them all to be and was ever clear why they were not. His ideal image of himself – and it is his best single trope ['figure of speech', 'literary metaphor'] for the new Adam – was that of a live oak he saw growing in Louisiana:

All alone stood it and the mosses hung down from the branches
Without any companion it grew there uttering joyous leaves of
dark green,
And its look, rude, unbending, lusty, made me think of myself.

But at his most honest, he admitted, as he does here, that the condition was somehow unbearable:

I wondered how it could utter joyous leaves standing alone there
without a friend near, for I knew I could not. ...
And though the live-oak glistens there in Louisiana solitary in a
wide flat space,

Uttering the joyous leaves all its life without a friend a lover near,
I knew very well I could not.

Adam had his moments of sorrow also. But the emotion had nothing to do with the tragic insight; it did not spring from any perception of a genuine hostility in nature or lead to the drama of colliding forces. Whitman was wistful, not tragic. We might also say that he was wistful because he was not tragic. He was innocence personified.

... Whitman's dominant emotion, when it was not unmodified joy, was simple, elemental loneliness; it was a testimony to his success and contributed to his particular glow. For if the hero of *Leaves of Grass* radiates a kind of primal innocence in an innocent world, it was not only because he had made that world, it was also because he had begun by making himself. Whitman is an early example, and perhaps the most striking one we have, of the self-made man, with an undeniable grandeur which is the product of his manifest sense of having been responsible for his own being – something far more compelling than the more vulgar version of the rugged individual who claims responsibility only for his own bank account.

... Whitman began in an Adamic condition which was only too effectively realised: the isolated individual, standing flush with the empty universe, a primitive moral and intellectual entity. In the behavior of a 'noiseless, patient spider', Whitman found a revealing analogy:

A noiseless, patient spider
I mark'd, where, on a little promontory, it stood out, isolated,
Mark'd how, to explore the vacant, vast surrounding,
It launched forth filament, filament, filament, out of itself,
Ever unreeling them – ever tirelessly speeding them.

'Out of itself.' This is the reverse of the traditionalist attitude that, in [T. S.] Eliot's phrase, 'home is where one starts from' [In section v of 'East Coker', one of his *Four Quartets*]. Whitman acted on the hopeful conviction that the new Adam started from himself; having created himself, he must next create a home. ...

And the process of naming is for Whitman nothing less than the process of creation. This new Adam is both maker and namer; his innocent pleasure, untouched by humility, is colored by the pride of one who looks in his work and finds it good. The things that are named seem to spring into being at the sound of the word. It was through the poetic act that Whitman articulated the dominant metaphysical illusion of his day and became the creator of his own world.

... Take, for example, 'Crossing Brooklyn Ferry':

Flood-tide below me! I see you face to face!
Clouds of the west – sun there half an hour high – I see you also
                                                                    face to face.
Crowds of men and women attired in the usual costumes, how
                                                        curious you are to me!

On the ferry-boats the hundreds and hundreds that cross,
　　　returning home, are more curious to me than you suppose,
And you that shall cross from shore to shore years hence are more
　　　to me, and more in my meditations, than you might suppose.

This is not the song of a *trovatore*, a finder, exposing bit by bit the substance of a spectacle which is there before a spectator looks at it. It is the song of a poet who creates his spectacle by 'projecting' it as he goes along. The flood tides, the clouds, the sun, the crowds of men and women in the usual costumes: these exist in the instant they are named and as they are pulled in toward one another, bound together by a single unifying eye through the phrases which apply to them severally ('face to face', 'curious to me'). The growth of the world is exactly indicated in the increasing length of the lines; until, in the following stanza, Whitman can observe a 'simple, compact, well-join'd scheme'. Stabilized in space, the scheme must now be given stabilizing relations in time; Whitman goes on to announce that 'fifty years hence, others will see them as they cross, the sun half an hour high' (the phrase had to be repeated) 'a hundred years hence, or ever so many hundred years hence, others will see them'. With the world, so to speak, a going concern, Whitman is able now to summon new elements into existence: sea gulls, the sunlight in the water, the haze on the hills, the schooners and sloops and ships at anchor, the large and small steamers, and the flags of all nations. A few of the conspicuous elements are blessed and praised, in an announcement (stanza 8) not only of their existence but now rather of the value they impart to one another; and then, in the uninterrupted prayer of the final stanza (stanza 9 – the process covers nine stanzas, as though it were nine months) each separate entity is named again as receiving everlasting life through its participation in the whole:

Flow on river! flow with the flood-tide, and ebb with the ebb-tide!
Frolic on, crested and scallop-edged waves!

And so on: until the mystery of incarnation has been completed. □
　　　　　　　　　　　　(R. W. B. Lewis, The *American Adam: Innocence,*
　　　　　　　　Tragedy and Tradition in the Nineteenth Century, 1955)[7]

The contention that Whitman, like Adam, was 'creating a world' though often sounding as though 'saluting a world that had been lying await for him' can, perhaps, be seen as analogous to Lewis' own critical position. In *The American Adam,* Lewis makes an important, 'classic' even, contribution to the fledgling academic discipline of American Studies by delineating the terms (in his case, mythic) for an examination of America and its culture. Along with Roy Harvey Pearce, whose reading of Whitman is to follow in this chapter, and Henry Nash Smith, Lewis is one of a handful of literary and cultural critics who were responsible for the growth and development of American Studies.

Writing in 1957, Henry Nash Smith set out some of the key issues in American Studies. He noted that American Studies represented the 'desire to study American culture as a whole', rather than within discrete disciplines that are (particularly) sociological or literary.[8] Because, Nash argues, of its attempts to assess the 'ambiguous relation between works of art and the culture in which they occur', American Studies must develop a new method of inquiry, one of 'principled opportunism' that draws from a variety of different disciplinary methods and resources.[9] He calls, then, for an American Studies that is as heterogeneous as American culture itself. What underpins this study of America 'as a whole' is a belief that myth and symbol are cultural phenomena. The underlying pattern of American culture can therefore be discovered through the proper reading and analysis of its dominant myths and symbols.[10] Given the steady growth of academic – and general – interest in *Leaves of Grass* after the Second World War, and the boost this received with the 1955 centenary of its first edition, it is not surprising that across the 1950s critical discussion of Whitman became increasingly important in the growth and development of American Studies. In this period of its critical history the emphases and concerns of the readers of Whitman's poetry shifted and seemingly became more adequate to the task of dealing with its expansiveness, sprawling poetic forms and provisionality. Indeed those very things in Whitman that had previously alienated readers and critics alike – the ambiguity and ambivalence, the reliance upon myth and symbol, the drawing upon Emerson and the apparently opportunistic use of heterogeneous sources (as highlighted by Emerson's famous comment that *Leaves of Grass* seems 'a remarkable mixture of the *Bhagvat-Geeta* and the *New York Herald*') – finally became the foci of a plethora of literary, cultural and sociological interpretations.

The second extract of this chapter is taken from the book *The Continuity of American Poetry* by Roy Harvey Pearce. For Lewis, Whitman is central to American sensibility through his poetic proposing of the idea of a mythical America. Pearce's book is one of the first to attempt a systematised theory of American poetry. It asserts that American poetry has a continuity of tradition and of theme, and – following Lewis – argues that the major constituent of this continuity is what it terms the 'Adamic poem'. As with Lewis, then, the biblical myth of Adam creating a new world in Eden, is, for Pearce, the one that underpins American consciousness. The notion of an Adamic poem is one that is based in this myth and which sees language itself as essentially creative, a poem that realises, as Pearce puts it, the 'fecundative power of language'.[11] The extract below deals less, though, with Whitman's use of Adamic myth than with the sorts of literary and cultural relationships that his poetry made possible. From a consideration of the fecund relationship between

Emerson's thought and Whitman's poetry and poetics, Pearce raises questions about the cultural and ideological force of Whitman as a representative American figure. What Pearce discovers in Whitman is a poetics of transformation, the power of the poetic to give the world a new meaning. For Pearce, Whitman's poetics resonates equally with America's struggles in the nineteenth century to assert itself as a new nation, and with the myth of Adam naming the world and thereby bringing it into being.

■ Whitman is the supremely realized Emersonian poet – the simple, separate person sufficiently free of theoretical concerns to let his ego roam (or as he put it, loaf and lean and invite) and endow the world with its utterly human perfection. Mastering the words which stand for the elements of his world, his sensibility transforms them into something unmistakably his own, but in the nature of the transformation does not deny them to other men. Rather, as though for the first time, it makes them available to other men. Discovering itself, it would discover the world and reveal it to all comers. Both the preface to the 1855 *Leaves of Grass* and 'By Blue Ontario's Shore', its poetic counterpart, are essentially expansions of 'The Poet.' And Whitman's conception of the forms of love whereby one is to discover oneself in myriad aspects of the cosmos – this is a development of the Emersonian conception of the power of the poet as universal man. ...

The effect of Whitman's poems is in the end akin to that of Emerson's. The poet glories in his discovery of the sheer creative, individualizing power of his egocentrism, yet at the same time tries (not quite successfully, I think) to demonstrate somehow that the way into egocentrism is also the way out of it. Emerson had achieved at best a perilous balance here. But his example freed Whitman to be a poet, as it were, beyond balance – a poet who saw that if he were to be a poet, such balance was out of the question. In this may well lie his main claim to glory. In any case, it is at this point, in this light, that Whitman most fully assumes that poetic set by Emerson's example and demanded by the nature and need of his culture.

In Whitman's poetry, the ego is made not only to assert but to preserve itself. Its tremendous creative powers somehow militate against that fusion of ego and cosmos (that eventual desire to build a cathedral) which seems to have been a major need of the later Whitman. Emphasizing the desire and the need (sharing them, perhaps?), we have too often tended to mistake them for the effect, and also the meaning, of the poetry itself.

The ego asserts itself Adamically, by naming. The poem is a titanic act of adoption. The poet is a father, giving his name to all he sees and hears and feels. His office is to make everything part of the community of man; the sense of community is revealed as he discovers, and then yields to, his infinite sense of himself. He puts things together as they never have been before; they are related only by the force of the poetic ego operative on them. There is little or no dramatic effect in the poems, even those with huge casts of characters; for the items which are named in them do not interact, are not conceived as modifying and qualifying one another, so as to make for dramatic tension. They are referred back to their creator, who does with them as his sensibility wills. If we see a relationship, it is because Whitman has made it, not because it was already there for him to discover and report. The great catalogues are inevitably the principal expressive form for one who would define himself as 'Kosmos.'

Whitman glories almost exclusively in the first-person singular – and in this is a more complete Emersonian than Emerson himself, who trusts it but would discover it more explicitly in the third-person too. Whitman said of *Leaves of Grass* that it was an attempt 'to put *a Person*, a human being (myself, in the latter half of the Nineteenth Century, in America) freely, fully and truly on record'. There can be no third-person in his world; and the second-person must necessarily be at the loving mercy of the first. What is true of *Song of Myself* is also true of all the poems: There is no formal control in them but that which stems from the self in the act of revealing the world to itself. ...

All experience, all thought, all belief, all appearance are referred back to the ego:

And I know that the hand of God is the promise of my own,
And I know that the spirit of God is the brother of my own,
And that all the men ever born are also my brothers, and the
                              women my sisters and lovers,
And that a kelson of the creation is love,
And limitless are leaves stiff or dropping in the fields,
And brown ants in the little wells beneath them,
And mossy scabs of the worm fence, heap'd stones, elder, mullein
                              and poke-weed.

Here ... the world is described as it exists apart from the poet; yet he can name and collocate its potentially infinite aspects only so that he may discover and define his relationship to it. His objectivity is that of an impressionist, and so finally an aspect of his subjectivity. He may aspire to achieve some sort of identity with this world; yet his power of naming, describing and collocating is such that a reader cannot but be overwhelmingly, even uncritically, aware of the single ego, the self, which generates it. The power is that of a lover who rather drives himself than is drawn to love the world. A Father Adam who bids men listen to him so that they might hear their proper names and so come alive – this is how Whitman images himself. He does not fear his power, but knows that others may. And he must quiet their apprehensions. One short poem says it all:

As Adam in the morning,
Walking forth from the bower refresh'd with sleep,
Behold me where I pass, hear my voice, approach.
Touch me, touch the palm of your hand to my body as I pass,
Be not afraid of my body.

Whitman knew that his fellows *did* live in a paradise, only they could not bring themselves to acknowledge the fact. In that paradise, the soul was the body. In the voice and its use lay proof of their quintessential identity. His subject, as he wrote in a preliminary note for the first section of *Leaves of Grass*, was 'Adam, as central figure and type'.

But Whitman would go farther than this. Having established the identity of the body and the soul by expressing it, he would establish higher and more inclusive levels of identity, until his voice should become all voices and all voices become his. Herein lies his special hubris, born of the over-confidence and euphoria which came after he had once and for all discovered his own identity. He did in fact discover his own identity, and he taught other men to discover theirs. But always he was tempted, sometimes fatally, to try to go on and establish a single identity for all – simple, separate, *therefore* democratic, en-masse. He failed. But then: he could not succeed unless he tried to do so much that he inevitably failed.

In 'The Sleepers' – to take a great but insufficiently noticed example – the ego is shown celebrating its oneness with all other egos. In the night, in sleep, the poet is able to lose his sense of individuated self and make vital contact with all other selves. Yet in the poem there emerges a sense of creativity so strong as to argue against the very oneness which is the poet's intended subject.

The poem begins thus:

I wander all night in my vision,
Stepping with light feet, swiftly and noiselessly stepping and
                                                    stopping,

Ending with open eyes over the shut eyes of sleepers,
Wandering and confused, lost to myself, ill-assorted, contradictory,

Pausing, gazing, bending, and stopping.

'My vision' is the key phrase here. For as the poem develops, the night is conceived of as the poet's lover, rendering him utterly passive. In this state he envisions himself as possessing and possessed by all men and all women, good and evil, now so undifferentiated as to be universally beautiful. He comes to see that it is 'the night and sleep [which have] liken'd them and restored them'. The night then is given its richest definition:

I too pass from the night,
I stay a while away O night, but I return to you again and love you.

Why should I be afraid to trust myself to you?
I am not afraid, I have been well brought forward by you,
I love the rich running day, but I do not desert her in whom I lay
                                                    so long,

I know not how I came of you and I know not where I go with you,
                    but I know I came well and shall go well.
I will stop only a time with the night, and rise betimes,
I will duly pass the day O my mother, and duly return to you.

It is thus a primal source of creativity, lover and genetrix, to which the poet must return, even as he must leave it for his daytime life. Most important, it is a source within the poet, the deepest aspect of himself as authentic person. Returning to his mother, he returns to himself as dreamer-creator, returns to the act with which the poem begins; for it is he who has 'liken'd ... and restored' all to beauty.

The passage is often read as involving a notion of the transcendental source of being, so that 'night' equals death-in-life and life-in-death, dissolution of the temporal into the eternal, and the like. Yet the form of the poem, its movement from the picture of the envisioning poet to a series of catalogues and narratives of what he envisions, to the discovery that the act of envisioning makes all beautiful, then finally to the realization of the source of the envisioning power – all this demonstrates a Whitman sufficiently conscious of his own commitment to isolated, egocentric creativity to manifest it even as he tries to transcend it. Lacking a hard-edged respect for the 'other', he is more Emersonian than Emerson. If the soul is always beautiful, it is so because Whitman can envision it and thereby make it so, as he yields to the night-time power of his genius. For us, the poem is the act of the envisioning. The account of the source of the vision, its meaning and rationale, is part of the act and derives its power from the actor, not from the transcendental, pantheistic world-view toward which he seems to aspire. Whereas in 'The Sleepers' Whitman argues for a transcendent One which would per se universalize the ego, he expresses the act of the ego striving to universalize itself by recreating the world in its own image. ...

Sometimes, as in 'Out of the Cradle Endlessly Rocking,' he establishes his relation to the cosmic process by developing in an argument a series of carefully defined, clearly symbolic, ego-centred relationships. In 'Out of the Cradle....,' the adult makes a poem which is his means to understand a childhood experience. The firm control in the poem (it is extraordinary here, especially for Whitman, but nonetheless it is not always a sign of the highest achievement of his poetry) is managed through the manipulation of this double point-of-view. Initially we are told of the range of experiences out of which this poem comes: the song of the bird, the place, the time, the memory of the dead brother, and the as yet unnamed 'word stronger and more delicious than any' which gathers unto itself the meaning of the whole; this is an introductory overview. Then we are presented with the story of the birds, the loss of the beloved, and the song sung to objectify this loss and perhaps make it bearable. Always we are aware that the poet-as-adult, the creative center of the poem, seeks to 'word stronger and more delicious' which will be his means finally to understand his reminiscences.

These points of view of child and adult are kept separate until the passage which reads:

Demon or bird! (said the boy's soul,)
Is it indeed toward your mate you sing? or is it really to me?
For I, that was a child, my tongue's use sleeping, now I have heard
you,
Now in a moment I know what I am for, I awake,
And already a thousand singers, a thousand songs, clearer, louder
and more sorrowful than yours,
A thousand warbling echoes have started to life within me, never
to die.

Here the points of view are hypnotically merged. In the 'boy's soul' the poet discovers a child's potentiality for adult knowledge. Having discovered the potentiality, he can work toward its realization, confident that the one will follow automatically from the other. He asks for 'the clew', 'The final word, superior to all', which will once and for all precipitate the meaning he has willed himself to create. And it comes as he recalls that time when the sea, manifesting the rhythm of life and death itself,

Delaying not, hurrying not,
Whisper'd me through the night, and very plainly before daybreak
Lisp'd to me the low and delicious word death,
And again, death, death, death, death ...

The merging of the points of view occurs as not only past and present, child and adult, but subject and object (i.e., 'The Sea ... whisper'd me' – not 'to me') are fused. The poet now knows the word, because he has contrived a situation in which he can control its use, having first re-created himself as both boy and man, and having then fused the two phases of his life into one. If the end of the poem is to understand cosmic process as a continual loss of the beloved through death and a consequent gain of a positive sense of life-in-death and death-in-life – if this is the end of the poem, nonetheless it is an end gained through a creative act, an assertion of life in the face of death. This act is that of the very person, the poet, whom death would deprive of all that is beloved in life.

'Out of the Cradle ... 'is typical of those poems of Whitman's we tend most to admire, 'When Lilacs Last in the Dooryard Bloom'd' being the other chief example. Most of all, it is *structurally* typical of such poems. The structure is one of relationship, in which the poet, through his control of two or more points of view, manages to pull his world together. Yet the relationship is of a particularly limited sort. The points of view are always aspects of the poet's creative self and are manipulated as such; they are in no sense dramatic, much less novelistic. ... In the end, his poems always return to him as maker. This is so because in the beginning his problem was to make sure that any poem he made was an authentic poem; and in the world in which he lived, which could not quite fit poems into its scheme of things, his sense of himself furnished him the sole means for testing authenticity.

Yet Whitman had always wanted more than this. Like Poe and Emerson, he was not altogether happy in his knowledge of the divisiveness for which his role as poet made him the speaker. Such knowledge made possible a conception of man as being necessarily defined by man – simple, separate man. His hope was always that, coming to know this much, he might come to know more. The momentum built up in the poetic act might be sufficient to take him who had initiated it into such knowledge as would make for a transcendence of divisiveness. To discover the simple and separate and to celebrate it would then necessarily be to define the democratic – man en-masse. The dilemma was inevitable, perhaps the product of the American poet's discovery that the alienation which was a condition of his writing his kind of poetry was too great to bear. Like Emerson and Poe, in the end Whitman wanted to be something of a 'philosopher'; and he came to write poems in which integrating argument is set against, not transformed by, sensibility and imagination. ...

A sense of ... limits saved Whitman from the sort of grandiose mysticism for which he so often yearned and also from the excesses of the 'Personalism' which he as often preached. That he was, in spite of his wide-ranging reading, cut off from large areas of knowledge and large forms of discipline ... is obvious enough. This is a weakness not only complementary but necessary to the strength of his poems. His conception of poetry not only made for his poems; it also protected him from the world to which he addressed them. For it demanded that the anti-poetic world be at the most translatable into, at the least congruent with, the concept of self, or have no claim to reality at all. This is to a degree a mutilating conception of reality. Yet it is at the same time a source of strength. The lesson is by now an old one: the miracle of the achieved poetic act is that by imaginative transformation it can derive its characteristic strength from the characteristic weakness of the culture in which it is performed. □

(Roy Harvey Pearce, *The Continuity of American Poetry*, 1961)[12]

Pearce, like Lewis, signals the critical realisation that Whitman's poetry must be taken seriously, and both extracts show that, through Whitman, critics were discovering ways of reading beyond the narrowly doctrinaire tenets of New Criticism. In many ways, Lewis and Pearce use Whitman in order to help them realise Henry Nash Smith's aspirations for American Studies. The controlling myth of both these pieces, in which Americans are seen as Adams in a new Garden of Eden, is one felt to be fundamental to American culture as a whole. And by this stage in its critical history, there seems little doubt that *Leaves of Grass* is a masterpiece of extraordinarily powerful, American, expression. Exactly what it expresses is, as we have seen again and again throughout its history, largely dependent upon assumptions about literature, culture and America that are brought to the text by each particular critic.

If the history of Whitman criticism in the mid-twentieth century tells us anything, it tells us that despite the best efforts to read American culture as a whole – a single unified body – that finds expression through a set of shared myths, symbols and assumptions, that culture is, in fact, one of dis-unity and competing myths, all of which struggle to express the particular idea of America held by each critic. And in the final three chapters of this Readers' Guide we will turn to more recent readings of Whitman, and their attempts to seek a critical accommodation between Whitman's poetry, his culture and his ideological assumptions.

CHAPTER FIVE

Whitman, Cultural Materialism and 'Reconstructive' Readings

The final three chapters of this book are, in many ways, closely linked. Taken together they chart some of the major directions taken by Whitman criticism in more recent years. They illustrate a fundamental change of direction – not only in Whitman criticism, but in critical practice generally – towards reading practices that are more ideologically aware. Such a tendency leads, in this chapter, to a series of essays which can be broadly termed 'cultural materialist', in that they examine the way in which Whitman's poetry is a product of the cultural materials of mid-nineteenth-century America. These essays assert that *Leaves of Grass* is defined by the ideological conditions of America in the nineteenth century, and any understanding of Whitman, they would argue, depends therefore upon recreating and examining, so far as this is possible, the cultural environment from which his poetry was produced. The essays in the final two chapters push this mode of critical enquiry further. Both seek to 'deconstruct' the ideological conditions that underpin Whitman's text, and in so doing raise questions about the extent to which Whitman's poetry can be seen as a product, not simply of the cultural forces at play in America during the nineteenth century, but also of the structures of ideological power that have determined the ways in which Whitman's poetry has been read throughout the course of its critical history. The essays in the next chapter look to Whitman's sexual politics, and the vexed question of his supposed homosexuality, whilst those in the final chapter seek to read Whitman's poetry through overtly politicised (and 'deconstructive') critical practices. In short, then, the essays which comprise these final three chapters bring Whitman criticism up to date by emphasising that the act of reading Whitman is never ideologically innocent. They stress that the ways in which Whitman's poetry is read betray ways of reading America and its culture.

In all cases, the critical pieces in this chapter are important in that they challenge us to return to Whitman's poetry and to read it afresh. The essays that follow signal a new – or revived – sense of excitement in the face of the radical challenges that Whitman offered to his culture. For these critics, Whitman's poetry provides an opportunity for rereading nineteenth-century America and its cultural conditions. These interpretations of Whitman derive from a belief, therefore, that the power and importance of Whitman's poetry results from its ability to offer some radical and invigorating insights into American culture, into our own liberal humanist assumptions, and, indeed, into our own reading practices. These analyses (especially in comparison with the essays that comprise the final chapter of this Reader) are at the 'softer' end of the critical-theoretical spectrum. Rather than out-and-out post-structuralist deconstructions of the text, they are better thought of as 'reconstructive' readings. David S. Reynolds, whose essay on Whitman and discourses of sex and gender in antebellum popular culture closes this chapter, describes what he terms 'reconstructive criticism' in the *Epilogue* to his book *Beneath the American Renaissance* (1988). According to Reynolds, such 'reconstructive criticism' brings together the best practices of close textual reading with a scholarly knowledge, and examination, of the sociopolitical environment from which the text is produced:

■ Applied to the internal workings of literary texts, reconstructive criticism views the literary work as simultaneously self-sufficient *and* historically shaped by environmental factors in society and personal life. In the case of the literary masterpieces of the American Renaissance, textual self-sufficiency does not constitute a rejection or evasion of socioliterary forces but rather a full assimilation and willed transformation of these forces. This process of assimilation and transformation – which might be called artistic or aesthetic – is another important aspect of reconstruction. The literary text reconstructs disparate socioliterary elements from its contemporary culture. In effect it tries to save the society by giving certain popular elements new emotional resonance and artistic meaning. □
(David S. Reynolds, *Beneath the American Renaissance*, 1988)[1]

Such a 'reconstructive criticism' does not hide its humanist agenda, then. Indeed, its persuasive power lies in its ability to see the materials of a literary text's contemporary culture transformed within that text, given a depth that is 'universal,' something that, it is assumed, speaks to the human condition. Reynolds continues: 'The "meaning" of a text lies in the richness of its texture, the emotions its stirs, the metaphysical speculations it instigates.'[2] Theoretical objections may be raised to this way of thinking by arguing that the very notion of a universality of human experience – especially literary experience – is, in itself, ideologically determined. But, objections to such a belief in literature's humanising power notwithstanding, Reynolds' critical model does seem to re-open the radical and subversive potential of texts such as Whitman's. He notes, further, that

■ The literary text can be distinguished from other types of text both by its openness to the most subversive forces in its immediate socioliterary environments and by its simultaneous endeavor to lend depth and artistry to these forces. Both the radical openness and the instinct to restructure must be present, or the literary text will not appear. The literary text fully confronts the subversive – plunges wholly into it, as it were – but at the same time it removes itself through an assertion of the humanizing artistic imagination. □

(David S. Reynolds, *Beneath the American Renaissance*, 1988)[3]

Though the relationship between 'literature' and 'the subversive' that Reynolds sets up here seems rather fraught and uneasy, it conveys, perhaps, an accurate sense of the pressures from which *Leaves of Grass* and other works of the American Renaissance were produced. Whereas Matthiessen's model of the American Renaissance dealt exclusively with works of 'high' literary merit, Reynolds' critical model prises open such exclusivity. This allows him to get beneath, so to speak, the surface of the culture which gave rise to the American Renaissance. Not only, therefore, does this provide him with a critical model for reading Whitman's poetry as deeply influenced by the popular culture of his day, but it also shows how other critics may usefully read *Leaves of Grass* as a product of ideological and cultural forces in nineteenth-century America that extend beyond the exclusively literary. And though earlier criticism had noted the influence of American popular culture on Whitman (and in many cases used this as a means of attacking Whitman with charges of barbarism, or lack of 'proper' culture), this had been seen to mark the poetry as anomalous, a strange and eccentric oddity. The cultural hybridity of Whitman's poetry had thus been read as problematic and ambiguous, something that distinguished it from 'proper' literature. Taken as illustrating a wider concern, this sort of difficulty in approaching Whitman seemed to embody the lack of a critical language for talking about American literature itself. In a sense, then, Reynolds' 'reconstructive' model discovers a critical language, so long lacking, for discussing the Americanness of American literature in general, and, as we shall see at the end of this chapter, of *Leaves of Grass* in particular.

The three essays from which this chapter draws seek to reconstruct and examine the cultural environment from which *Leaves of Grass* arose. The first extract, from M. Wynn Thomas's groundbreaking study, *The Lunar Light of Whitman's Poetry* (1987) examines Whitman's poetry in the light of specific crises of identity and representation in nineteenth-century America, crises, Thomas argues, that resulted from far-reaching economic changes in The United States as it moved from an artisanal to a post-artisanal phase of capitalism. The remaining essays, by Ed Folsom and David Reynolds, focus on the relationship between Whitman's poetry and a specific topic or discourse of nineteenth-century America. All three essays, however, are at some pains to use such readings to throw light upon the wider culture of Whitman's America. In their specific and general terms of inquiry, they show some of the ways in which Whitman has been mobilised as a means of re-reading nineteenth-century America.

In the introduction to *The Lunar Light of Whitman's Poetry*, M. Wynn Thomas is careful to emphasise that his reading of Whitman is not based in any generalised notion of Whitman as America's grand bard, someone who embodies 'the essential spirit of America'. Rather, his study shows Whitman to be the product of a very specific cultural moment, and of a very specific set of discourses. His book represents an attempt, therefore, to read Whitman back into those particular circumstances:

■ Instead of accepting that his poems embody the essential spirit of America, I have concluded that they are the products of what was for Whitman, as it was for the artisan class with which he was closely associated, a historically specific period of social crisis. In his own case not only did poetry surface in him under this pressure, his poems were also instrumental in enabling Whitman to adapt, or to temper his ideals (themselves partly historical in origin; the residue of an earlier period) to the sometimes harsh requirements of a new environment. At the same time, poetry was his indispensable means of stating his *own* requirements, allowing him to address the contemporary situation in terms and tones that were, not infrequently in one and the same poem, critical, celebratory, and visionary. □
(M. Wynn Thomas, *The Lunar Light of Whitman's Poetry*, 1987)[4]

Here, Thomas effectively draws a line under previous Whitman criticism and signals a new phase in ways of reading Whitman. Rather than the overarching and all-encompassing rhetoric of earlier evaluations of Whitman's importance, Thomas seeks to establish a more nuanced and subtle appreciation of Whitman's place in American culture.

In the following passage, Thomas is perhaps the first Whitman critic to examine in any great detail the impact of a rhetoric of labour and capital on Whitman's poetry. And from such rhetoric Thomas is able to describe and evaluate a quite startlingly new version of Whitman. Under Thomas' keen critical eye Whitman emerges as a rather troubled and embattled poet, less the mythic bard and more an index of complex and subtly disconcerting times in American history. In this respect Thomas' book is crucial to the developing critical history of Whitman's poetry. Though after Thomas we see Whitman in a colder – less effusive – light, we also see him as more fundamentally challenging, more poetically realised and textured than earlier assessments of him allowed. Quite simply, Thomas makes it possible for us to understand Whitman's poetry, and nineteenth-century America, better.

■ 'I celebrate myself.' The beginning of 'Song of Myself' has become so disastrously familiar that it has lost its original brash power to provoke the reader into a constructive misinterpretation. By failing nowadays to recognize and react to Whitman's perfect imitation of the tone of voice characteristic of a struttingly aggressive individualism, we may also fail to appreciate how subtly he suggests the limitations of that tone and that voice. But he goes further than this. By means of the lines that follow, he incorporates the phrase into a sentence which, read complete, puts a very different complexion on this 'self' that is celebrating and being celebrated. That solitary, egotistical phrase, placed in this redeeming social context, is reclaimed for use in the service of a radically different conception of the glories of individual existence:

I celebrate myself, and sing myself,
And what I assume you shall assume,
For every atom belonging to me as good belongs to you.
    (Sculley Bradley et al., Leaves of Grass: A Textual Variorum, 1980)[5]

The last line is encouraged by the rest of the poem to bear two different but corroborative meanings. It tells us that 'your atoms are every bit as good as my atoms'; just as later Whitman speaks of 'opposite equals advanc[ing]' and instructs us that 'All I mark as my own you shall offset it with your own'.[6] But it can also be understood as making us an extraordinary offer, in the same spirit as the one made later in the poem when the thoughts of great men are described as being 'yours as much as mine'.[7] Whitman is actually offering to share every atom of himself with us.

These two meanings, brought like a single pair of eyes to bear upon the opening phrase, give a stereoscopic prominence to its hitherto concealed meaning. Thomas Stone, writing in The Dial, complained that in contemporary society 'the permanent I subjects and enthrals itself to the changeful MINE, all which can be brought within the compass of this same MINE is sought rather than the being and growth of the MYSELF'.[8] It is precisely this distinction which Whitman is implicitly making at the very beginning of what is very pointedly a 'Song of MYSELF'. And it is a distinction by which the whole poem is significantly governed. ...

The word 'myself' in 'I celebrate myself' can ... be understood as existing in what structuralists would call a 'vertical' or 'associative' relationship with the word 'mine', which had in contemporary life effectively usurped its place at the center of people's conception and definition of themselves. The word 'mine' has a kind of absent presence in the first sentence, which 'partly creates and certainly winnows and refines the meanings of [the word] that is present' (Terence Hawkes, Structuralism and Semiotics, 1977).[9]

But that term 'myself' is further charged with an additional discriminatory force which Emerson can ... help us to feel. 'Men', he remarks in 'Self-Reliance', 'have looked away from themselves and at things so long that ... they measure their esteem of each other by what each has, and not by what each is' (*The Riverside Edition of Emerson's Complete Work,* 1883).[10] In such a social context, to 'celebrate myself' on Whitman's terms is indeed therefore to look in a radically new direction and to speak in a new way. ...

Whitman's poem is also conceived and presented in terms of the act of love it can perform for the reader. The first evidence of this love is negative – Whitman's refusal to let his poem provide the reader with the kind of acquirable content of meaning and message that other books provide. Negatively considered, then, 'Song of Myself' frustrates the reader's wish to make the content of books, like the books themselves, a form of ... 'portable property'. It is interesting to note that, despite all critics have said about Whitman's approaches to the reader, insufficient work has been done on 'Song of Myself' from the point of view of the difficulties and challenges with which, in the name of love, it confronts the reader. Instead, it has been readily taken at its face value – as the proclamation and demonstration of a unique self – and discussed chiefly in terms of expressive theories of literature. But passages such as the following seem rather to invite a different kind of approach:

The smoke of my own breath,
Echoes, ripples, and buzzed whispers ... loveroot, silkthread,
                                                 crotch and vine,
My respiration and inspiration ... the beating of my heart ... the
                              passing of blood and air through my lungs,
The sniff of green leaves and dry leaves, and of the shore and
                   darkcolored sea-rocks, and of the hay in the barn,
The sound of the belched words of my voice ... words loosed to the
                                                 eddies of the wind,
A few light kisses ... a few embraces ... a reaching around of arms,
The play of shine and shade on the trees as the supple boughs wag,
The delight alone or in the rush of the streets, or along the field
                                                 and hillsides,
The feeling of health ... the full-noon trill ... the song of me rising from
                              bed and meeting the sun.[11]

The point and power of this verse paragraph lies in its not having a main verb – which is, of course, something the unwary reader is likely, on a first reading, to spend his time expecting in vain. The discovery when it finally comes, and the rereading that must hastily follow, involve much more than the noting of a grammatical peculiarity. They involve a realization that these descriptive phrases are not simply a preparation for action, subject to and therefore subordinate to the directing presence of the verb. They are grammatically an end in themselves, thereby creating a physical world in which experiences such as 'The smoke of my own breath... The sniff of green leaves and dry leaves... The sound of the belched words of my voice' become vividly foregrounded. Filling the whole picture, they become significant and satisfying experiences in themselves. In other words, as the reader adjusts so as finally to find meaning in the verbless 'sentence', so too does he simultaneously reorient himself in relation to himself and his world, and engage in a revaluation of life itself. It is a fine example of the quiet subversiveness of Whitman's writing – the way the 'new free forms' of the poetry constitute what he himself called a 'silent defiance' (Floyd Stovall, ed., *Prose Works*, 1892).[12]

... It is surely significant that specifically in 'Song of Myself' – and not, sadly, in most of his poetry thereafter – Whitman is supremely [D. H.] Lawrence's poet of 'the quivering nimble hour of the present', revelling 'in the sheer appreciation of the instant moment, life surging itself into utterance at its very well-head' (Anthony Beale, ed., *D. H. Lawrence*, 1961).[13] He is addicted to the present tense and the present participle, and his descriptions of people always catch them in the very act of living. 'The pavingman leans on his twohanded rammer... The canal-boy trots on the towpath... / The drover watches his drove, he sings out to them that would stray... / Off on the lakes the pikefisher watches and waits by the hole in the frozen surface.' By so catching them and isolating their actions from questions of motive, purpose, and consequence, he manages to recreate an idealized form of the comfortably blended urban and rural worlds of his childhood. Yet the whole panorama is implicitly presented as a celebration of the free spirit of economic liberalism, the laissez-faire capitalism of the mid-nineteenth century. It is of course nothing of the sort. Whitman replaces the pleasure of acquiring and the acquiring of pleasure which was becoming the real business of his time, with the pleasure of simply being and living. His poem translates a having world into a being world, which appears to obey the biblical injunction to 'serve the Lord your God with joy and gladness of heart, in the midst of the fullness of things' (Deuteronomy 28: 47). America so transfigured becomes a psalm of life.

... Whitman's attempt, in 'Song of Myself', to unfreeze [the] body and to nerve it again for joy, is part and parcel of his anatomy of psychic health:

> If I worship any particular thing it shall be some of the spread of
> my body;
> Translucent mould of me it shall be you,
> Shaded ledges and rests, firm masculine coulter, it shall be you,
> Whatever goes to the tilth of me it shall be you,
> You my rich blood, you my milky stream pale strippings of my life;
> Breast that presses against other breasts it shall be you,
> My brain it shall be your occult convolutions,
> Root of washed sweet-flag, timorous pond-snipe, nest of guarded
> duplicate eggs, it shall be you,

Mixed tussled hay of head and beard and brawn it shall be you,
Trickling sap of maple, fibre of manly wheat, it shall be you;
Sun so generous it shall be you,
Vapors lighting and shading my face it shall be you,
You sweaty brooks and dews it shall be you,
Winds whose soft -tickling genitals rub against me it shall be you,
Broad muscular fields, branches of liveoak, loving lounger in my
                    winding paths, it shall be you,
Hands I have taken, face I have kissed, mortal I have ever touched,
                    it shall be you.[14]

This is a dramatic substantiation of his creed: 'I believe in the flesh and the appetites, / Seeing hearing and feeling are miracles, and each part and tag of me is a miracle.'[15] Accordingly, there is a naming of parts – not by repeating the familiar terms of physical identification so as to draw up an inventory of the commonplace, but by finding a language of wonder that can express his body's own intricate, independent existence, and so bring him to a fuller identity. What Whitman is doing in joyfully tracing the mysterious contours, excrescences, and organic processes of this 'foreign' body is accepting the spread of his personal being beyond the area dominated and controlled by the ego. The 'I' extends itself to, and through, a recognition of this 'you' which nevertheless is still decidedly *my* body'. Here the 'my' is clearly not a simple possessive. It does not mean this body belongs to the 'me'. Rather, as the whole passage makes clear, Whitman is communicating a satisfying experience of the self as indwelling everywhere in the body. Whereas the passage starts by registering details of the body as if they were features of the natural environment, it then proceeds to treat the natural world as if it were sentient and sensuously organized like the human body, so that it is through the body that man best gains entry to an understanding of the real nature of this world. Moreover, Whitman's corporeal identity is strengthened by the world's delighted physical recognition of *him*. Nor is its response only one of intimate sexuality. The sexuality is integrated with other aspects of the world's approaches to Whitman. And in its conduct towards him it, too, recognizes his body (inclusive of its sexuality) as having the status of a person. The sun is generous, the vapor implicitly considerate, and the liveoak is a 'loving lounger in my winding paths'. Even his sweat is provided with a new meaning in being seen as the counterpart of brooks and dew. That it is misleading to talk dismissively of all this as 'narcissism' (at least in the ordinary sense of the word) is shown by its outcome in the final sentence: 'Hands I have taken, face I have kissed, mortal I have ever touched, it shall be you.' The affectionate, sympathetic relationship with another, does not simply follow what has preceded: it flows directly from it. Whitman's security of personal being – incorporated as it is in a complex state of physical well-being – leaves him free to reach out, literally and metaphorically, to acknowledge the being of others. By rejecting possessiveness, with all its aggressions and defences, he has entered into fuller possession of himself.

Whitman's observations on the proprietorial and acquisitive self, whether in his notes or in 'Song of Myself', are frequently infused with the values and expressed in the language of a venerable Christian and biblical tradition. But they are also addressed very directly to, and deeply affected by, the special circumstances of his own age. Emerson characterized that age as one in which 'A selfish commerce and government have caught the eye and usurped the hand of the masses. It is not to be contested that selfishness and the senses write the laws under which we live, and that the street seems to be built, and the men and women in it moving not in reference to pure and grand ends, but rather to very short and sordid ones' (Emerson, *The Dial*, 1961).[16] And contemporary observers, domestic and foreign, almost without exception seconded Emerson's opinion, seeing the average American of this period as one 'striving every fibre to accumulate the things he covets and amoral about the methods to be used' (Edward Pesson, *Jacksonian America*, 1969).[17]

... It is obviously true that 'Song of Myself' does not concern itself with the detailed socioeconomic causes and results of Jacksonian capitalism; but it is a reaction – and as valid and constructive a reaction as the political radicalism in which the younger Whitman engaged – to the widespread human world produced by this process. ...

[The] early Whitman lived through and was closely identified with a decisive transformation in the social character and structure of New York and Brooklyn. From the twenties onwards, the work conditions of the self-employed craftsmen, artisans, and tradesmen – the solid bulk of the population of the cities – changed very markedly in what has been variously described as a period of 'epochal historical transformations', or, quite simply, 'the great transformation' (Sean Wilentz, *Chants Democratic*, 1984).[18] This was due to the advance from the artisanal to the post-artisanal phase of capitalist production (Raymond Williams, *Culture*, 1981).[19] Under the former, the producer, although ultimately subject to local market forces, is still able to retain a considerable amount of control over his work, including the eventual terms and conditions of sale. Consequently the process is not one easily construed by the participants as a purely financial transaction, as there is much more at stake, at every stage, than the accumulation of capital. ... But in the post-artisanal phase the function (and with it the whole status) of the producer is fundamentally altered. He now produces for a middleman who deals in a complex, increasingly remote, and demanding market. In the first instance this intermediary may be only the distributor of the product, but even then he soon comes to dictate the terms of production. Alternatively, he may himself be a large producer, who uses the small producer only as a profitable source of supply. Under this arrangement the former artisan, now effectively a supplier or hirer of labor in return for money, finds himself deeply implicated in a system of relations which alters his whole conception of himself and his work. In short, his consciousness is changed in the ways Whitman explores so critically in 'Song of Myself'. He lives by the competitive accumulation of capital, rather than by virtue of what he produces through the exercise and public demonstration of patiently acquired skills.

The change from the artisanal to post-artisanal system of production contributed very largely toward the making of a commercially dynamic mid-nineteenth-century America. But from the beginning this transition caused a serious, and in some cases traumatic, upheaval, whose effects continued to be very widely felt throughout the fifties, not least in Whitman's poetry. ...

Exceptionally sensitive to all the different issues involved, and to the different levels of those issues, Whitman turned to poetry to resolve him of his ambiguities. In 'Song of Myself' he makes contemporary capitalism, with all the freedom and variety of existence it quite genuinely seems to him to promise, the ostensibly simple subject of his celebrations, while at the same time he attacks the very spirit of selfhood, which in historical fact animates and agitates this new world – pulling down its vanity by means of his very different pride in himself. It is almost as if he were trying to bring the artisanal and post-artisanal phases he had known together into a single imaginative synthesis, in which each of the two elements is used to criticize and transform the other. In this he is perhaps a fascinating example of how poetry made a visionary out of 'the schizophrenic Jacksonian, the man who looks backward while plunging forward' (Bernstein ed., *Towards a New Past*, 1970).[20] And it was this visionary who, in 'Song of Myself', produced his own distinctly American view of what Marx, at virtually the same time and with tragic splendor, was calling the simultaneous 'birth and decline' of the individual. □

(Thomas, *The Lunar Light of Whitman's Poetry*, 1987).[21]

A similar desire to explore Whitman's entanglements in the culture of his day is found in the following extract from Ed Folsom's *Walt Whitman's Native Representations* (1994), a book that traces and assesses Whitman's relationship to his native culture. Like Thomas, Folsom finds Whitman drawing from the reserves of a rich and diverse popular culture in order to produce a nuanced and complex poetry. Rather than simply dismissing Whitman and the culture that produced him as 'barbaric', such interpretations contend that reading Whitman must inevitably be an exercise in reading culture, in reading America. Dissatisfied with the rather sweeping terms of earlier critics – 'Democracy', 'Individualism', 'Personality', 'Adamic myth' – more recent Whitman criticism has attended to particular details of Whitman's participation in American culture in order to investigate his Americanness. Concomitantly, Whitman's poetry seems far more subtle and delicately poised than in the broad brushstroke accounts of it in the middle years of the twentieth century.

Like many other readings of Whitman, Folsom's book represents an attempt to reconstruct some of the cultural circumstances of Whitman's time, through analysis of his poetry. Unlike many other such critical dealings with Whitman, this attempt is highly successful. The book's arresting power lies in the apparent simplicity of its methods, and its tight focus upon specific topics. Rather than seeking to document the range of Whitman's borrowings from nineteenth-century American popular culture, the book is highly selective. Successive chapters deal with Whitman's relationship to American dictionaries, to American sport, to (representations of) American Indians and to photography. Folsom notes in his preface that rather than being all-inclusive, the book's method might be seen as 'a kind of metonymic criticism' in which its particular points of critical focus come, metaphorically, to stand-in for an analysis of the whole of Whitman's poetic achievement. Folsom's reading of Whitman is one, therefore, that draws a wider cultural significance from very specific moments documented in the poetry.[22] The book does indeed achieve Folsom's aim of 'discover[ing] how almost any cultural activity could help [Whitman] form his poetry and enable him to define a distinctive American poetics.'[23] Fascinatingly, perhaps a little surprisingly, but certainly convincingly, the extract from Folsom's book that follows traces connections between Whitman's poetry and Baseball.

■ [It] is ... significant that when a British writer like Virginia Woolf mentions Walt Whitman, the subject of baseball naturally pops up. In 1925 Woolf wrote that 'the only American writer whom the English wholeheartedly admire is Walt Whitman' (Woolf in *The Movement and other Essays*, 1948).[24] He was, she said, 'The real American undisguised', the true original who certainly did not imitate any figure in English literature; in Whitman, the 'English tourist in American literature' would find no writer more 'different from what he has at home'. For Woolf, Whitman is the pure example of a writer who took 'the first step in the process of being American – to be not English', 'to dismiss the whole army of English words which have marched so long under the command of dead English generals'.[25] And it is baseball, 'a game which is not played in England',[26] that she finds to be the perfect American farm club [in baseball (and other sports) a club that has its own training programme to induct 'home grown' youth talent into its senior team] for a new poetic language, a native activity with its own built-in localized slang and its own essential connections to American culture. It is a game, she says, 'indigenous to the soil'. Woolf points out that the English tradition is measured on a small scale; it assumes a small familiar country, and 'its centre is an old house crammed with objects and crowded with people who know each other intimately, whose manners, thoughts, and speech are ruled all the time ... by the spirit of the past'. 'But in America', Woolf suggests, 'there is baseball instead of society', and this peculiar national sport magically incorporates the vast space and uneven pace of 'a new land, its tin cans, its prairies, its cornfields flung disorderly about like a mosaic of incongruous pieces waiting order at the artists' hands'. Furthermore, the game generates its own language, a way of talking, a slang in America, and so 'the Americans are doing what the Elizabethans did – they are coining new words', and 'when words are being made, a literature will be made out of them'.[27]

Woolf's analysis of American literature is incisive; she was not aware that Whitman had direct and long-standing associations with the game of baseball … but she intuitively senses the connection between the national poet and the national sport, a connection that was more direct and more fertile than she imagined. Other writers sensed the connection, too; John Dos Passos wrote an essay in college called 'Art and Baseball', identifying Whitman as the model writer of precisely the kind of vitality that baseball represented (Michael Clark, *Dos Passos' Early Fiction*, 1987),[28] and Michael Gold, writing in the *New Masses* in 1928, noted how America's true poets learned from Whitman 'to see America for the first time … to walk in their own strong American sun, to push and crowd with the American mobman at baseball games and picnics',[29] to come down off the pedestal in an act of linguistic and experiential democracy – poetry embracing the life of the great mass of people. And from the 1840s on, baseball became the emblem of that emerging American spirit. Baseball, Whitman said, is 'America's game: has the snap, go, fling, of the American atmosphere – belongs as much to our institutions, fits into them as significantly, as our constitutions, laws …' (Horace Traubel, *With Walt Whitman in Camden*, 1953).[30] Whitman did indeed assimilate the lingo of baseball into his poetic vocabulary, appropriating its essentials as key metaphors, recognizing that a defining trait of American democracy was precisely the fact that we had 'baseball instead of society'. …

What, then, was Whitman's actual connection to the game? How significant was baseball to his life and to his work? It is notable that baseball as we know it began when Whitman was a young man, and it began almost literally in his back yard. …

Ball games were more than an exalted metaphor for Whitman; they were an integral part of his day-to-day life. They seemed, in fact, repeatedly to mark important moments of his experience. In Boston in April 1860, for example, just after Whitman had had his famous stroll with Ralph Waldo Emerson when Emerson tried to convince him to tame his poetry by removing some of the more explicitly sexual poems, Whitman noted the emerging spring by writing of the reemergence of sports:

> Thursday, the grass begins to look green on the common, the buds on the elms are russet, the young fellows are playing football. Football! A noble and manly game – there they are in their shirt sleeves, running, crowding, tumbling together, quite an inspiring sight.[31]

As he rejected Emerson's advice to reduce the physicality of his poetry, Whitman turned to the inspiring sight of physical contact, Americans at play developing their bodies and their character.

At various times over the years, Whitman would extol wrestling, track, quoits, sailing, and other sports, but there was only one sport he would return to throughout his life and that was baseball. Even when he was a virtual invalid in his final years, he still kept up with the sport, reading baseball reports in the newspapers; he often testified to his status as a baseball fan. In 1889, he told his young friend Horace Traubel, 'I still find my interest in the game unabated: I suppose it's so with you, too: I can't forget the games we used to go to together: they are precious memories.'[32]

...[Whitman's] lifelong interest in baseball is significant... because his adult life coincides, geographically and temporally, with the development of American baseball from its birth to its maturity. Whitman, growing up with the sport, eventually came to see baseball as an essential metaphor for America.

Baseball as we know it was born in 1845 with the formation of the Knickerbocker Club in New York, where the first recognizable baseball rules were set down in writing, including a key new rule that prohibited throwing the ball at the runner in order to put him out. This change immediately allowed for the use of the hard, lively ball that altered the nature of the game drastically – speeding things up, increasing distances, requiring quicker reflexes, and promptly turning a children's game into a full-fledged sport. On June 19, 1846, the Knickerbockers played the first game of baseball (under the new rules) at Elysian Fields in Hoboken. And only a month later, Whitman, young editor of the *Brooklyn Daily Eagle*, wrote an editorial entitled 'Brooklyn Young Men – Athletic Exercises':

In our sun-down perambulations, of late, through the outer parts of Brooklyn, we have observed several parties of youngsters playing 'base', a certain game of ball. We wish such sights were more common among us. In the practice of athletic and manly sports the young men of nearly all our American cities are very deficient – perhaps more so than any other country that could be mentioned.

We can see, even this early on, why more than forty years later Whitman would be excited and proud about America's manly baseball players demonstrating to the world their athletic skills; for in this early editorial, Whitman exhorts the youth of the country to 'enjoy life a little. ... Let us go forth awhile, and get better air in our lungs. Let us leave our close rooms.' Exercise was essential for success on the open road, and of all forms of sport, Whitman from the start was most attracted to the young game of baseball: 'The Game of ball is glorious' (C. Rogers and J. Black (eds), *The Gathering of Forces*, 1920).[33] As baseball was born, then, it immediately was bound up in Whitman's mind with qualities he would endorse his whole life: vigor, manliness, al fresco health. ...

...In the notebooks he kept during the 1850s, Whitman made long lists of young men he had met, affectionate catalogues of America's strong democratic workers; he described their jobs and characteristics... and he specifically identified many of the men as ball players: 'Bill – (big, black round eyes, large coarse ... Irish descent playing ball).' So it is not surprising that in 'Song of Myself', after we have been through a catalog of carpenters, pilots, farmers, printers, machinists, paving men, canal boys, and conductors, we come upon (in the vast catalog of Section 33) an image of baseball. At this point in the poem, Whitman is 'afoot with [his] vision', spanning the continent with his rolling catalogue, when he records a refreshing group of manly pursuits:

Upon the race-course, or enjoying picnics or jigs or a good game of
base-ball,
At he-festivals, with blackguard gibes, ironical license, bull-dances,
drinking, laughter.

And in his vast, loving catalog of America working (the poem that would come to be entitled 'A Song of Occupations'), Whitman included baseball in the list of activities that defined his wondrously variegated vision of democracy:

The ladders and hanging ropes of the gymnasium, manly exercises,
the game of base-ball, running, leaping, pitching quoits.

Whitman eventually removed this line when he altered the poem to emphasize occupations more than activities; he always remained ambivalent about baseball becoming an 'occupation'. The professionalization and specialization of the sport (which occurred largely in the 1870s and 1880s) cut against the grain of his ideal vision of a skilled society of individual artisans who used sport to keep themselves healthy for their crafts, not those who used sport to *replace* or displace their crafts.

...There is [another] aspect of baseball behaviour that would have appealed to Whitman during the late 1850s when he was writing his *Calamus* poems, and that is the sport's sanctioning of open expressions of male–male affection. Early baseball clubs were very close fraternities, sites of intense male bonding. Descriptions of early games often include mention of a physical and spiritual closeness among players, as in an 1860 description of players leaving the field, 'many of them arm in arm with each other'. (W. Goldstein, *Playing for Keeps*, 1989).[34] This tendency of players to express their camaraderie in physical terms would have struck Whitman, of course, as a healthy sign of the kind of intense friendship – he called it 'fervid comradeship' – that he believed had to evolve in America to 'offset...our materialistic and vulgar American democracy'. Democracy, he argued, would be 'incomplete, in vain, and incapable of perpetuating itself' without the 'threads of manly friendship...carried to degrees hitherto unknown' that would rival 'amative love' (Floyd Stovall ed., *Walt Whitman*, 1963).[35] Baseball remains in American culture one of the few public sites where men embrace, pat other males' rears, drape their arms around male teammates, without causing homophobic reactions. From the beginning, then, Whitman would have appreciated the possibilities for the game to produce the kind of comradeship that he believed would eventually lead to real democracy.

...The emerging role of the spectator was one of the most significant developments in American sports during the last third of the nineteenth century. Whitman's well-known stance of being 'Both in and out of the game' reflects the spectators' evolving sense of their duties and responsibilities (*Leaves of Grass* in Norton Critical Edition).[36] Allen Guttmann notes how a 'historically unprecedented code of spectatorship' developed during the Victorian era, a code that 'was never perfectly institutionalized', but which nonetheless set certain standards of expected behaviour, including the acknowledgement of outstanding play by opponents. The vast crowds, largely male, immigrant, and lower class that Whitman reported seeing at baseball games were potential challenges to democracy: they could easily become vicious mobs, ruled by violence and prejudice, so the code of spectatorship served a civilizing function: 'The spectators' passions were to be governed by strict rules of conduct analogous to the rules of the game (and also analogous to the behaviour of middle-class concert and theater audiences' (A. Guttmann, *Sports Spectators*, 1986).[37] As American sports developed specializations leading to the separation of professional athletes and paying spectators, most Americans who cared about baseball were involved in the game as observers rather than as active players. As active observers, they had to find ways to channel their passionate but necessarily passive involvement into behaviour that would allow the game to proceed fairly but would still allow them to feel they were helping their team to victory; they had to figure out, in other words, how to maintain a stance of being simultaneously both in and out of the game.

Whitman's poetry, of course, was precisely the poetry of the crowd; his infamous 'catalogs' became the poetic equivalent of a turnstile admitting a diverse group of individuals into one arena, where each detail retained its uniqueness yet all worked together as they focused on one action – a democratic diversity responding to the same sweep of energy. The baseball crowd, then, one of the evolving common aspects of American experience in the late nineteenth century, came to be a gauge of the democratic experience, a visible measure of the success of the attempt to meld the individual and the 'En-Masse'. The baseball crowd came to be the cultural icon for democracy; as the *Boston Globe* noted in 1883, 'Every class, every station, every color and every nationality will be found at a ball match.'[38] But such democratic ideals were undermined by the entrepreneurship of the growing baseball business; rising and differentiated ticket prices (the bleachers ['a usually uncovered stand of tiered planks providing seating for spectators' (Webster's)] became the cheap seats) led to an intensification rather than an obliteration of social and economic distinction. In 1877, turnstiles were introduced at National League baseball parks, just as Ladies' Days were becoming common: these were the first signs of 'crowd control', as baseball magnates attempted to diminish the potential problems of a lower-class male rowdiness by diluting the crowd with a gender and a class that would provide good behavioral examples.

... But toward the end of his life, as crowd violence began to be a problem in baseball, as fans began taunting black players, Whitman saw that baseball was beginning to reflect some unsettling cultural changes. Not only the crowds, but the game itself seemed to be conforming to anti-democratic tendencies in the culture.

...[However,] Whitman persisted in holding on to an idyllic vision of the game: baseball as something essentially bound up with the best of America. Some of Whitman's last outdoor excursions were to watch the national sport, which he seemed to associate with Nature itself; for him, watching baseball was as natural and exhilarating as breathing fresh air. Traubel notes how in the early 1890s Whitman 'is taken out regularly in his chair, perhaps to the outskirts of the town, where he may scan the free sky, the shifting clouds, watch the boys at base-ball, or breathe in drowsily ... the refreshing air'.[39] Traubel recalls Whitman talking about one of his favorite topics in the last years – the idea of 'free Sundays', with no blue law[40] restrictions on activities (like the ones that prevented Spalding's international team from playing in Hawaii when they arrived on a Sunday): 'W. believes in "free Sundays." The boys should have their ball or any frolic they choose.'[41] Whitman here is entering into a raging controversy in the 1880s, as two baseball leagues, the American Association and the Union Association, directly challenged Sunday blue laws by scheduling games on the one day of the week that workingmen could easily attend (and by serving beer as well). Such actions led to widely publicized arrests of managers and players in Baltimore, Washington, and Cincinnati in the last two summers of Whitman's life and led to widespread denunciation of the sport by priests and preachers, one of whom sermonized that baseball was 'a travelling contagion that should be quarantined for the public good'.[42] Whitman remained firmly in support of the baseball interests, though he never admitted the pecuniary interests the club owners had in challenging blue laws (Sunday games drew larger crowds); he argued instead on the basis of freedom from priestly and puritanical authority:

> Talking of Sunday agitation generally and Gloucester [New Jersey] baseball in particular W. said: 'I believe in all that – in baseball, in picnics, in freedom: I believe in the jolly all-round time – with the parsons and the police eliminated.'[43]

Whitman here gives early voice to what would become an American cliché: 'baseball, picnics, and freedom' formed a commonplace nexus of American values. ... So it comes as no surprise to hear Whitman express his despair in late autumn in the last years of his life as he is taken outside in his wheelchair on a restricted Sunday and finds the day hollow and cold as baseball has disappeared from the land:

> I was out in my chair yesterday – Warrie [Warren Fritzinger, Whitman's nurse] took me and we went up towards the city hall. Generally, on weekdays, there are boys playing base ball – a fine air of activity, life, but yesterday everything was glum – neither boy nor ball to be seen. I thought then – told Warrie, too – how much better the play, the open air, the beautiful sky, the active movement, than restriction, Sabbathism.[44]

Whitman, then, resisted the lingering power of the Puritan suspicion about sport and the cultural perpetuation of the Puritan ban on Sunday recreational activity. ... Baseball, the American game with its American pace, had replaced the church as the source of morality, value, and vitality, and the spirited national debate in the 1880s and 1890s about Sunday baseball provided Whitman one final opportunity to give voice to his desire to see a country in which 'There will soon be no more priests' and where the crowds will replace them: 'A superior breed shall take their place. ... the gangs of kosmos and prophets en masse shall take their place.'[45]

... Baseball for Whitman was the emblem and enactment of straightforwardness, and its pace and heritage made it the ideal athletic backdrop against which his poetry could be read. Even the baseball field itself was the manifestation for Whitman of how America should occupy the continent, joining with but not arrogating the natural landscape: 'The desired thing was not an absolute cutting away but modification – nature not all wiped out, as if ashamed of.'[46] Whitman dreamed of the United States reaching a communal culmination in the 'Prairie States' where the vast open spaces would allow for huge populations without congestion, allow for human landscapes to merge with natural ones, where neither man nor nature would 'wipe out' the other:

A newer garden of creation, no primal solitude,
Dense, joyous, modern, populous millions, cities and farms,
With iron interlaced, composite, tied, many in one.[47]

The baseball field, long viewed as a microcosm of America with its congested infield arching around home and its vast and underpopulated outfield expanding in an ever-widening arc beyond the congestion, was part of Whitman's memory of his own childhood relations to America's changing landscape:

I remember – it is quite vivid – a spot off on Long Island, somewhere in the neighborhood of our old home – rough, uncultivated, uncared for – choked with underbrush – forbidding: people coming would avoid it – it was that kind of place: put to no practical uses, untouched. ... I left the neighborhood – was away for years: wandering seeing: living: went back again: the whole face of it was changed: now a base ball ground, a park ... yet it had required but little work to effect the transformation – simply clearing away the brush: now it is a perfect spot of its kind – a resort.

A wilderness had been transformed into a habitable place, a place of American activity, yet in the process the natural had not been destroyed, only enhanced. Whitman was quick to draw the lesson for his own poetry: 'Carry the thought along: there is an art in such a situation – an art of not doing too much.'[48] It would be another way Whitman's poetry and his country would imitate each other, transforming uncharted experience into form, but doing so gently, allowing the experience itself to generate the form, learning, with words or plans or tools, the 'art of not doing too much', of nudging a baseball field out of the brush.

... It's important, then, to realize that Walt Whitman, our most essentially American poet, was one of the first of our writers, perhaps *the* first, to recognize the vital significance of baseball to America. ... Clearly for Whitman, baseball was the sport that came to coincide with the best aspects of the American character and eventually came to absorb its worst aspects, too; like some cultural litmus paper, the game absorbed events and attitudes, and it altered its appearance to reflect changes in the national environment. It was the sport that was precisely about Americans, and as such, it became for Whitman an analogue for his poetry, which he hoped would be the literary equivalent of baseball – a cultural structure guided by a set of rules peculiarly American, paced according to American needs and customs, available to all, somewhat incomprehensible to other cultures. Whitman's baseball credo could only have been spoken by a man who grew up with the sport; saw it develop from its slower, more sedate forms into a demanding game of hardball with 'snap and go'; saw the democratic demands of skill force gentlemen to give way to young roughs; saw the baseball team itself become an image of America, accepting and absorbing men from all walks of life, immigrants from all over the world, molding them into one body, a union committed to a common purpose; saw the sport, starting from Manhattan, spread westward and eventually be played from coast to coast, affirming America's secure occupation of the continent; saw baseball, finally, become an athletic image of his soul, accomplishing the rondure of the world, spreading 'America's game' and 'the American atmosphere' to Australia, Asia, Africa, and Europe, then returning home in triumph and comradeship. ☐

(Ed Folsom, *Whitman's Native Representations*, 1994)[49]

Folsom's examination of Whitman stresses that the importance of his poetry lies in its ability to reflect some of the specific ideological conditions from which it arose. Though the vehicle for his examination of Whitman in the above extract is baseball, Folsom's concern is ultimately with the power of Whitman's poetry to provide us with a means of understanding nineteenth-century America in richer and more nuanced detail. This aim is shared by the final essay of this chapter which turns to an examination and 'reconstruction' of another specific aspect of nineteenth-century American culture as a means of reading Whitman. In the essay that follows, David S. Reynolds draws on his extensive scholarly researches into the popular writing and culture of antebellum American in order to consider Whitman's dealings with issues of gender and sexuality. Though perhaps more concerned than both Thomas and Folsom with the cultural circumstances as such, he nevertheless signals a new way of approaching Whitman via the materials of his culture. In fact, Reynolds' grand aim of setting Whitman in his cultural context is carried out in his magnificent *Walt Whitman's America: A Cultural Biography* (1995). Published a year earlier than this book, the essay that follows originally appeared in a book marking the centennial of Whitman's death, *Walt Whitman of Mickle Street: A Centennial Collection*, edited by Geoffrey Still, an important collection of readings and re-readings of Whitman from broadly cultural materialist perspectives. It is reproduced here in its entirety.

■ Studying Whitman against the background of nineteenth-century views of gender and sexuality reveals that Whitman's erotic images were, in large part, a poetic response to representations of sexuality in American popular culture. In an essay entitled 'A Memorandum at a Venture', Whitman identified two predominant viewpoints toward sexuality in America. The first, he wrote, was 'the conventional one ... of good folks and good print every where, repressing any direct statement' of sexuality and viewing it as something 'sneaking, furtive, mephitic ['offensive to the smell' (OED)].' The second view, 'and by far the largest', he emphasized, was visible in the 'wit, of masculine circles, and in erotic stories and talk', stories that dwelt on 'merely sensual voluptuousness'. Denouncing both views, Whitman declared that sex was a proper literary theme only when it was what he called 'normal and unperverted', and asked for 'a new departure – a third point of view', one that placed sex in the realm of 'sanity' and 'nature'.[50]

Whitman's description of two conflicting viewpoints was in fact quite accurate. Having surveyed the total range of popular novels and newspapers in antebellum America, I have found that there were two main types of popular literature, what I call the conventional and the subversive, which represented opposing views of sexuality and gender issues. Conventional literature – such as popular domestic novels, religious tracts, and genteel poetry – typified that sensibility attacked by Whitman as prudish, repressive, and furtive. Designed mainly for a female audience, conventional literature valorized woman's powerful role as mother and moral exemplar and made little mention of her sexuality or her need for greater political or social rights.

As popular as this literature was, it is misleading to say, as many scholars have, that it dominated the literary scene in Whitman's day. Whitman was justified in claiming that 'by far the largest' point of view toward sexuality was embodied in the 'erotic stories and talk' of masculine circles. I have found that, in the fifteen years just prior to the first edition of Leaves of Grass, the highly wrought, adventurous volumes published in America actually outnumbered the conventional ones by nearly two to one. In the hands of such popular writers as George Thompson and George Lippard, this literature became notably subversive in its nightmarishness, its political radicalism, and its rampant eroticism.

The subversive writers were generally working-class advocates driven by a ferocious impulse to expose the American upper classes as rotten to the core. In order to do this, they wrote scathing novels and journalistic pieces that pictured the so-called 'idle' rich engaged in various forms of sexual misbehavior. Many subversive novels pictured upper-class men, such as clergymen or lawyers, who used every tool of manipulation and treachery to seduce young women, whose physical charms were inevitably described in detail. Others dramatized the intrigues of wealthy, sexually insatiable women, who demanded many lovers. There was nothing clean or genuine about relations between the sexes for subversive radical democrats like George Thompson, who in his nearly one hundred novels portrayed all varieties of sex: incest, sadomasochism, homosexuality, group sex, child sex, mass orgies. In the twisted world of subversive fiction, sex was unconnected with love. Instead it was governed by violence, entrapment, and manipulation.

Whitman feared that such popular literature was contributing to what he regarded as America's alarming moral decline. He once wrote in his notebook: 'In the plentiful feast of romance presented to us, all the novels, all the poems really dish up only one … plot, namely, a sickly, scrofulous [Adj. from "Scrofula": "A constitutional disease characterized mainly by chronic enlargement and degeneration of the lymphatic glands." (OED)], crude, amorousness.'[51] …

In opposition to this sensational popular literature, he wanted to treat sex as natural and genuine, free of hypocrisy and gamesmanship. He wrote in *Democratic Vistas* that the test of the great writer is 'the absence in him of the idea of the covert, the lurid, the maleficent, the devil' – all of which Whitman saw in American sensational writings.[52] American culture could be rescued, he believed, only through a new generation of poets who absorbed their culture but at the same time purified it and transformed it into something better.

To counteract what he saw as the corruptions and inhumanity of the love plot, Whitman borrowed sanitizing images from modern sciences and from new American religious movements that permitted a spiritual redefinition of sexual mores. The most useful sciences for him were physiology and phrenology. The 1840s and 1850s produced several books on human physiology that lent a new objectivity to the exploration of human sexuality. As editor of the *Brooklyn Daily Eagle*, Whitman approvingly reviewed several physiological books, and in his poetry he tried to supplant the grotesque distortions of the love plot with the frank freedoms of physiology. … The first full passage on sex in 'Song of Myself' shows Whitman taking care to place his persona in the objective, clean realm of physiology, distant from what he considered the nasty arena of sensational sex:

> Welcome is every organ and attribute of me, and of any man
>   hearty and clean,
> Not an inch nor a particle of an inch is vile, and none shall be less
>   familiar than the rest.[53]

Throughout his poetry, his exploration of sexual organs and functions is guided by his impulse to remove sex from the lurid indirections of the popular love plot. When in his poetry he sings praise for thc naturalness of copulation, to jetting sperm or cohering wombs, or when he lovingly records the private parts of men and women, he displays his prevailing interest in ushering sex from the coarsely sensational to the honestly physiological. …

Of equal use to Whitman in combating the luridness of popular romances was phrenology, the pseudoscience that attributed human impulses to distinct organs of the brain. Leading phrenological theorists, such as Whitman's friends Orson and Lorenzo Fowler, had underscored the natural-ness of sexuality when they had argued that the two most powerful brain organs were amativeness (sexual love between men and women) and adhe-siveness (comradely affection between people of the same sex). For Whitman, phrenology provided another means of dealing with sex with combined can-dour and tact. He wrote confidently: 'I know that amativeness is just as divine as spirituality – and this which I know I put freely in my poems.'[54] Elsewhere he wrote that the underlying qualities of his poetry were 'a powerful sense of physical perfection, strength and beauty, with great amativeness, adhesive-ness'.[55] He justified his most openly sexual poetry sequences, 'Children of Adam' and 'Calamus', by specifying that the former was designed to illustrate 'amativeness', or heterosexual love, and that the latter focused on 'adhe-siveness', of comradely fellowship.[56]

Whitman also profited from another antebellum phenomenon associ-ated with sexuality, what I call sexual antinomianism – that is, the effort to redefine sexual norms according to moral or religious belief. This period was a particularly fertile one for sexual antinomians of various kinds; the Mormons, the spiritualists, the Oneidan perfectionists, the Fourierists, and the free-love advocates all introduced highly unconventional sexual codes based upon personal belief. Varied as these groups were, all of them were convinced that bold sexual experimentation could go hand in hand with spiritual righteousness. They introduced a special vocabulary that described sexual experience in terms of mysticism and electrical, magnetic attraction. Often in his poems Whitman uses the mystical or electrical terminology of the sexual antinomians to uplift passages that otherwise might be scabrous ['Risky, bordering upon the indelicate' (OED)]. In 'Song of Myself', in his famous self-portrait of his persona as 'hanker-ing, gross, mystical, nude', the word 'mystical' gives a spiritual tinge to this otherwise shocking line. The free fusion of the sexual and the spiritual is evident in many Whitman poems, such as 'I Sing the Body Electric', which begins with the sexual antinomian lines:

I sing the body electric,
The armies of those I love engirth me, and I engirth them,
They will not let me off until I go with them, respond to them,
And discorrupt them, and charge them full with the charge of the
soul.[57]

The images in 'Children of Adam' and 'Calamus' of the 'divine nimbus' around the human form, or the 'divine list' of female body parts, or 'the divine wife' and 'the divine husband' engaged in 'the act divine' all fuse intense spirituality and sexuality, in the vocabulary of the sexual antinomians.

Whitman's unifying imagination not only produced inventive combina-tions of popular sexual beliefs, but it also engendered a wholly original fusion of sexual and nature images. Since his overriding goal was to absorb his culture's shocking images but at the same time to purify them, he repeatedly used what might be termed *cleansing rhetoric* – that is, the yoking together of refreshing nature images and sensational ones in an effort to overcome prurient sexuality. Cleansing rhetoric dominates the famous opening section of 'Song of Myself', in which the poet moves from a rejection of 'houses and rooms full of perfumes' ... through a cleansing line that fuses sexual and nature images ('Echoes, ripples ... loveroot, silk-thread, crotch and vine') to a tentative sexual passage ('A few light kisses ... a few embraces ... the reaching around of arms') to a completely joyous picture of health in nature ('The feeling of health ... the song of me rising from bed and greeting the sun').

Cleansing rhetoric also uplifts the long sexual passage in 'Song of Myself' (section 11) describing the rich woman's erotic fantasy about the twenty-eight young men she sees bathing in a nearby stream. This scene might be viewed as Whitman's cleansing of popular sensational images, for many sensational novels of the day depict wealthy women who fantasize about having numerous lovers. Like the sensationalists, Whitman stresses that the woman is wealthy, that her sexual fantasies are secretive, that she fantasizes about many lovers. But Whitman revives the voyeuristic eroticism of the popular writers in ways that make it natural and redemptive rather than selfish and destructive. There is absolutely no seduction or manipulation involved in the scene of the woman viewing the bathers. Indeed there is no sexual contact, since the bathers do not even see her staring at them. Voyeuristic fantasy is stripped of malice and is conveyed through refreshing, baptismal images of nature. Not only are the splashing men the picture of fun and health, but the woman's rising orgasmic excitement is made pure and beautiful because it is adeptly fused with cleansing nature images. Whitman writes:

> The young men float on their backs, their white bellies bulge to the
> sun ... they do not ask who seizes fast to them,
> They do not know who puffs and declines with pendant and
> bending arch,
> They do not think whom they souse with spray.[58]

The carefree sport of the bathers precludes any sort of machination or intrigue, and the dazzling final image, in which the spray of water is fused metaphorically with the spray of orgasm, weds the sexual act with frolic in nature.

Throughout his poetry, Whitman adopts sexual images common in sensational literature but converts them into lovely metaphors for his aesthetic enjoyment of nature. Instead of gloating lasciviously over a woman's 'snowy globes,' as did many popular writers, he writes, 'Press close bare-bosomed night!' Instead of smacking his lips over a voluptuous woman, he declares himself the lover of the 'voluptuous coolbreathed earth'. Instead of portraying sex as a violent game that thrives on sham and broken homes, he emphasizes that his rapturous union with nature is a consecrated marriage in which the partners 'hurt each other as the bridegroom and bride hurt each other'. This fusion of sex and nature is equally evident in many other images in his poetry, such as the 'winds whose soft-tickling genitals rub against me', the 'clasping and sweet-flesh'd day,' or 'the souse of my lover the sea, as I lie willing and naked'.

In his most daringly sexual poems, such as 'From Pent-Up Aching Rivers', 'A Woman Waits for Me', and 'Spontaneous Me', Whitman inter-weaves images from phrenology, physiology, sexual antinomianism, and nature in a wholesale effort to use *all* his cultural arsenal for ridding sex of tawdriness and overcoming the iniquities of the popular love plot. His intention to revise the treatment of sex is made clear in the opening lines of 'Pent-Up Aching Rivers', in which he calls sex that which 'I am deter-min'd to make illustrious, even if I stand sole among men.' Sex does become illustrious in the poem, which is earnestly passionate instead of licentious, when he sings praise to the phallus and procreation in physio-logical terms, which celebrates 'the act divine' by 'divine' husbands and wives in the spiritual language of sexual antinomianism, which creatively mixes frankly sexual images of fondling and copulation with exhilarating pictures of the sights and smells of nature. 'A Woman Waits for Me' adver-tises sex 'without shame' for both men and women, as Whitman tries mightily to overcome prurient furtiveness by glorifying healthy sexuality, in which sexual prowess is fused with patriotism: 'I pour the stuff to start sons and daughters fit for these States, I press with slow rude muscle.' In 'Spontaneous Me', Whitman again weaves a subtle tapestry of sexual and nature images, creating a dialectic between the two and, above all, omit-ting any reference to the popular love plot that he so fiercely detested.

In conclusion, Whitman's treatment of sex can be profitably viewed as a response to the literary context within which he was writing. Realizing that 'by and far the largest' view toward sex was expressed in the 'merely sensational voluptuousness' of 'erotic stories and talk', he succeeded in creating what he called 'a new departure – a third point of view', one that placed sex in the realm of natural passion and aesthetic perception. By creating rich poetic alternatives to the sensationalized eroticism of his day, Whitman became our most *genuinely* erotic poet.[59] □

(David S. Reynolds, 'Whitman and Nineteenth-Century Views of Gender and Sexuality', 1994)[59]

The next chapter develops themes raised by Reynolds by examining three (out of many) readings of Whitman's poetry that attend to the vexed, and at times extremely heated, critical debate over Whitman's sexuality.

CHAPTER SIX

Ideology and Desire: Whitman and Sexuality

C ritical discussion of sex and the body, sexuality and desire in relation to Whitman's poetry has a surprisingly long history. Emerson himself attempted to step back from his initially positive position towards *Leaves of Grass* on the publication of its second edition by declaring himself wary of the passages dealing with sex. And other, more dismissive critics, declared the book to be monstrous by clearly implying that questions of sex, and more particularly of Whitman's own sexual ethics, rendered the book morally reprehensible and poetically redundant.[1] As we saw in Chapter 2, Symonds displayed an almost prurient fascination with questions of Whitman's sexuality, eliciting from Whitman his famous response about having fathered six children. Despite Whitman's denial of what lay beneath Symond's line of questioning, the issue of Whitman's sexuality has been a common and recurring theme throughout Whitman criticism. Ever since its first publication, *Leaves of Grass* has caused more than a few raised eyebrows amongst its readers. Whitman's poetic method of 'indirection' has been the focus of numerous studies that claim to have understood his dark 'secret', having 'cracked' what they see as the great code of the poetry. Invariably, though, such readings have done little to illuminate the real forces operating behind Whitman's poetry and often make it seem little more than a riddle designed to disguise titillating gossip.

More recently, critical debate about Whitman's sexuality has been used as a means of reevaluating his contribution to American poetry, as well as of opening up wider-reaching investigations into the ideological conditions of Whitman's America (and, interestingly, of the particular critic's own perspective). One of the first full-scale studies to tackle head-on the fraught question of Whitman's sexuality and its relationship to his poetry was Roger Asselineau in his massive doctoral dissertation *L'Évolution de Walt Whitman* (1954). This was published in two volumes in English translation in 1960 and 1962. Asselineau argues that Whitman's homosexuality is central to an understanding of his poetry. Whitman's poetry, Asselineau contends, emerges directly out of his struggle with his own homosexual desires. In fairly classic Freudian terms, then, Whitman's poetic impulse sublimates his homosexual desire into an act of aesthetic compensation. Asselineau claims therefore that the turbulent passions of the poems are the product of Whitman's deeply repressed sexual drives. This leads Asselineau to a detailed and complex examination of the tensions and instabilities of Whitman's poetry, and furnishes us with a picture of Whitman as a profoundly troubled and fraught poet. Clearly this is a far cry from the simplistic image of Whitman as poet of American optimism and openness that was still – in the 1950s – being propounded amongst critics and general readers alike.

Asselineau's examination of Whitman's sexuality allows him to open up Whitman's poetry to a more searching analysis. The issue of sex discovers a different Whitman, one whose actual and imagined poetic circumstances do not necessarily tally. And in thus letting us see beneath the surface of Whitman's carefully mythologised image, attention to questions of Whitman's sexuality can be seen as a tool for analysing the ideological circumstances that produced a poet such as Whitman. Indeed, in their attempts to get beneath the surface of underlying assumptions about poetics and culture that have been, perhaps, suppressed by Whitman and his critics, the essays in this chapter signal a new direction in critical thought about Whitman.

The extracts that follow can all be seen as attempts to free Whitman from what the cultural theorist Louis Althusser has called 'the grip of ideology'.[2] Indeed Althusser's notion of ideology adds a useful gloss on the ways in which the critical pieces of this chapter read how Whitman's poetry inscribes its particular ideological gesture. For Althusser, ideology is 'the representation of the subject's Imaginary relationship to his or her Real conditions of existence'.[3] Within this concept of ideology, then, what we believe our social and political relationships to be as subjects within a particular culture, and what they actually are, become divorced from each other. Ideology, according to Althusser and other Marxist critics following his lead, performs a crucial political function of disguising and deterring a full understanding of the conditions of our existence by providing a convenient set of beliefs that *seem* (but only seem) to explain those conditions.[4] It is to the ways in which Whitman's dealings with sex and sexuality carry out such an act of disguising and deterring that the critical pieces in this chapter pay attention. And in this sense, by asking what version of culture is disguised within the difficulties and evasions of Whitman's sexually fraught poems, they represent some of the first critical attempts to 'deconstruct' both Whitman's poetry and the culture from which it arose.

The first extract is taken from Malcolm Cowley's essay, of 1948, entitled 'Whitman: The Poet and the Mask'. In this essay Cowley attends to the ways in which Whitman's poetry, and the myths about himself promulgated by Whitman, perform a function of 'disguising and deterring' a full understanding of the 'real' Whitman. Cowley goes on to argue that this is because of Whitman's homosexuality, and suggests that the genesis of the poem lies in some homosexual encounter – never disclosed, but often elliptically alluded to by Whitman – of Whitman's early adulthood. As Asselineau was to argue just five years later, the source of Whitman's poetry is, for Cowley, his homosexuality. Such a reading may rely, ultimately, too much on hearsay, gossip and unsubstantiated biographical speculation, but it does mark a crucial turning point in critical appreciation of Whitman.

■ I haven't always been an admirer of Whitman's poetry. In the past when I tried to read *Leaves of Grass* from beginning to end, I always stopped in the middle, overcome by the dislike that most of us feel for inventories and orations. Even today, after reading all the book as Whitman wished it to be preserved and after being won over by what I think is the best of it – till I am willing, if not for the usual reasons, to join the consensus that regards him as our most rewarding poet – I still feel that *Leaves of Grass* is an extraordinary mixture of greatness, false greatness, and mediocrity. Whitman designed it as his monument, but he made the book too large and pieced it out with faulty materials, including versified newspaper editorials, lists of names from the back pages of a school geography, commencement-day prophecies, chamber-of-commerce speeches, and sentimental ballads that might have been written by the Sweet Singer of Michigan, except that she would have rhymed them. The fire bells ring in his poems, the eagle screams and screams again, the brawny pioneers march into the forest (décor by Currier and Ives ['lithographers whose prints were among the most popular wall hangings in 19th-century America.' *Encyclopedia Britannica*]), and the lovely Italian singer gives a concert for the convicts at Sing Sing, her operatic voice

Pouring in floods of melody in tones so pensive sweet and strong
                    the like whereof was never heard.

In no other book of great poems does one find so much trash that the poet should have recognized as trash before he set the first line of it on paper. In no other book, great or small, does one find the same extremes of inspiration and bathos. It is as if Whitman the critic and editor of his own work had been so overawed by Whitman the poet that he preserved even the poet's maunderings as the authentic record of genius. He did not succeed – though he worked on the problem all his life – in giving an organic form to the book as a whole. It doesn't grow like a tree or take wing like a bird or correspond in various sections to the stages of the poet's life; instead it starts with a series of twenty-four 'inscriptions', or doctrinal pronouncements, almost like twenty-four theses nailed to a church door. It reaches an early climax, with the 'Song of Myself'. It continues through celebrations of 'woman-love', as Whitman called it a little coldly, and passionate friendship for men. Then, after a series of set-pieces – some of them magnificent, like the 'Song of the Open Road' – after the Civil War sketches and the big symphonies of his Washington years, it dwindles away in occasional verses and old-age echoes. ...

... We might find it easier to picture the complexities of [Whitman's] character if we imagined that there were at least three Whitmans existing as separate persons. There was Whitman I, the printer and small politician and editor, always described by his associates as indolent, timid (except when making public speeches), awkward, and rather conventional in his manners. He disappeared from public sight after 1850, yet he survived for more than thirty years in his intimate relations with his family. Then there was Whitman II, the *persona*, who characterized himself as 'one of the roughs, large, proud, affectionate, eating, drinking and breeding, his costume manly and free, his face sunburnt and bearded, his posture strong and erect, his voice bringing hope and prophecy to the generous races of young and old'. This second Whitman, ripening with age – and becoming much more discreet after he moved to Washington and went to work for the government – at least merged blandly into the figure of the Good Gray Poet. He wrote poems, too, as part of his role, but most of them were windy and uninspired.

The real poet was still another person; let us call him Whitman III. He never appeared in public life; he was hardly more than a voice from the depths of the subconscious; but the voice was new, candid, powerful; and it spoke in different words not only from Whitman the young editor but also Whitman the gray bard of Democracy. Whitman III was boastful but often tender and secret where Whitman II was bluff and lusty. He was feminine and maternal rather than physically adventurous; but at the same time he was a revolutionist by instinct where Whitman I was liberal and Whitman II merely sententious. He appeared from nowhere to write the 'Song of Myself' and the other poems published in 1855. He had little to say after 1860 and fell silent for ever in 1874, whereas the *persona* lived after him till 1892; yet during his brief career he wrote – or dictated to the other Whitmans – all the poetry that gave *Leaves of Grass* its position in world literature.

But what explains the mystery of the poet's birth? There was an apparently quite ordinary fellow named Walter Whitman who wrote editorials and book reviews and moral doggerel; then there was an extraordinary showman named Walt Whitman who peddled his personality as if it were a patent medicine; but there was also for six years, and at intervals thereafter, a poet of genius known by the same name. How did he come to exist? Was it merely because Whitman the editor visited New Orleans, had a phrenological reading, was inspired by Emerson's doctrine of the representative individual, and tried to make himself over into a character by

George Sand? Is there any other case for what we must still regard as the Whitman miracle?

The only evidence that bears on this question consists of Whitman's early notebooks and of the poems themselves, which are of course a less trustworthy guide. Still, they return so often to one theme that its importance in his life seems fixed beyond dispute. Whitman had apparently been slow to develop emotionally as well as intellectually. The poems suggest that, at some moment during the seven shadowy years, he had his first fully satisfying sexual experience. It may have been as early as his trip to New Orleans in 1848, to judge from what he says in a frequently quoted poem, 'Once I pass'd through a Populous City', which, incidentally, has more biographical value in the early draft discovered by Emory Holloway than it has in the altered and expurgated version that Whitman published. Or the Louisiana episode, if real, may have been merely an introduction to his new life, and the decisive experience may have come later, during his carpenter years in Brooklyn.

Whenever it occurred, the experience was so intense that it became an almost religious ecstasy, a moment of vision that wholly transformed his world. Whitman describes such a moment in the marvelous fifth section of 'Song of Myself':

Swiftly arose and spread around me the peace and knowledge that
                    pass all the argument of the earth,
And I know that the hand of God is the promise of my own,
And I know that the spirit of God is the brother of my own,
And that all the men ever born are also my brothers, and the
                    women my sisters and lovers,
And that a kelson of the creation is love,
And limitless are leaves stiff or drooping in the fields,
And brown ants in the little wells beneath them,
And mossy scabs of the worm fence, heap'd stones, elder, mullein
                    and poke-weed.

After this experience Whitman had to revise not only his general and philosophical picture of the world but also his private picture of himself. 'I am not what you supposed', he would say in one of his 1860 poems, 'but far different'. The discovery of his sexual direction must have been a shock to him at first; but he soon determined to accept himself with all his vices and 'smutch'd deeds', just as he accepted everything in the universe. He wrote: 'I am myself just as much evil as good, and my nation is – and I say there is in fact no evil.' All his nature being good, in the larger view, he felt that all of it should be voiced in the poems he was planning to write.

At first his revelations concerning one side of his nature were made obliquely, in language that could be easily understood only by others of his own type. By 1860, however, when he was preparing the third edition of his poems, the impulse to confess himself had become so strong that he was no longer willing to speak by indirection. 'Come', he said, 'I am determin'd to unbare this broad breast of mine, I have long enough stifled and choked.' And in the first of his 'Calamus' poems, written for that edition, he proclaimed his resolve 'to sing no songs today but those of manly attachment':

I proceed for all who are or have been young men,
To tell the secret of my nights and days,
To celebrate the need of comrades.

There has been a long argument about the meaning of the 'Calamus' poems, but it is or should be clear enough from the title under which they were published. Whitman is sometimes vague and hard to follow in his metaphysical symbols, but his sexual symbols are as simply conceived as an African statue of Potency or Fertility. The calamus root is one of those symbols...

The sweet flag or calamus root, the 'growth by the margin of pond-waters,' was simply Whitman's token or symbol of the male sexual organ. 'This,' he said in a poem, 'O this shall henceforth be the token of comrades, the calamus-root shall.' The poems under this general title were poems of homosexual love, in its physical aspects and with its metaphysical lessons. They were 'blades' or 'spears' or 'leaves' of the calamus, to use another of Whitman's favorite symbols; and, as he said in his letter to Rossetti, they were bigger and hardier than all the other leaves of grass.
...

After the concealments, evasions, and apologies of the poet himself and most of his critics, it is time to restore this living figure, so far as we can find him in the records. He was not 'emotionally versatile' in the sense in which some of his recent biographers have used the phrase. They imply that he could turn his affections from one sex to the other, but the evidence fails to show that Whitman was ever sexually attracted by women. There was no romance in his life with a highborn Creole lady; nor was there any other romance (except with young men like Peter Doyle, the Washington horsecar conductor) that careful students have been able to trace. He was not 'unconsciously' or 'half-consciously' homosexual; after 1855, and perhaps as early as 1847, he was completely aware of his own nature. His abnormality was not an 'unhealthy mood' that passed after 1860; it continued for the rest of his active life. And it was never something that could be overlooked by his critics as having a merely private or biographical interest; on the contrary, it was part of the impulse that set him writing poetry; it served as theme for a whole section of Leaves of Grass, besides being a minor theme in other sections; and it became curiously interwoven with Whitman's notions about a future democracy, which would have to be based, he said, on manly comradeship or adhesiveness.

...There is only a footnote in Democratic Vistas that mentions [Whitman's] central idea about the basis for democracy. To find that idea expressed at length, we have to turn ... to the 'Calamus' poems and, after the symbolical interpretations offered by a hundred critics, we have to read them with the notion that Whitman meant in them exactly what he said. In the 'Calamus' cluster we find him acting as prophet and proselytizer for his doctrine of fervent manly comradeship or adhesiveness. ... [We] begin to see that Whitman is trying to identify, or at least confuse, homosexuality with Americanism. The intention becomes clearer in [the] passage:

I believe the main purport of these States is found a superb
                              friendship, exalté, previously unknown,
Because I perceive it waits, and has always been waiting, latent in
                                                            all men.

And this strange confusion at last develops into a definite political program, perhaps the only one of its sort since Plato.

... Once seized upon, this notion of the close relation between homosexuality and democracy seems to have been retained as a central point in Whitman's thinking. He hadn't surrendered it in 1871, when he published *Democratic Vistas*. There it appears only in a footnote, as I said, but Whitman states the notion clearly: he tells us that manly friendship, 'fond and loving, pure and sweet, strong and life-long, carried to degrees hitherto unknown', will be found 'to have the deepest relations to general politics. I say democracy infers such loving comradeship' ...

The picture of Whitman as a democratic sage and prophet, the healthy, sane and purely native embodiment of his own poems, has been convenient to historians and flattering to the national spirit, but it will have to be abandoned. It has led in the past to illusions, apologies, and a red-faced unwillingness to admit that he often lied about himself. It has led to serious misconceptions of American literature and whole bookstacks full of third-rate critical and creative writing. It has led to the notion that the ideal American poet or novelist is a rough-hewn aboriginal creature tallying in his works – as Whitman would say – the geographical features of the country: high as its mountains, broad as its prairies, tangled as its swamps. But American writers have rarely been lettered savages or extroverts flinging their arms right and left to embrace multitudes; they have been, for the most part, hurt and lonely men – as Whitman was hurt and lonely when he wrote his first great poems; and they have been more concerned in their works with depth than with breadth of emotion; more interested in achieving psychological truth and honest craftsmanship than in reproducing the sweep of the continent as seen from a train window. 'Great are the myths,' I might say to those friends, chiefly in academic circles, who still believe in this legendary Whitman, 'but they shouldn't be confused with history. This rugged and masculine poet who embodied the aspirations of American democracy, this father image of yours, was a fictional or dramatic creation that belongs in the same category as Rip Van Winkle and Leatherstocking and Huckleberry Finn. ...'

'He created and dressed and acted a part', I would say, 'and always when acting he was a bad poet who wrote chamber-of-commerce speeches and cried, "O Pioneers!" but invoked the pioneers in flat images and awkward rhythms, without the grace that comes from intimate belief. What we have to rediscover is the Whitman who wasn't acting, who spoke from the depths of his nature and wrote the greatest poems of his time. We have to rescue him from the pundits and politicians and give his work back to poetry.'

...So many misconceptions about Whitman to be cleared away! The real but almost unknown poet was American, not by thesis or proclamation, but because he was born in America, absorbed it with his ears and eyes, and gave back honestly what he heard and saw. He was democratic, not by his vagrant philosophy, but by instinct, inheritance; and he was a democrat, as it were, from below, feeling his brotherhood with the crippled and despised, rather than with the healthy average persons he later celebrated in his poems. He looked for companionship, not because he was grandly expansive by nature, but because he was wounded and alone. He presented a showman's mask to the world. He was a great poet behind the mask – not because he was wise, but because, at first, he was rash and unworldly enough to reveal the depths of his nature; and not because he celebrated 'the prairies, pastures, forests, vast cities, Kanada, the snows,' but because he wrote of his own Manhattan and Long Island as no other poet has ever done; and not because he soared ecstatically to the heights where people become abstractions, but because in his early work the ecstasy that was real – whatever its source – cleared his eyes so that he could see the infinite wonder of little and homely things. □

(Malcolm Cowley, 'Whitman: The Poet and the Mask', 1948)[5]

Given the date of Cowley's essay, 1948, it is perhaps a little surprising that there was not more written about Whitman's sexuality until the publication of Robert K. Martin's hugely influential and important book *The Homosexual Tradition in American Poetry* in 1979. From the very opening page of his study, Martin takes Whitman's homosexuality as a given. As Martin sees it, the struggle of Whitman criticism is a struggle to find a critical voice and tradition for a poetics of homosexuality. He begins his opening chapter by noting that, 'Although Whitman intended his work to communicate his homosexuality to his readers, and although homosexual readers have from the very beginning understood his homosexual meanings, most critics have not been willing to take Whitman at his word.'[6] By starting his examination of what he terms 'the homosexual tradition in American poetry' with a discussion of Whitman's poetry, Martin is, perhaps, being deliberately provocative. Although he sees Whitman as the father-figure for such a tradition, Whitman's homosexuality is, in fact, not at all as clear-cut as Martin makes it out to be.

Though Martin's assault upon some of the critical complacencies of Whitman scholarship in the late 1970s is timely, it is also rather reductive. It seems to narrow Whitman's poetry down to a sort of coded performance that only those in the know – 'homosexual readers' – can fully understand and appreciate. Within such a critical methodology it is not at all clear what Whitman's poetry might offer to heterosexual readers, both male and female, or even lesbian readers. Martin's reductiveness is troubled by at least two ironies that reflect upon the ways we approach reading Whitman. First, by implying that only homosexual readers can (or, indeed, have) *really* understood Whitman's message, Martin all but dismisses a history of powerful and important readings of Whitman by heterosexuals. What status, for example, would Malcolm Cowley's essay have? Though heterosexual, Cowley highlights Whitman's homosexuality, thereby pointing out the very thing in Whitman's text (his homosexuality) to which, according to Martin's formulation above, he (as a heterosexual) is blind. Even more concernedly, one might ask of Martin's model of homosexual reading practices, how does it accommodate a critic such as Matthiessen who was, in fact, homosexual, but for whom Whitman's homosexuality was simply not a critical issue? If Martin's 'tradition' replaces subtle, persuasive and landmark analyses of Whitman's poetry with an orthodoxy of solely gay readings of Whitman, then it clearly represents a diminishment of the range, complexity and, one might say, sexual ambiguity that characterise Whitman's poetry. A second irony lies in the fact that, of course, Whitman himself would simply not have understood the term 'homosexual'. As we saw in David Reynolds' essay in the previous chapter, nineteenth-century discourses of sex, sexuality and gender were far more fluid than those of the late twentieth century. What such ironies point to, then, is that Martin's 'homosexual tradition', with Whitman as its representative starting point, is an ideological product of late-twentieth, rather than nineteenth-century, America.

Clearly the dynamic behind Martin's model of a homosexual tradition in American poetry is emancipatory and is part-and-parcel of a particular cultural moment and rhetoric when 'Queer' Studies was just beginning to be recognised within academia, and the gay movement was gaining intellectual respectability and cultural power. In this sense, Martin's book acts as a vital 'coming-out' story for Whitman and Whitman studies. But it leaves more questions about Whitman's supposed sexuality unanswered than it resolves. However, Martin's clear and accessible reading of Whitman, coupled with his call for more tolerant reading practices, signal a refreshing and challenging new direction for Whitman studies.

■ Prior to Whitman there were homosexual acts but no homosexuals. Whitman coincides with and defines a radical change in historical consciousness: the self-conscious awareness of homosexuality as an identity. 'Calamus' is the heart of *Leaves of Grass*, as well as the root; it is Whitman's book of self-proclamation and self-definition. This does not imply, of course, that it is to be taken as direct autobiographical statement. Like any autobiography, it is fictional, an artful rearrangement of life in order to present oneself in a particular light. 'Calamus' does not describe an affair with a particular young man, nor does it deal with an emotional crisis that we may presume to have really occurred. Instead it offers a dramatized version of Whitman's acceptance of himself as a homosexual and his realization of the consequences of that acceptance.

The first poem of the 'Calamus' sequence announces the poet's purpose and indicates a major change of heart. ...

In paths untrodden,
In the growth by margins of pond-waters

This figure introduces a spatial element to the contrast ... between two points in time: the new space, like the new time, announces Whitman's conversion. The new man is to inhabit a new world. The 'untrodden' paths represent Whitman not only as the pioneer but also as the 'first man', as Adam. Whitman's dramatization of his conversion demands that he see himself as radically new, going alone into virgin land ... While Whitman makes use of the pioneer and explorer metaphor, it is significant that he does not situate himself in a western landscape. In Whitman space is not a territory to be conquered (as is characteristic of male heterosexual literature) (R. Slotkin, *Regeneration Through Violence,* 1973)[7] but a place 'by margins' to be explored, a 'secluded spot' which is not a territory beyond but alongside. Instead of an extension in length, as in the metaphor of conquest, there is a broadening, an extension in width to include what was once seen as 'marginal'.

The new territory of 'In paths untrodden' is an aspect of the self, not of the other. In the myth of the explorer (which is perhaps the quintessential male heterosexual myth) place is always outside, different, and alien to the self. But the place chosen by Whitman is isolated, suitable for meditation and self-exploration. ...

The setting of this first poem of the 'Calamus' cycle is reminiscent of one of the most famous of homosexual poems, Virgil's Second Eclogue, and the resemblances are sufficient to suggest that Whitman had Virgil in mind as he prepared the 1860 version of his text. In the eclogue Corydon withdraws from the world into a dark wooden undergrowth to sing his songs of unrequited love for Alexis ... The opening of 'In paths untrodden' echoes this scene, one of the best known in pastoral literature. Whitman, like Corydon, withdraws from the world to find solitude in dark places and to draw forth his art from his experience of impossible love (a theme made more explicit in the 1867 revisions of 'Calamus' 39, 'Sometimes with One I Love'). Like Virgil, Whitman uses the song of the abandoned lover as the type of all music and turns his suffering into a beautiful hymn in praise of love. ...

[The] suffering of the ninth 'Calamus' poem is ultimately a measure of the depth of [the poet's] love and the extent to which that love can inform his whole life. In this way the poem leads to the next, 'You bards of ages hence!' with its famous injunction, 'Publish my name and hang up my picture as that of the tenderest lover.' ... [Here] there is a contrast between the political poet and the personal. Whitman, who has just displayed his capacity for tenderness through his suffering, asks to be remembered in this way and not as the 'rough' of 'Song of Myself'. In order to understand the impact of this poem, it is necessary to place it in its historical context. Men in mid-nineteenth-century America did not cry, suffer, and languish for love; these reactions were deemed 'feminine'. Men were the aggressors in love; women waited and suffered. Against this orthodoxy of strict sexual delineation Whitman affirms his 'feminine' qualities. He argues that love between men implicitly challenges traditional Western ideas of male superiority and of male hardness and female softness. The homosexual, more than other men, can experience the world from the perspective of a woman. He knows the impotence of unreturned love, the inability to speak out, the need to bear everything quietly. To call oneself the 'tenderest lover' is to accept one's femininity or, more accurately, to challenge all social prescriptions of behaviour according to gender. Whitman's ideal is nonactive, nonproductive; his joy is in companionship, in being, not doing. He recalls his 'happiest days' in the past, 'wandering hand in hand', 'saunter[ing].' To wander, to saunter, is to move without purpose, to find one's satisfaction in the moment rather than the future. These views go directly against nineteenth-century (and American) ideals of progress, directed activity, and work. The organization of patriarchal society, psychoanalysis argues, rests upon the suppression of nonprocreative sexual behavior.[8] Competition between men ensures the maximization of productivity, while love between men represents a radical resistance to unnecessary productivity. If men walk arm in arm in the streets, they are not busy in the factory or begetting children. Hence their danger to society; and it is precisely thus, as an opponent of dominant social values, as an exponent of the 'feminine' in culture, that Whitman asks to be remembered.

... There is a constant ebb and flow through 'Calamus'. Each section of honesty and forthrightness is followed by one or more of hesitation and warning. To have written the first book in two thousand years in praise of homosexual love required a fortitude that must, even in Whitman, have occasionally wavered. Thus the announcement of his sexual nature is followed by a brief hesitation, 'O conscience-struck! O self-convicted!' No doubt Whitman passed through periods in which he accepted the prevailing social attitudes toward homosexuality and masturbation (the two were considered synonymous); 'Calamus', as a dramatization of the poet's acceptance of his homosexual self, includes portrayals of such moments of doubt and even despair. What is far more striking is Whitman's ability, without any external support, to overcome such despair. In each case he realizes that his sexuality is his nature and that it must be given expression. Whether it is right or wrong becomes absurd once he recognizes that it simply is: 'as if it could cease transpiring from me until it must cease'. If his love is 'wrong-doing', still it must be. Like Twain's Huck, Whitman learns that natural inclinations are often at odds with social definitions of good and evil. ...

Whitman's dream, although utopian, is not manifestly impossible. For it is based not on a transformation of men but on a realization of their potential. In 'To you of New England' Whitman expresses his view that 'the germs' (following the basic horticultural metaphor) 'are in all men'. He thus anticipates the theories of psychoanalysis, which, early in the twentieth century, suggested that all human beings are bisexual but that their homosexual impulses are arrested by social pressures. Whitman is not asking for understanding or tolerance for a minority. His position is much more radical: that all men are potentially homosexual and will be fulfilled only when their homosexual impulses are recognized and given expression. As in *Democratic Vistas*, he sees this latent homosexuality as the potential foundation of national and international unity and the essential condition for harmony among men. He ascribes divisiveness to the imposition of heterosexuality upon otherwise homosexual men, resulting in the frustration of their desires and the transformation of those desires (sublimation) into aggression. To express this view, he salvaged a line from the manuscript of 'Proto-Leaf' ('Starting from Paumanok') and placed it here, to suggest that his utopian vision need not await the end of time but might find a suitable home in the present. For it was to be in America above all that homosexuality should find its expression, as homosexuality was implied in the entire history of American experience; as he put in the manuscript, 'I believe the main purport of America is to be found in a new ideal of manly friendship, more ardent, more general.' This became, in the 1860 text, 'a superb friendship, exalté, previously unknown'. America's prophetic destiny was to be realized through the establishment of the 'new ideal'; since homosexuality is universal, America would again become a beacon for the world. Whitman would write, in *Democratic Vistas*, 'I say democracy infers such loving comradeship, as its most inevitable twin or counterpart, without which it will be incomplete, in vain, and incapable of perpetuating itself.' Whitman seems to have believed, like Melville in *Typee* [(1846)], that heterosexuality was the sexual expression of capitalism and of a society based on property. Homosexuality was for him the sexual expression of community, and would follow necessarily in a true socialist society.

... Of the last group of poems [in the 'Calamus' sequence] three celebrate love, while two deal with the relationship of love to art. 'Sometimes with one I love' suggests the importance of love as the basis of Whitman's art (an idea developed most fully in 'Out of the Cradle'): 'Doubtless I could not have perceived the universe, or written one of my poems, if I had not freely given myself to comrades, to love.' Love becomes essential to art, in this formulation, because art requires self-definition and self-expression. Had Whitman not given himself 'to comrades', he would not have developed the perception of self which underlies a work so self-examining as his. It will be remarked that this original formulation is quite different from the one finally adopted in the Blue Book revisions:

> (I loved a certain person ardently and my love was not return'd,
> Yet out of that I have written these songs.)

The revised version picks up the idea of 'return' for love and substitutes an artistic return for a more direct return of love (thus anticipating the Freudian view of sublimation); but it substitutes a more specific vision of unreturned love for an earlier expression of love freely given. The second version appears to be more personal and may reflect a greater ability, with the passage of time, to understand the origins of the 'Calamus' sequence. In either case the poem suggests strongly the need to love, regardless of the return that one may receive for one's love. 'Here my last words, and the most baffling' alludes again to the need to conceal, yet paradoxically states that even this concealed version 'exposes' most. Whitman's prediction is striking: the 'Calamus' leaves are 'the frailest leaves of me, and yet the strongest-lasting'. Their frailty is revealed by the attacks they have provoked and by Whitman's own difficulties with this section. But their ability to last, too, is demonstrated by the fact that poets of the twentieth century have found in them a source of strength as they have sought their own poetic and sexual identities, and the links between the two. While for some, sexual choice remains 'irrelevant', for others it is at least as important as nationality, religion, class, or any other factor that determines one's self. Whitman recognized that even as he 'shaded down' his thoughts in this section, they acted towards his exposure. To speak of such love is to reveal it, as Whitman knew when he undertook 'Calamus' as an act of self-definition.

... If Whitman begins his 'Calamus' with self-declaration, he concludes with an injunction. He has asked the reader to follow him through the presentation of the 'secret'; he has revealed the pleasures and the pains of life as a homosexual in nineteenth-century America. He has also offered a program for the future. Now it remains for the reader to fulfill that program. Whitman's address in the last poem is to the future – 'To one a century hence, or any number of centuries hence' – in recognition that the goals he has set cannot be fulfilled in his own lifetime. His poems were themselves roots, as he suggested in 'Calamus taste', which would require loving care in order to bloom. The burden falls upon the reader as the author departs. The work written, the author vanished, the dialogue is between text and reader. It is the reader who will 'realize' (fulfill, make real) the poems. Whitman offers that reader the assurance of his support and encouragement: 'Be it as if I were with you. Be not too certain but I am now with you.' The final lines return playfully to the tension of appearance and reality. Is the author alive 'now' when he writes, or 'then' when he is read? Is the author finally ever there? If the poems have succeeded, they have not merely evoked a poet. They will have used the persona of the poet to spur the imagination of the reader. Is Whitman the man present in his poems? We shall never know. Whitman the man is deliberately elusive, reminding us of his view that the end of art is to transform reality, through its action upon the reader.

Whitman's final dramatization of self is as an evanescent spirit ... This is not to suggest that he is coy or deceptive, but to realize that his 'exposure' has been a strategy, the results of which can only be seen in the future. The historical Whitman is of no literary interest. He can vanish and leave behind the spiritual Whitman, the eternal lover, the risen god of male love. Whitman predicted that of all his poems, 'Calamus' would be 'the last to be fully understood'. But he did not doubt that such understanding would come. □
(R. Martin, *The Homosexual Tradition in American Poetry*, 1979)[9]

In the essay from which the final extract of this chapter is taken, Nick Selby seeks to offer a corrective to Martin's rather too reductive analysis of Whitman's sexuality. He argues that a model of 'bisexual' poetics is more appropriate to the experience of reading Whitman's poetry, and to the ideology of nineteenth-century capitalism which produced that poetry. The extract seeks to demonstrate this by close readings of some of those Whitman poems that deal with the issue of sex.

■ It has become a critical commonplace to view ... Walt Whitman ... as [a] gay poet ... whose [work] demonstrate[s] and develop[s] a gay poetic.[10] Indeed, [his] homosexuality and [his] radical poetic agenda [is] seen as inseparably bound together with [his] status as [a] rebel hero whose vision of America challenge[s] mainstream American ideology and culture. Robert K. Martin's notion of a (male) homosexual tradition in American poetry starts with Whitman, and describes him as an heroic father-figure against whom subsequent gay American poets have measured themselves. Whitman's position as the hero-poet of American romantic democracy is, argues Martin, a direct result of his oppositional sexuality. 'No other poet, until the present time', writes Martin,

has so clearly defined himself in terms of his sexuality and so clearly defined his poetic mission as a consequence of his homosexuality. This remains true despite the attempts Whitman made, late in his own life-time, to conceal his homosexuality from outsiders. It may be, of course, that in part he was telling the truth: that he never gave physical expression to his love for men. The textual evidence makes that seem unlikely, how-ever; Whitman was fully aware of the possibilities of sexual expression between men, and he celebrated them not only as an end in themselves but also as a means to a mystic penetration of the universe and a more democratic vision of the American future.[11]

It is the assumed clarity of such a connection between the production of Whitman as radical American poet and Whitman as the site for the production of a specifically gay poetic which this paper seeks to challenge. My aim is to ease the work of Whitman ... away from a poetic that places [him] exclusively within the canon of gay writing by emphasizing [his] importance in the theorization of a bisexual poetics. This can be seen by turning ... to two examples from Whitman. Both examples show how the operation of desire in Whitman's text becomes a site in which claims for America as a poetic democracy are contested. The first example records the type of same-sex desire which Martin designates homosexual, whilst the second records opposite-sex desire commonly designated heterosexual. ... [Such] poetic fluidity of desires, then, and how this is a product of Whitman's America, is the ground upon which I will investigate Whitman's mobilization of a bisexual poetics.

In the above quotation from Martin, for instance, the assumed clarity with which Whitman defined his sexuality and his poetic mission serves to illustrate Martin's desire to categorize Whitman within a gay aesthetic rather better than it illustrates the experience of reading Whitman's poetry. 'Textual evidence' does indeed show Whitman's awareness of 'the possibilities of sexual expression between men'. The poem 'When I Heard at the Close of Day' from the 'Calamus' section of *Leaves of Grass* clearly defines the poet's desire for the return of his male lover: 'And when I thought how my dear friend my lover was on his way coming, O then I was happy.'[12] The poem's conclusion is a clear celebration of homosexual love:

For the one I love most lay sleeping by me under the same cover in
the cool night,
In the stillness in the autumn moonbeams his face was inclined
toward me,
And his arm lay lightly around my breast – and that night I was
happy.[13]

Whitman's declaration of his homosexual desire becomes here (as throughout the 'Calamus' section generally) the means by which he generates his 'vision' of a 'more democratic ... American future'. The play of poetic, homosexual and political desires in the poem make it the site from which the terms of Whitman's democratic romanticism emerge. The poem itself mobilizes and satisfies those desires. In terms of poetic logic, the desire for completion, for narrative closure, that is set up in the opening line's 'still it was not a happy night for me' is satisfied by the final line's 'and that night I was happy'. It is thus that the poem is structured out of desire and its satisfaction. By making his poem into such a structure of desire Whitman is allowed to conflate his homosexual and his democratic desires. Not only does the poem, finally, satisfy the desire for the anticipated embrace of the poet's male lover, but in that embrace it engages Whitman's romance of American democracy. The poem's lovers are themselves held by the embrace of a primal romantic scene of 'autumn moonbeams', in a gesture that mirrors the comradely love described in the poem 'For You O Democracy' from earlier in the 'Calamus' section:[14]

> I will plant companionship thick as trees along all the rivers of America,
>   and along the shores of the great lakes, and all over the prairies;
> I will make inseparable cities with their arms about each other's necks,
> By the love of comrades,
> By the manly love of comrades.[15]

Whitman's homosexual desire is thus legitimized because it is seen, as here, to form the basis of his democratic conception of America.

The 'manly love of comrades', as with the two lovers earlier who incline towards each other in the moonlight, articulates a desire to embrace that which is not other. To desire, and thence to embrace, that which is the same produces the ideal of union that lies at the heart of Whitman's ideal of America. Whitman's generic notion of The Poem, in its embodying of such a principle of 'companionship' constitutes, and is constituted by, the constellation of desires that shape America into the *United* States. His poetic embracing of America thus renders cities 'inseparable', the 'continent indissoluble' in the poem's first line, and is underscored by a romantic reaching after a union of individual and democracy, of poem and nation....

For Whitman, however, selfhood is never ... assured or unified. This is precisely because it is raised on a poetics of desire, or more accurately, as I shall go on to argue, it is raised upon a bisexual poetics of desire. Thus, despite Robert K. Martin's insistence upon the clarity with which Whitman defines himself in terms of his homosexuality, what does become clear is that Whitman's poetics engages the idea of the self as fluid. This is reflected, as we shall see, in the embracing of both homosexual and heterosexual desire by his text. ... Whitman's text seeks actively, poetically, to mark the differentiations between which its desiring subject can flow in its act of adhesive union. ... His poetic self must distinguish between, in order to flow between, 'the great lakes' and 'the prairies'; between 'rivers,' 'trees' and 'cities'; between desire for men and desire for women.

I am thus arguing that, counter to traditional (i.e. Freudian) theories of bisexuality that are predicated upon a notion of undifferentiated desire, Whitman's bisexual poetics is one peculiarly reliant on acts of differentiation. The Freudian model of a primary 'full bisexuality' is built from an idea of essential similarity, not difference, wherein, as Martin Duberman notes, 'bisexuality ... [is] a biological universal'.[16] According to Judith Butler, Freud's theory of bisexuality abolishes difference by asserting 'the coincidence of two heterosexual desires within a single psyche'.[17] Freud's privileging of heterosexual desire abolishes homosexuality, as Butler notes, by asserting that 'only opposites attract'.[18] Initially, this notion of the attraction of opposites may seem to go against the grain of undifferentiated desire at the heart of Freudian formulations of bisexuality. However, we should note that the force of Butler's '*only* opposites attract' implies that in Freud's model, the possibility of same-sex (i.e. 'homosexual') attraction is excluded.

Differentiation of desires is thus effectively precluded by Freud's bisexual model. This is not the case with Whitman's bisexual poetics: its very fluidity between positions is an attempt to embrace the 'full range of sexual attitudes of his day' described by David Reynolds.[19] Whitman's bisexual poetics does not, then, see men and women as all essentially the same, undifferentiated. What it does display, though, is how such a poetic emerges from, indeed is produced by, an America in which sexuality was a relatively fluid concept able to embrace a range of differing and (to late-twentieth-century minds) contradictory emotional, psychological and sexual attitudes. Reynolds has further noted that Whitman's poetry is the product of a culture in which 'gender roles ... were fluid, elastic [and] shifting in a time when sexual types had not yet solidified' into the rigid categories demanded by increasing urbanisation, commercialism and the expansion of capitalism in the latter part of the nineteenth century.[20] Whitman's bisexual poetics is radical precisely because its fluidity represents an attempt not to surrender to a coercive universalism which ... abolishes difference at the same time that it seems to be being proclaimed. Yet to see Whitman's bisexual poetics working in these terms paves the way for a consideration of how that poetics is a product of capitalist discourses of exchange emerging in nineteenth-century America, and therefore offers a substantially less radical version of America than Whitman would have us believe.

When we turn to the poem 'A Woman Waits for Me' we find clear expression of heterosexual desire, a desire, moreover, that expresses the 'mystic penetration' at the heart of Whitman's vision of American democracy. The poem relies upon the productive interpenetration of various oppositions – 'containing all' / 'lacking'; 'bodies' / 'souls'; active poet / passive woman waiting; male / female – which are set up in its opening lines. Such interpenetration is not to be found in the comradely poems of the 'Calamus' section. It signals a desire for the embrace of otherness and difference in order to produce its democratic vision of America as a sexual melting pot. The man and woman of the following lines are caught in a poetic interplay of similarity and difference: 'without shame' both avow 'deliciousness' whilst the gender roles which underpin this democratic vision are, despite Reynolds' claims for fluidity noted above, fixed pretty firmly. The passivity of the woman's waiting is matched by a depiction of her sexuality as something so passive that it has to be assumed in grammatical parallel to that of the man:

A woman waits for me, she contains all, nothing is lacking,
Yet all were lacking if sex were lacking, or if the moisture of the right man
were lacking.

Sex contains all, bodies, souls,
Meanings, proofs, purities, delicacies, results, promulgations,
Songs, commands, health, pride, and maternal mystery, the seminal milk,

All hopes, benefactions, bestowals, all the passions, loves, beauties,
                                      delights of the earth,
All the governments, judges, gods, follow'd persons of the earth,
These are contained in sex as parts of itself and justification of itself.

Without shame the man I like knows and avows the deliciousness of
                                                  his sex,
Without shame the woman I like knows and avows hers.[21]

Given the expression of heterosexual desire here, as well as the sense of
rapidly shifting perspectives in poetic subjectivity, it is simply not possible to
read Whitman as clearly as Martin's model of him as the gay American
poet–hero *par excellence* demands. Martin's (re)production of Whitman
assumes, insists upon, a unity of self and sexuality where in fact there is
seen to be flux. Thus Martin's model resolves Whitman's sexuality into a
state of undifferentiated one-ness, whereas Whitman's own model of unity is
a state of combined differences, the 'en-masse' of his democratic 'song.' ...
Reading on further in the poem shows how such a complex of sexual,
poetic and political discourses is increasingly (as in American culture gen-
erally at this time) the subject of a capitalist discourse of production.
Whitman's poem becomes a reproductive economy based on heterosexual
desire. Within such a system, America, its poetry, and especially its sexu-
alities become cultural commodities. The mystic penetration of the uni-
verse that will engender a new American sense of nationhood becomes a
matter of saving and capital, of deposit and withdrawal. Semen, like
money, is spent and thus Whitman's democratic vision realizes itself as a
product of America's burgeoning commercialism.

I pour the stuff to start sons and daughters fit for these States, I press with
                                              slow rude muscle,
I brace myself effectually, I listen to no entreaties,
I dare not withdraw till I deposit what has so long accumulated within me.

Through you I drain the pent-up rivers of myself,
In you I wrap a thousand onward years,
On you I graft the grafts of the best-beloved of me and America,
The drops I distil upon you shall grow fierce and athletic girls, new artists,
                                              musicians, and singers,

The babes I beget upon you are to beget babes in their turn,
I shall demand perfect men and women out of my love-spendings,
I shall expect them to interpenetrate with others, as I and you interpenetrate
                                                  now[22]

Here the fluidity of poetic exchange that is deeply rooted in Whitman's sex-
uality begins to give way to a fixing of meaning within a capitalist discourse

of exchange. The process witnessed in the poem thus mirrors the claim of John D'Emilio and Estelle B. Freedman that 'sexuality ... moved into the world of commerce' over the course of the nineteenth century in America.[23] Such elision of Whitman's discourses of sexuality and repro-duction by that of commerce witnesses also what Stephen Heath has described as the way in which, in the Victorian age, '*sexuality*' and 'the sex-ual' were 'beginning to be named, and realized and pulled into a hesitant focus'.[24] It is against such a pulling into focus that the fluidity of poetic and sexual personae that mark Whitman's bisexual poetics attempts to work. ... Although a site for a radical critique of consumer capitalism as it was emerging in the nineteenth century, its reliance upon a model of exchange, and the way in which the reproductive economy of the passage above turns from the sexual to the financial indicate the degree to which it is a product of the increasingly dominant discourse of capitalism at the time. What we witness therefore in Whitman's bisexual poetics is not only the 'production of sexuality', as Foucault would have it, but also the pro-duction of the idea of 'American poet' as a kind of rebel-hero out of the capitalist discourses it seeks to challenge.[25]

... Throughout 'Song of Myself' Whitman's bisexual poetics becomes the site for an exploration of the complex and fluid interpenetration of ideas of personal identity, American democracy, and sexuality. ...

'Song of Myself' ... sets up the desire for an identity that it recognizes as fluid, that sees the body as the site in which apparently conflicting desires can reside to radical and liberating effect:

I am the poet of the Body and I am the poet of the Soul,
The pleasures of heaven are with me and the pains of hell are with me
The first I graft and increase upon myself, the latter I translate into a new
tongue.
I am the poet of the woman the same as the man,
And I say it is as great to be a woman as to be a man
And I say there is nothing greater than the mother of men[26]

The identity of the poet is built here ... not from a hopelessly universalist poetics of desire, but from the fluid interpenetration between seeming opposites. Whitman here becomes the poet of a radical re-vision of America because his bisexual poetics allows, or even demands, that his identity as the 'poet of the Body' is in fluid and productive exchange with the body of his text, and with America's body-politic. When the poet finally names himself more than a third of the way through 'Song of Myself', the constellation of somatic, poetic and democratic concerns is marked by Whitman's radical construction and voicing of sexuality in the poem

Walt Whitman, a kosmos, of Manhattan the son,
Turbulent, fleshy, sensual, eating, drinking and breeding,
No sentimentalist, no stander above men and women or apart from them,

No more modest than immodest.

Unscrew the locks from the doors!
Unscrew the doors themselves from the jambs! ...

Through me the afflatus surging and surging, through me the current and
index.
I speak the password primeval, I give the sign of democracy,
By God! I will accept nothing which all cannot have their counterpart of in
the same terms. ...

Through me forbidden voices,
Voices of sexes and of lusts, voices veil'd and I remove the veil,
Voices indecent by me clarified and transfigur'd.[27]

The poetic self here opens up the poem as a discursive and desiring site
through which surge many different voices that, taken together, constitute
'the sign of democracy'. Whitman's fluidity of language and voice, his poetic
lists, and his radical defiance of rigid patterns of thought all point to a bisex-
ual poetics that conforms to Paglia's fluidity model of bisexuality.[28] In this
sense, then, his poetics struggles with his concept of American Democracy.
Whilst seeking to preserve difference, to plot a range of desires, it seems
also to be at the point of surrendering to the erasure of social, ethnic and
sexual difference implied by America's ideological conception of itself as
melting pot.

Such fluidity of identity and sexual desire is explicitly presented in
Section 11 of the poem. The poet watches the desiring woman in her 'fine
house by the rise of the bank' as she watches, desires and (in her imagi-
nation) passes her hand over the 'Twenty-eight young men [who] bathe by
the shore.' The desire of the lonesome woman and the desire of the poet
become one within the poem's imagery of fluidity:

The beards of the young men glisten'd with wet, it ran from their long hair,
Little streams pass'd all over their bodies.

An unseen hand also pass'd over their bodies,
It descended tremblingly from their temples and ribs.

The young men float on their backs, their white bellies bulge to the sun, they
do not ask who seizes fast to them,
They do not know who puffs and declines with pendant and bending arch,
They do not think whom they souse with spray.[29]

Whitman's bisexual poetics thus becomes the means through which can
flow a complex of meanings which extend outwards from the purely sexual.
It is possible to see the woman as a figure of fate, or death; she is the
figure for women's emancipation; and she signals male desires, or female.
The spermatic imagery of her being 'soused with spray' represents the
creative poetic act, the procreative sexual act, as well as signalling a
wasted 'expenditure' on pleasure of Whitman's precious 'fatherstuff of

nations'. The passage also generates a specifically American political meaning, by representing the admitting of the twenty-ninth state, Texas, into the Union in 1845. As a rich and complex vehicle of several interpenetrative meanings Whitman's poetics thus allows him to sing and celebrate his democratic American self. His allegiance is to a radicalized vision of America that, like his bisexual model, 'contain[s] multitudes'.[30]

In his poetic efforts to 'contain multitudes', though, Whitman can be seen very much to be the white man. In the passage above the woman's role (as in 'A Woman Waits for Me') is passive. Her desire to escape the class-bound decorum by which she finds herself contained in her 'fine house' is radical only in her imagination. She remains contained by images of her status and sex: 'She hides handsome and richly drest aft the blinds of the window.' And blind, too, seems Whitman to the full implications of the whiteness of the twenty-eight young men. His vision of American Democracy is severely limited if what it contains are multitudes of white men surprisingly similar in looks, with their beards and flowing hair, to Walt himself as he appears in the daguerreotype frontispiece to the 1855 edition of Leaves of Grass. Even though Whitman details his harbouring of a runaway slave in lines immediately preceding these, the radicalism of this gesture is somewhat undercut by its sentimental paternalism: '[I] gave him some coarse, clean clothes, / And remember well his revolving eyes and his awkwardness, / And remember putting plasters on the galls of his neck and ankles.'[31] Thus Whitman's bisexual poetics registers a radicalism that its production out of the discourses and ideology of white nineteenth century America violates. □

(Nick Selby, The Bisexual Imaginary, 1997)[32]

The suggestion here that Whitman's apparently radical poetic agenda may in fact disguise a far more deeply embedded 'traditional' or 'conservative' ideological agenda is one that is taken up by the essays in the final chapter of this guide.

CHAPTER SEVEN

Ideology and Deconstruction: Whitman and 'New Americanist' Critiques

W e turn, in this final chapter, to readings of Whitman that might, broadly, be seen as 'deconstructive'. The following three critical pieces all share a postmodern concern with language and ideology as a system of power, one that can be unpicked through a detailed critcal examination of Whitman's poetry. The sort of deconstructive critical practice that operates, to a greater or lesser degree, in these essays is perhaps best summed up by Jonathan Culler in his book *On Deconstruction* (1983). Culler writes that

> to deconstruct a discourse is to show how it undermines the philosophy it asserts, or the hierarchical oppositions on which it relies, by identifying in the text the rhetorical operations that produce the supposed ground of argument, the key concept or premise.[1]

This closing chapter, then, provides a sampling of the ways in which *Leaves of Grass* is being read by yet another new generation of critics. Whilst charting the impact of postmodern thought on the process by which both Whitman's poetry and contemporary America can be read critically, it also points to some of the political gains that can be made through a critical practice that calls for a readjustment of our assumptions about texts and the role they play in marking out a particular cultural and ideological territory. In fact it is the calling for such a process of critical readjustment that most clearly unites the strategies of these three essays. As we shall see, for all these critics, Whitman's poetry remains a text that is central to the act of reading and understanding America. However – and in quite different ways for each of the critics – Whitman's centrality comes to signify an America that is far less radical, far less democratic and far more vexed than could ever have been supposed by earlier, more traditional, readings which strove to assert Whitman's position as *the* representative poet of America.

The extracts in this chapter, then, challenge the responsive reader of Whitman's poetry to re-think their political and ideological position, by demonstrating Whitman's complicity with a coercive Americanist ideological agenda. For Karen Sanchez-Eppler this takes place at the level of the bodily. She sees Whitman's poetic display and dispersal of concerns with the bodily as the means by which he both signals *and* writes over that most disruptive and disturbing of discourses in nineteenth-century America, slavery. Allen Grossman's brilliant reading of the continuities between Whitman's rhetoric and that of President Lincoln, urges a reconsideration of the connection in American thought between poetry and policy. In a sense, he revisits Emerson's notion of America as a poem but delivers back a startlingly new assessment of what such an entanglement of American as poem and as political reality might entail. And in the final essay of this chapter and of this Readers' Guide, Jonathan Arac carefully unpicks one of the most strongly held critical assumptions about Whitman, that he wrote in a vernacular (and therefore 'deeply American') tradition, until he is able to read Whitman not as the exclusive poetic property of America, but as the product of emerging forces of global capitalism in the mid-nineteenth century. All these pieces demonstrate that Whitman's poetry will continually be re-read and re-interpreted in terms of the struggles for power, dominance and the survival of a particular set of national myths upon which American ideology is grounded.

Like the essays in the previous two chapters, these pieces strive to return *Leaves of Grass* to its cultural setting by seeing it as a product of mid-nineteenth century America. But what they do with this setting is rather different from how it is treated in the two previous chapters. Arac and Grossman especially seem to want to ease readings of Whitman away from the liberal humanist perspective implied by the 'reconstructive' practices of critics such as Thomas, Folsom and Reynolds. And although Sanchez-Eppler shares many common concerns with the critics in the last chapter (most notably Selby), her ultimate focus is not so much Whitman as such but the antebellum ideology he has come to signify, and its crisis over the issue of slavery. As she notes at the close of her essay,

> if Whitman's poetry does absorb the social divisions of antebellum America, and particularly the crisis over slavery, it is also absorbed by it. Thus the poet, the person whom Whitman imagined as capable of mediating between the social divisions exemplified by American slavery, finally comes to incarnate those divisions.[2]

The critics in this chapter all stress Whitman's enormous cultural power and influence. Most especially for Grossman and Arac, though, Whitman's importance is not just because his poetry seems so clearly to reflect the state of American culture in the mid-nineteenth century.

Leaves of Grass, they argue, has been used by each succeeding generation of critics to portray an image of America that is particularly conducive to that specific generation of readers. If Whitman's poetry has come to be read as an archetypal American text, they argue, then this is because the tensions and struggles within nineteenth-century America have come to be seen as epitomising American identity and culture generally. Both of these essays may therefore be described as 'New Americanist' because they seek to deconstruct the key concepts and premises upon which traditional readings of American literature and culture are grounded.

In the first extract that follows, Karen Sanchez-Eppler challenges those sorts of ideas about American culture of the last century that Mathiessen puts forward in his *American Renaissance*. Implicit in her argument is a reading against his claim that Whitman and other writers of the antebellum period were 'devoted to the possibilities of democracy'. In fact her argument implies that such an assumption about Whitman, the sort of assumption through which *Leaves of Grass* and other 'classic' American texts have traditionally been read, promotes an agenda of white cultural superiority. What her essay points out, through its close examination of tropes of the body in Whitman's poetry, is that *Leaves of Grass* discloses the underlying faultlines in an American ideology brought to crisis point by issues of slavery, abolition and national consensus.

■ At that moment in his early notebook jottings when Whitman first assumes his new voice and verse form, he defines what it means to be a poet, and specifically to be the poet of the body, in terms provided by American slavery. Claiming to reconcile racially distinct bodies, Whitman locates the poet in the sexually charged middle space between masters and slaves:

I am the poet of slaves and of the masters of slaves
I am the poet of the body
And I am

I am the poet of the body
And I am the poet of the soul
I go with the slaves of the earth equally with the masters
And I will stand between the masters and the slaves
Entering into both so that both shall understand me alike[3]

Only two of these lines are actually preserved in *Leaves of Grass*: 'I am the poet of the body, / And I am the poet of the soul' introduces the twenty-first section of the poem Whitman eventually called 'Song of Myself', offering a self-defining summation that has informed most subsequent readings of Whitman's poetics.[4] Slavery is not mentioned in any published version of section 21; it has disappeared leaving the pairing of body and soul as its only trace. A sense of the political import of Whitman's poetics of embodiment is similarly absent from most critical assessments of his work. Yet in these notebook lines Whitman depicts his strategy of singing the body as a practice derived from the dynamics of American slavery. My discussion of Whitman's poetics reassesses the political sources and implications of his corporeal poetry, demonstrating that his celebration of the body not only reinterprets the body but also uses that reinterpretation to redefine the political. Even Whitman's effacement of the political origins of his poetics, as in his deletion of master and slave from these lines, ultimately serves not to dismiss the political in favor of the personal and bodily, but rather to absorb each into the other, to demonstrate that the same issues that inform political practice also designate individual identity.

In locating the poet between master and slave, and between body and soul, Whitman attempts to claim for his poetry the power to mediate oppositions. Able to speak for both sides, the poet alone seems capable of overcoming both the difference between slave and master that divides American society and the division between body and soul that makes the identity of each individual problematic. Moreover, in locating the poet between these two concerns, Whitman proposes to equate political questions with the question of the body, and hence to relate the structure of social practices to the structure of personal identity. What I call Whitman's poetics of merger and embodiment refers, then, both to his poetic goal of healing racial divisions, social and personal, and to the poetic strategies by which he attempts to effect that goal.

Merger and embodiment are linked strategies in this poetics: merger, the perfect melding of opposites into a complete undifferentiated oneness, is best exemplified for Whitman in the physical imagery of the sexual embrace. What Whitman seeks in his poetry simultaneously to express is the particularity of bodily experience – he frequently compares his poetry to the human body – and to promote the healing sameness of merger. The practice of miscegenation or racial amalgamation associated with plantation slavery thus provides within Whitman's writings an historically resonant vocabulary with which to examine his poetics: in the scene of miscegenation racially distinct bodies merge. Presenting the poet as standing between master and slave, body and soul, the political and the personal, the ideals of merger and of bodily specificity, Whitman asserts the power of poetry, but such a presentation also inadvertently reveals the limitations of that power, the ways in which such poetry must remain contingent upon the very divisions it claims to heal.

... 'I Sing the Body Electric' comprises Whitman's most insistent demonstration of his ideal of poetic embodiment, that the supple, flexing body of the 'wellmade man', 'conveys as much as the best poem ... perhaps more' (l. 11). His claim that the wellmade body and the best poem are equally expressive suggests that flesh and words can serve as substitutes for each other. The programmatic aim of this poem is to collapse the two meanings of *convey*: to present what is carried by the body and what can be communicated by words as the same. Significantly, Whitman fashions this 'Poem of the Body', as it was perhaps more appropriately entitled in 1856, out of the least celebratory, most exploitative of discourses on the body: the chant of the auctioneer hawking slaves.

> A slave at auction!
> I help the auctioneer.... the sloven does not half know his business.
> Gentlemen look on this curious creature,
> Whatever the bids of the bidders they cannot be high enough for him,
> For him the globe lay preparing quintillions of years without one
> > animal or plant,
> For him the revolving cycles truly and steadily rolled.
> > (ll. 83–7)

Like the poet, the auctioneer stands between slave and master, product and buyer; the business of both is to sing the value of the thing at hand and to extract the assent of purchase from their audience. In usurping the place of the auctioneer, Whitman is, of course, criticizing his office, demonstrating that even the hyperbole of the auctioneer's pitch grossly understates the value of the item on the block: the human body, he opines, is hardly paid for by all time and the entire world. But he is also inadvertently demonstrating the uneasy parallels between his poetics and the practices of American slavery, the ways in which the act of celebrating a body resembles the act of selling one so that his task as poet corresponds to that of the auctioneer. The parallels prove even closer, for Whitman's concept of embodiment is delimited by the body of the slave.

On the auction block, regardless of any other claims to identity a slave might express, he or she is nothing but body, flesh for sale. The slave at auction provides the quintessential instance of what it means for one's identity to be entirely dependent upon one's body. Though many other human bodies are celebrated in this poem, and throughout Whitman's poetry, to a significant degree Whitman's fundamental image of the body remains that of the slave: one central example of the completely corporeal person. The description of the negro driver in 'Song of Myself' suggestively matches in the details of dress and posture the drawing of Whitman that replaces his name on the title page of the 1855 *Leaves of Grass*.

> The negro that drives the huge dray of the stoneyard ... steady and
> > tall he stands poised on one leg on the stringpiece,
> His blue shirt exposes his ample neck and breast and loosens over his
> > hipband,
> His glance is calm and commanding ... he tosses the slouch of his hat
> > away from his forehead,
> The sun falls on his crispy hair and moustache ... falls on the black of
> > his polish'd and perfect limbs.
> > (ll. 220–3)

Whitman's placement of the drawing, as has often been argued, privileges flesh, or at least the image of flesh, over name or word as pointer to identity. It is the first instance of the book's complex and self-conscious strategies of self-incarnation: 'Whoever touches this book touches a man.' The substitution of a portrait for his name, and the similarities between that portrait and his description of a black man indicate comparable efforts on Whitman's part to assert the corporeality of his own identity.

To argue that in Whitman's poems the challenge of bodiliness gains its absoluteness and urgency from even an indirect comparison of the black salable body of the slave and his own is, however, to tell only half the story. Whitman proposes to unify a discordant America by creating a poetry that would reconcile bodily differences. The intense bodiliness of the slave at auction thus simultaneously initiates Whitman's poetic project and poses the major obstacle to its achievement. The auction block initiates Whitman's poetic project by staging his attempt to negotiate the space between master and slave. It poses the major obstacle to the achievement of this project of poetic reconciliation because, though Whitman insists on the materiality of all being, and particularly of our sense of otherness, he can find no way to heal these divisions that does not dissolve the bodies out of which his poetry is made. Despite his exuberant rhetoric of celebration, despite his insistence that in singing the body this poem overcomes all bodily differences, the costs and contradictions inherent in his double goals of merger and embodiment remain visible. So, as auctioneer in 'I Sing the Body Electric', Whitman gradually strips off the slave's skin, dismembering the body in the act of celebrating it, until all that is left is eternal and ubiquitous blood.

> Examine these limbs, red black or white ... they are very cunning in tendon
> and nerve;
> They shall be stript that you may see them.
> Exquisite senses, lifelit eyes, pluck, volition,
> Flakes of breastmuscle, pliant backbone and neck, flesh not flabby,
> goodsized arms and legs,
> And wonders within there yet.
> Within there runs his blood ... the same old blood ... the same red
> running blood;
> (ll. 91–6)

Here Whitman evokes blood as a physical equalizer: something of the body that is, nevertheless, not implicated in the bodily differences of skin 'red, black or white'. In asking us to imagine this blood as distinct from the bodies that contained it, Whitman nevertheless insists that it serve as a metonym for those bodies, recalling them even as it would replace them. The refrain of blood promises to function as refrains usually do, to promote the comfort of repetitive, nostalgic sameness. Yet Whitman's reliance on blood in his effort to merge the body of the slave into a generalized humanity is, to say the least, disturbing. From the auction block an appeal to blood too easily recalls the bloody backs of whipped slaves. In the lore of plantation slavery, as well as in racist discourses, blood is precisely where race dwells, and the genealogy and value of light-skinned slaves is traditionally measured in drops of black and white blood.[5] Whitman's poetics of merger and his poetics of embodiment both initiate and contradict each other. For just as Whitman's celebration of the body results in pulling apart the slave's flesh to facilitate the slave's notoriously difficult body into a vision of human sameness, Whitman's chorus of merger and inclusion repeats the bloody, physical differentiations of plantation life.

... The mergers Whitman seeks in his lyrics first require the recognition of discord. The stable opposition between lyric mergers and narrative difference cannot be ... easily maintained. Within *Leaves of Grass* the determinate relations between moments of merger and moments of difference, and between lyric and narrative modes that Whitman seems to propose, do not hold. Instead these concepts and the relations between them constantly require renegotiation. ...

In describing Whitman's vision of the mediating poet in terms of interacting lyric and narrative modes, I am suggesting that the choice and manipulation of poetic style can exert political force. Thus Whitman's conception of the poet as mediator itself establishes connections between literary and social practices.[6] Such connections function not only to expand the notion of poetic efficacy but also to redefine what constitutes political action. What I have been calling Whitman's poetics of embodiment amounts to the aspect of his poetic style most deeply implicated in this process. For Whitman, the human body serves as the site where the issues of representation and the questions of political power intersect, and so it is in his treatment of the human body that Whitman most explicitly establishes links between poetry and politics and most radically revises the assumptions and practices of both.

In 'I Sing the Body Electric' Whitman presents the body of the slave as an exemplary instance of embodiment: the salable flesh of the slave attests to the role of the human body in designating identity. It is not surprising, therefore, that Whitman's depictions of the slave serve to ground the poetics and politics of embodiment developed in 'Song of Myself'. Though other black bodies – most notably the negro driver and his team of horses – appear in the 1855 version of this long poem, and more are added in the new catalogues of the 1856 edition, the figure of the fugitive, of the black body in transition between slavery and freedom, predominates. Just as the slave on the auction block, a piece of merchandise, appears to encapsulate the materiality of being, the transitional status of the fugitive seems to denote the fluidity of identity.

Yet as we have seen, Whitman's celebration of corporeality in 'I Sing the Body Electric' strips away the flesh it claims to sing, while here the slave's attempt to change his condition, to disentangle blackness from slavery, is represented through brutal marks upon his body. Moreover, the two scenes in 'Song of Myself' in which Whitman depicts an escape from slavery to freedom also involve a transformation of the relation between the poet and his subject, a gradual elimination of the initial distance between the 'I' that speaks and the body of the fleeing slave. In short, the transition of the fugitive from slave to freeman manifests the structure and implications of Whitman's poetics of embodiment from a variety of perspectives: individual, aesthetic, and political. The relation between identity and the human body, the relation between the poet and his subject matter, and the relation between poetry and political practice all cohere in Whitman's representation of the fugitive.

The figure of the runaway slave first appears in a series of verse paragraphs that pose varying personae for the poet: he is the solitary hunter, the ecstatic sailor on a Yankee Clipper, the playful companion of boatmen and clamdiggers, the witness of a marriage between a trapper and a squaw, and finally the host of a fugitive slave. As such a list makes clear, by the time the story of the slave is told, the flexibility of the poet's identity, the ease with which his 'I' can be transferred from one subject to the next, has already been well established. Such metamorphoses are so characteristic of Whitman's verse that readers generally take them for granted. In the depictions of the fugitive slave in 'Song of Myself', however, Whitman carefully details this usually instantaneous transformation, laying bare some of the contradictions it entails. Anticipated by the fugitive 'I' of Whitman's poem, the figure of the fugitive slave makes evident the predicament of that 'I'.

> The runaway slave came to my house and stopped outside,
> I heard his motions crackling the twigs of the woodpile,
> Through the swung half-door of the kitchen I saw him limpsy and weak,
> And went where he sat on a log, and led him in and assured him,
> And brought him water and filled a tub for his sweated body and bruised feet,
> And gave him a room that entered from my own, and gave him some coarse clean clothes,
> And remember perfectly well his revolving eyes and his awkwardness,
> And remember putting plasters on the galls of his neck and ankles;
> He staid with me a week before he was recuperated and passed north,
> I had him sit next me at table ... my firelock leaned in the corner.
>
> (ll. 183–92)

While the fugitive remains outside of the house, the speaker retains the fixed integrity of an observing 'I' clearly distinct from what it observes: 'I heard his motions', 'I saw him'; but once the speaker begins to tend the slave, he relinquishes this self-defining pronoun. In washing and clothing and giving and remembering, the unique identity of the server is gradually absorbed by the body being served as each 'and' further separates the act that follows from the 'I' that designates the actor. Only after the fugitive leaves for the north, becoming, for the first time since entering the house, an actor rather than a body acted upon, does the speaker again assert his 'I'. Whitman's deployment of pronouns presents physical contact as capable of holding the differentiations of identity in abeyance.

Whitman claims in this passage that the slave's body not only represents but is the locus of social divisions, so that healing the galls caused by the physical iron fetters of slavery actually sutures the divisions between the enslaved and the free, black and white. The healing of the slave's body enables him to claim a free identity and become a grammatical subject. In this passage physical contact merges the identities of host and slave, but the successful outcome of this merger, the slave's transformation into a freeman, requires that the barriers of pronomial difference be reerected. If the assertion of a separate 'he' and 'I' is necessary for the achievement of freedom, it nevertheless reinscribes the divisions emancipation hoped to remove. The 'firelock leaned in the corner' offers a sad reminder of the violence those divisions produced within antebellum society. Indeed the question of the host's relation to the fugitive gains urgency from the presence of the gun: how secure is their merger, how wary is their difference?...

Over six hundred lines later, the figure of the fugitive re-appears, and this time Whitman attempts a more radical union, as if to demonstrate the limitations of his earlier strategy.

> The hounded slave that flags in the race and leans by the fence,
> > blowing and covered with sweat,
> The twinges that sting like needles his legs and neck,
> The murderous buckshot and bullets,
> All these I feel or am.
>
> I am the hounded slave ... I wince at the bite of the dogs,
> Hell and despair are upon me ... crack and again crack the marksmen,
> I clutch the rails of the fence ... my gore drips thinned with the ooze
> > of my skin,
>
> I fall on the weeds and the stones,
> The riders spur their unwilling horses and haul close,
> They taunt my dizzy ears ... they beat me violently over the head
> > with their whip-stocks.
> > (ll. 830–9)

The transference of the poet's 'I' to the figure of the hounded slave, and the consequent merger of these two identities, is marked by the drip and ooze of wounded flesh. Here Whitman employs a manifestly corporeal vocabulary to articulate the union of poet and fugitive, demonstrating how his poetics of merger depends upon the notion of embodiment. There is a Doubting Thomas quality to this passage, as if probing the fugitive's wounds would assure the veracity of Whitman's poetic miracle: he would become the other, and so otherness would be eliminated. The fugitive's attempt to change his status and the poet's attempt to write this poem share, for Whitman, the same assumptions about the corporeality of identity: for the slave, escaping to freedom or returning to captivity entails a harrowing of his flesh; for the poet, telling this story involves representing that flesh as his own. Whitman's equation of poetry with bodily experience strives to defy any distinction between the written and the physical world. ... The case of the fugitive slave provides Whitman with an extreme and definitive instance of the problematics of embodiment characteristic of his poetry as a whole. Whitman's focus on the body has a political as well as a poetic meaning. He proposes in *Leaves of Grass* that the divisions in the social fabric, the nature of identity, and the relation of the poet's word to the external world are not simply analogous, but finally identical questions. For in trying to reconcile an embodied and a disembodied conception of identity, Whitman makes clear that the divisions between self and other (white and black, master and slave) that inform the political delineations of personhood can be located with equal force within each person and within every act of utterance. I have suggested as much already in arguing that Whitman's first notebook poetry presents the relation between slave and master as an alternative means of articulating the relation between body and soul and in showing that Whitman's most powerful image for the commingling of body and soul reiterates the scene of miscegenation. The import of bodily difference manifested by American slavery challenges not only national unity but also any unitive conception of identity. By literalizing this challenge Whitman dismantles traditional distinctions between what is a personal and what a political issue: each stands equally well as an emblem for the other. Moreover, Whitman finds that poetry is constituted out of the same divide between the disembodied and the embodied, the intangible words that demand to be felt as a palpable world. ...

In reading the relation Whitman traces between body and soul ... as reinscribing the problematics of a corporeal identity characteristic of American slavery, I am, therefore, also examining the erasure of such historical markers: Whitman's consistent decontextualizing of his imagery. ... Whitman concluded his preface to the 1855 edition by setting up a criterion by which to judge the poems that follow: 'The proof of a poet is that his country absorbs him as affectionately as he has absorbed it.' The claim of affection acknowledges the erotic nature of this standard. Whitman's ideal of absorption is fulfilled. For if Whitman's poetry does absorb the social divisions of antebellum America, and particularly the crisis over slavery, it is also absorbed by it. Thus the poet, the person whom Whitman imagined as capable of mediating between the social divisions exemplified by American slavery, finally comes to incarnate those divisions. □

(Karen Sanchez-Eppler, 'To Stand Between', 1997)[7]

Sanchez-Eppler's reading of Whitman traces the political pressures embedded in Whitman's attention to matters of the personal and the bodily. For her, his poetry therefore incarnates those cultural and political divisions its rhetoric of democratic optimism seeks to erase. In the next critical extract, Allen Grossman asserts that the troubled relationship between the personal and the political is, in Whitman, attended to at the very level of his poetic line, in his struggles to find a poetic rhythm and measure for his 'Democratic' expression. Grossman claims, further (and in a fascinating comparison), that the divisions of mid-nineteenth century America are made incarnate in Lincoln's political rhetoric and Whitman's poetics. Both Whitman and Lincoln, he argues, are 'captives of a system of representation'. Thus, whilst claims are regularly made for these two being the prime agents in America's assertion of unified and democratic nationhood, Grossman demonstrates how they are actually the subjects of an American rhetoric of cultural expansion and political union. The book of essays from which Grossman's essay is taken (*The American Renaissance Reconsidered*, first published in 1985) is the first significant publication employing revisionist and deconstructive ways of reading the 'American Renaissance'. It is the starting point, therefore, for 'New Americanist' criticism, a way of thinking about America and its culture(s) that has had a profound effect on American Studies. Such New Americanist reconsiderations of America and its meaning have recently led, in publications such as the journal *boundary 2* and the 'New Americanists' series for Duke University Press edited by Donald Pease, to a serious questioning of the applicability of the very notion of nationality to a country as culturally diverse as the Unites States of America. Predictably, *Leaves of Grass* remains a central text in such re-evaluations. Grossman's essay is therefore crucially important in the history of both Whitman criticism, and of critical thinking about America.

■ ... When Matthiessen named Whitman 'the central figure of our literature affirming the democratic faith', he did so because he saw Whitman as the champion, not only of liberty and equality, but also (unlike Emerson, Thoreau, and even Melville) of fraternity – the master of union as social love.[8] But Lincoln was the great speaker of the American Renaissance whose imagination empowered the democratic faith. Its way, he said, is 'plain, peaceful, generous, just'. In the 1850s, both Whitman and Lincoln held more or less the same politics, including the view that slavery *and also abolition* were barbarisms: abolition because it interrupted contract and exchange without which there was no social world in which anyone *could* be free; slavery because, as an impermissible variation of the practice of liberty (you cannot choose to enslave), it destroyed the value both of labor and leisure without which freedom was empty of praxis ['The practice or exercise of a technical subject or art, as distinct from the theory of it' (OED)].[9] Lincoln's characteristic strategy for freeing slaves was *compensated* emancipation, the completion of the Revolution by the co-optation in its service of the constitutional principle of contract – the justification, in effect, of logical discourse. Whitman supposed that the same result could only be obtained by a more fundamental revision of the central nature of relationship – the establishment of a new basis for speaking in the counterlogic, and infinite distributability, of the affectionate presence. Both Lincoln and Whitman intended the same thing. The two systems (the closed and the open) that they sponsored aspire each to specify the inclusion of the other as the best outcome of its view of nature. ...

Whitman's policy was to establish a new principle of access that would effect multiplication, or pluralization (the getting many into one), without the loss entailed by exchange – the glory of the perfect messenger. In the chronology of Whitman's work, the 'open' line as formal principle appears simultaneously with the subject of liberation, and is the enabling condition of the appearance of that subject. That is to say, his first poems in the new style are also his first poems on the subject of slavery and freedom (specifically, 'Resurgemus', 'Blood-Money', 'Wounded in the House of Friends'). His first lines in the new style altogether (so far as I can tell) are recorded in a notebook as follows:

> I am the poet of the slave, and of the masters of the slave
> ....
> I am the poet of the body
> And I am the poet of the soul
> I go with the slaves of the earth equally with the masters
> And I will stand between the masters and the slaves,
> Entering into both, so that both shall understand me alike[10]

... Instead of a 'poetic language' (always a mimetic version of the language of one class) Whitman has devised a universal 'conjunctive principle' whose manifest structure is the sequence of end-stopped, nonequivalent, but equipollent ['Equal in power, effectiveness, or validity' (OED)] lines. ... His poetic authority is J. S. Mill's 'overheard' soliloquy of feeling, and his physicalist basis is the phrenological continuity between inner and outer mind. The drama of translation is enacted at the beginning of an early poem, 'The Answerer':

> Now list to my morning's romanza, I tell the signs of the Answerer,
> To the cities and farms I sing as they spread in the sunshine before me.
> A young man comes to me bearing a message from his brother,
> How shall the young man know the whether and when of his brother?
> Tell him to send me the signs.
> And I stand before the young man face to face, and take his right hand
>   in my left hand and his left hand in my right hand
> And I answer for his brother and for men ...

By curing the human colloquy, the poet (the translator, answerer, perfect messenger, better president) intends to establish a boundless resource of the central acknowledgement-value, and to rid sociability of death by overcoming the scarcity of fame, a process that requires the mechanical checks and balances (reifications of the competing will of the inaccessible other) in the poetics of Lincoln's constitutionalism. But Whitman's new principle of access – his line – is not 'organic' in Matthiessen's ... sense. It has the virtuality of a paradigm; and the negotiation of its actualization against the resistances of history and mind is Whitman's major subject.

The primal scene of that negotiation is the 'transparent morning' of part 5 of 'Song of Myself.' It is the inaugural moment of Whitman's candor, and as such it recapitulates the first subject matter liberated by his line. The form is the confession of a creed:

I believe in you my soul, the other I am must not abase itself to you
And you must not be abased to the other.

The rewriting of hierarchies – soul/body, collective/individual, nation/state – as equalities, and the rewriting as identities of conventional dualities, above all the self and the other, is the task of the 'translator', whose goal is union as the fraternalization of the community ... What follows in Whitman's creed is the greater mystery of the mortal union of two, the competent number of acknowledgement, and the archetype of all political relationship. For Lincoln, labor is prior to capital and is the praxis of the individual will by which all selfhood, and therefore all value, is produced.[11] It is indistinguishable from the act of clarification (the intention of the lawgiver) by which univocal meaning is derived, many made one. To loaf ('Loafe with me on the grass ...') is to exchange the posture of hemeneutic attention for the posture of receptivity, the unity of all things in the last sorting category of mere consciousness prior to interpretation ('the origin of all poems') of which the voice is the 'hum', the sound of the blood doing the cultural work of God ... the doggerel of life. What follows, then, is the sexual union reconstructed as a moment of primal communication, the tongue to the heart. The principle of the language of the soul is the deletion, as in Whitman's metricality as a whole, of centralizing hypotactic ['in grammar: ... a subordinate construction' (OED)] grammar, and the difference-making prosodies both of individual meaning–intention and abstractly patterned (stress/no stress) metricality. What is obtained is an unprecedented trope of inclusion – the sign, embodied in that revision of primary human relationship ('gently turned upon me'), of which the greater inclusions of emancipation and union are the things signified:

And limitless are the leaves stiff with drooping in the fields
And brown ants in the little wells beneath them
And mossy scabs of the worm fence, heap'd stones, elder, mullein and
poke-weed.

But what is created, paradoxically, is a new slave culture. The Whitmanian voice, like the slave, is uncanny – a servant of persons, but not itself personal – a case of delegated social death: 'A generalized art language, a literary algebra' (Sapir). 'Comradeship – part of the death process. The new Democracy – the brink of death. One identity – death itself' (Lawrence). 'To put the paradox in a nutshell, he wrote poetry out of poetry writing' (Pavese).[12] There is truth in these judgements. The logic of presence, Whitman's 'profound lesson of reception', has its own violence. The Whitmanian convulsion ('And parted the shirt from my bosom-bone, and plunged your tongue to my bare-stripped heart') attendant upon the reduction of all things to appearance, is the counterviolence to that which flows from the logic of clarification, the reduction of all things to univocal meaning. The tongue of the soul is the principle of continuity figured as the 'hum' of subvocal, absorbed, multitudinous, continuously regulated 'valved voice', or 'this soul', as Whitman elsewhere says, '... its other name is Literature.'[13] The tongue sacrifices the subject of justice in the interest of a personal immediacy that overcomes the difference of the social body, but at the same time destroys (tongue to barestripped heart) the destiny of the secular person which the social body is.

In a tract Whitman wrote in 1856 on behalf of Fremont (whom Lincoln also supported), Whitman produces his model of the 'Redeemer President' whose nay will be 'not exclusive, but inclusive' (J. Furness, 'The Eighteenth Presidency' 1928)[14] Lincoln was not Whitman's redeemed president. Lincoln was the type of the 'unknown original' (Sapir's expression) from which, as from the utterance of the hermit thrush of the elegy, Whitman translated his song. Whitman's taxonomic line runs 'askant' history (the abstract pattern he deletes is precisely the element of the line that has a history). That variation produces the infinite access he required for his 'peace that passes the art and argument of earth'. In Lincoln's terms such a variation is as transgressive (and of the same nature) as ... slavery itself.

Lincoln's sentence, by contrast, prolongs the history of each soul beyond mortality in a never-darkened theater of judgment. In the midst of an argument in his 'Second Annual Address' (1862) in support of compensated emancipation, Lincoln inserts the following sentence: 'In times like these men should utter nothing for which they would not be responsible through time and in eternity.'[15] In the straightening of choice, Lincoln in his language grows thick with character, the pure case of tragic personhood enacting the indissolubility of a moral identity that persists across eschatological boundaries in space and time (the cosmological expression of ethical contract) – unmistakable, eternally situated, judged. The peroration of the same speech begins; 'Fellow citizens, *we* cannot escape history. We of this Congress and this administration, will be remembered in spite of ourselves. No personal significance, or insignificance, can spare one or another of us. The fiery trial through which we pass, will light us down, in honor or dishonor, the latest generation.'[16] By deleting the abstract pattern of internal marks that closes the traditional line and carries it across time, Whitman deleted history, founded an infinite resource of acknowledgement, dissolved the moral praxis of the singular individual, and 'launched forth' (as he says at the end of the 'Song of the Answerer') into the destitute universe of transparent minds, generated by an open metrical contract, 'to sweep through the ceaseless rings and never be quiet again'. Lincoln's language, unlike Whitman's, is empowered because it is of the same nature as the institutions that invented him, and his space and time are institutional space and time. In such a world, judgement and acknowledgement are inseparable; and the economy of scarcity is reconstituted in the oldest economic terms of our civilization – honor or dishonor.

Both Whitman and Lincoln are captives of a system of representation, which they are commissioned to justify and put in place as an order of the human world – a policy for union. Are there two policies, or only one? On the one hand, a Whitmanian policy – open, egalitarian, in a sense socialist (as Matthiessen thought it to be), generalized from the fame–power of art, and darkly qualified by that abjection of the subject of value which is the other side of receptivity; and, on the other hand, a Lincolnian system – closed, republican, capitalist, a regulative policy driven by the logic of clarification, and darkly qualified in its turn by the obliterative implications both of moral exclusiveness and the delegatory economies of labor? We have seen that the centered, hierarchical, Lincolnian ethical rationality is precisely the enemy element from which Whitman is bent upon exempting his human world. We see also that the resonant, scale-finding, integrative vocality of Lincoln is the most severe criticism our literature affords of Whitman's indeterminate realization of the person – 'You whoever you are'. Whitman's 'Word over all, beautiful as the sky' reconciles what Lincoln's ethical dualism drives into division, yet only at that distance; Lincoln's sentiment of ethical difference cruelly specifies the limit of variation in which regulative rationality can produce the actual life of all men. But despite the reciprocally canceling nature of Whitman and Lincoln as liberators, the gravity of representation itself unites them in a common conservatism. ... ☐   (Allen Grossman, 'The Poetics of Union')[17]

Grossman's reading of Whitman is compelling because it locates his poetry within specifically American political circumstances. Whitman's poetics, Grossman is claiming, cannot be separated from the history out of which it arises. In contrast, then, it is perhaps fitting that the essay that concludes this guide to critical readings of Whitman should assert that Whitman is best read in an international, as opposed to a narrowly nationalistic (American) perspective. Jonathan Arac's reading of Whitman's poetry is a bold and challenging attempt, therefore, to wrest Whitman away from the dominant critical tendency that we have witnessed throughout this guide, namely the attempt to read Whitman as a product of – or even, producer of – American ideology. It is fitting too that Arac's critical tool for doing this should be a notion of the 'creole', or culturally mixed, character of American language. For if one thing is apparent from the critical history of Whitman's poetry, it is precisely a creolised sense that its legacy is 'vast' and that it 'contains multitudes'. It is a poetry of mixtures, of possibilities and of ambiguities, not of exclusions. Arac's model for reading Whitman, then, pushes critical enquiry of his poetry in new directions. It discovers new ideological and cultural occasions for Whitman's poetry, and finds it to be adequate to those occasions.

■ Let me start well within bounds, with a commonplace. Someone eager to learn about the author of *Leaves of Grass* could turn to recent works of good repute and find that Whitman is notable for his use of 'the American vernacular', that he was the 'first genuine master of the American vernacular'.[18] But what is meant by this laudatory description? How did this term *vernacular* come to occupy a key place in discussions of Whitman? What is the value of maintaining it? The term was not part of nineteenth-century discussions of what Cmiel (1991) calls 'popular language' in the United States, nor does it figure in the path-breaking discussion of Whitman's language in F. O. Matthiessen's *American Renaissance* (1941).[19] So far as I can tell, the term begins to play its current role in the early postwar period, functioning among the founding premises for the institutionalization of literary American Studies. The specific premise is that Whitman, together with Mark Twain, inaugurated what Henry Nash Smith in the 1948 *Literary History of the United States* called, in praise, 'the intrusion of the vernacular into consciously literary usage'. A decade later, Leo Marx developed this claim in 'The Vernacular Tradition in American Literature', which as late as 1988 Marx placed first in the warmly reviewed volume of his collected essays.

Departing from this well-established view, I explore conceptual problems in the notion of *vernacular*, especially its frequent linkage to nationalist myths of purity. I argue instead for a comparatist perspective that emphasises *mixture*: a 'creole' mixture associated with the Black Atlantic (Gilroy) or 'Circum-Atlantic Performance' (Roach); the heterogeneity of life and language associated with the big city, whether Whitman's New York or Baudelaire's Paris; and finally even the impurity that joins this self-consciously American writer to the literary practices of British romanticism.[20] ...

[Leo] Marx's essay on 'The Vernacular Tradition' begins from the question of national cultural identity. He claims that before 1850 'the boundary between British and American literature remains uncertain'.[21] So it is apt in this volume to note that the topic of vernacular may involve establishing bounds more than breaking bounds. Walt Whitman and Twain are 'the two great seminal figures of modern American writing' because in 'Song of Myself' and *Huckleberry Finn*, the line between British and American becomes 'much more distinct'.[22] These works 'establish once and for all the literary usefulness of the native idiom'.[23] Because they 'fashioned a vernacular mode', they made possible a 'national style'.[24] Vernacular, Marx explains ... stands in contrast to what George Santayana had called the 'genteel tradition', the traditional mentality from which a younger generation had diverged. For Marx, then, the vernacular tradition is not only a matter of characteristic language; it also carries with it social, specifically political, values: 'the core of the American vernacular ... is not simply a style, but a style with a politics in view'; its 'political ideal is freedom'.[25]

To make his point, Marx compares a poem by Longfellow ('The Slave in the Dismal Swamp') with these lines from section 10 of 'Song of Myself':

The runaway slave came to my house and stopt outside,
I heard his motions crackling the twigs of the woodpile,
Through the swung half-door of the kitchen I saw him limpsy and weak,
And went where he sat on a log and led him in and assured him,
And brought water and fill'd a tub for his sweated body and bruis'd feet,
And gave him a room that enter'd from my own, and gave him some
                                                coarse clean clothes,
And remember perfectly well his revolving eyes and his awkwardness,
And remember putting plasters on the galls of his neck and ankles;
He staid with me a week before he was recuperated and pass'd north,
I had him sit next me at the table, my fire-lock lean'd in the corner.[26]

Marx claims that Whitman 'imagines a completely different kind of relationship to the black man' from that in Longfellow's poem, achieved through the 'extraordinary sense of immediacy that the vernacular mode conveys'.[27] Marx praises the 'indirection by which Whitman's speaker at the end ... casually mentions the gun in the corner'.[28] For Marx, here, 'the image *is* the meaning; it is a perfect example of the democratic hero's relaxed but militant egalitarianism'.[29] Stylistically, Whitman 'anticipates the kind of ironic understatement' that would flourish in the twentieth century.

However, I find it painfully evident that the aesthetic principles of American new-critical modernism – an emphasis on irony and imagery, on 'showing' rather than 'telling' – have saturated Marx's socially, culturally, and politically concerned argument, and further, that those principles underwrite a Cold War, American Century stance even in this leftist critic. Whitman's speaker's soft talk and big stick form a recognizable style of boasting, later brought by Teddy Roosevelt from his macho western experiences to the stage of world diplomacy and reinforced in the days of massive deterrence when Marx wrote. ...

As I consider Marx's argument further, I an struck by the instability of the key term *vernacular*. Marx does not remark upon its etymological history, which, however, seems to predict his examples. *Vernacular* comes from Latin *verna*, a slave born in the master's house, and it thus carries from its beginnings the problematic of domination and domestication.[30] ...

The current senses in the *American Heritage Dictionary* for the noun *vernacular* suggest the problems I find. Sense one is 'the standard native language of a country or locality'; sense two is the 'nonstandard or substandard everyday speech of a country or locality'. In considering these senses, we might think of the model of Latin vis-à-vis the emerging

Romance languages (the 'vernaculars'). From the point of view of the Roman empire, the second sense (substandard, everyday) predominated, but from the point of view of nations in formation the first sense (standard, native) prevailed. The distinction between standard native language and non- or sub-standard everyday speech throws back into crisis the bounds of American literary nationality: is there a standard 'American' national language of the 'country' or are there only innumerable everyday variations differing by 'locality'? What does it mean to imply that, as masterpieces of 'the vernacular', *Leaves of Grass* and *Huckleberry Finn* have the relation to past British and future American languages that the *Divine Comedy* and the *Decameron* do to past Latin and future Italians [meaning 'Italian languages of the future']? At least it makes us ask whether Marx's praise of vernacular does not in fact work to fix a vernacular *standard*, as the great Renaissance writers did for their European cultures through the prestige they were accorded in critical and educational practices. That is, having been used to define one set of bounds (America versus the Old World), vernacular becomes a means for drawing further bounds within the United States, as to what will count as authentically 'American'. The third sense of *vernacular* in the *American Heritage Dictionary* further emphasizes this problem of representativeness: 'the idiom of a particular trade or profession'. In other words, here *vernacular* means much the same as *jargon*, not what is common, but what is peculiar or particular to a closed group, although that group may claim for itself, or have claimed for it, the right to stand for the whole.

Marx's usages display the complications that the dictionaries make explicit. He wrote of the vernacular as an American 'native idiom' and thus the basis for a 'national style'. But what is the relation of native and national here? To begin, we may note that the dictionaries mention vernacular as not only *native* but also *indigenous*. The difference between these terms lies precisely in the historical depth of settlement. While the U. S.-born children of immigrants might be native, and proudly called themselves so, they were not indigenous. In the earlier nineteenth-century discussions of the possibilities of an American literary nationality for the United States, this problem was directly addressed, namely, that the Indians, the historically rooted inhabitants of what had become the United States, spoke as their mother tongues languages that were not the English language of the politically dominant culture. The opposite problem, certainly by the time Whitman was writing, was felt even more immediately, that is, the problem of nonanglophone immigrants. Marx's discussion of vernacular seems to leave no room for either of these features of the language and life of the United States.

Whitman, with whatever success, did deliberately incorporate non-English words into his poetry, and many twentieth-century students of American English have found much of its distinctive difference from British English to spring precisely from idioms (words, inflections, syntactic patterns) drawn from other languages. The example of Whitman moves me to claim that the 'creolization' of American English is what produces its difference from the English that served as the standard of literary language. ...

... *creole* might be a more useful term than *vernacular* for thinking about American language. This terminological shift would start to place less weight on distinguishing the culture of the United States from the cultures of Britain and Europe and more on relating, both as similar and different, the cultures of the United States to those of other areas once held as colonies of Britain and Europe. Moreover, in recognizing that questions of empire were not terminated by the Revolution War, a 'creole' perspective would foster the understanding of the United States not only as itself a postcolonial nation but also as itself an imperial nation. ... Although the notion of creole has at times been used as part of an ideology of racial purity, its wider connotations, as seen in its usage as a term of linguistics, suggest 'mixture' rather than 'purity'. Thus I find the term especially apt for the figure of Whitman I am delineating, since the journalistic practice and language of Whitman have also been understood as impure ..., in contrast to ... the national-racial identitarian purisms of 'vernacular'.

Thus a 'creole' perspective encourages thinking about Whitman and the emergence of American literary nationality not as something in the first place unique and exceptional, but instead as one among many occasions – around the globe and over centuries – where colonialism precipitated resistances that became nationalism. ...

I am about to discuss Whitman further as a poet in the culture of newspapers and the economy of capitalism, and I will connect him back to Europe, not as an argument for influence, but in order to redefine the grounds for transatlantic comparative study of Whitman. In pursuing this argument, I will make use of the work of Walter Benjamin, a great critic of the thirties. ... If we define for Whitman the historical ground he shares with his French contemporary Charles Baudelaire, what interesting differences will then emerge? ...

It requires fresh thought to consider why Whitman and Baudelaire alike make seriously moving poetry out of the materials of life which had long been thought least propitious for great art. Baudelaire did not believe in democracy or progress; indeed he polemicized against such ideals and the view of human nature that supported them. Precisely this difference between Whitman and Baudelaire arises once as a disturbing question in a notebook of the interpreter of Baudelaire whose work has meant the most to me, Walter Benjamin: 'That Baudelaire was hostile to progress was an indispensable condition of his being able to cope with Paris in his poetry. Compared to his, later city poetry must be accounted feeble, and not least where it sees the city as the seat of progress. But Walt Whitman?'[31]

It has been usual to compare the social significance of mid-nineteenth-century American literature with that of transatlantic writings by contrasting the American concern with freedom to Old World concerns with poverty: Victor Hugo's Jean Valjean in *Les Misérables* [(1862)] first goes to prison for stealing a loaf of bread; the death of Dickens' Jo in *Bleak House* [(1852–53)] speaks to the national urgency of assisting those who lack food, housing, and health care; but Stowe's Eva dies in *Uncle Tom's Cabin* [(1852)] because the national sin of slavery is too great to bear, and the fates of George Harris and Uncle Tom no less testify that freedom far outweighs economic issues. The force of Benjamin's work is to help make understandable a fundamental structure by which the same economic system that produced European (and of course American) poverty also established the basis for fierce concern with human equality in freedom. The replacement of what had been considered 'organic' bonds of hierarchical interdependency left every individual in principle free, and the poor free to starve; the transformation of patterns of work on the model of mass production, of the analytical separation of tasks, made it increasingly likely that a worker performed the same repetitive action rather than being responsible for producing a whole; the growth of commercial-industrial urban centers on a new scale brought people together who showed themselves to each other in anonymous, heterogeneous, fascinating masses; and newspapers became the newly dominant medium for the linguistic exchange of information. Benjamin understood the condition of possibility of Baudelaire's poetry as the Paris of crowds and of newspapers that cut up the doings of the world into atomized bits, each equal and isolated, like members of a city crowd. Benjamin helps us imagine that the journalistic, along with its appeal to self-remaking, rather than some 'native' vernacular, may join Whitman to his age, and not necessarily specifically to his nation.

What, then, if we question Whitman under the rubric of Benjamin's study of Baudelaire, as a poet 'in the age of high capitalism', a system that a later student of the mid-nineteenth century has characterized as 'unification through monetarization'?[32] The measure of Whitman's verse is a syntax which poses an equation between elements that would conventionally be understood as different from each other in as many ways as possible. To Leo Marx and American Studies this is radical democracy. To Roman Jakobson, it lays bare the poetic principle of projecting equivalence from the axis of combination to the axis of selection.[33] But to Karl Marx it is the logic of the commodity: 'Just as every qualitative difference between commodities is extinguished in money, so money, on its side, like the radical leveller that it is, does away with all distinctions.'[34] This principle of uniformity, which makes possible modern industry as well as politics, in Benjamin's analysis also encompasses the crowd and the newspaper and sets the challenge to old models of experience that Baudelaire brings into his poetry.

... This line of speculation brings me to a text. Benjamin offers a strong reading of Baudelaire's sonnet 'A une passante' ('To a Passing Woman', in my very literal translation).

The deafening street howled around me.
Tall, slim, in deep mourning, majestic sorrow,

A woman passed, with a stately hand
Lifting, balancing the scallop of her hem;

Quick and noble, with her leg like a statue's.
Me, I drank, twisted like a madman,
Deep in her eye, ashen sky where hurricanes grow,
The sweetness that binds and the pleasure that kills.

A flash ... then night! – Transient beauty
Whose look has brought me suddenly to rebirth,
Will I not see you again except in eternity?

Somewhere else, far from here! Too late! *Never* perhaps!
For I don't know where you're fleeing, you don't know where I'm going,
O you I would have loved, O you who knew it!

Number 22 of the 1860 'Calamus' is the sonnet-sized poem that begins, 'Passing stranger!' ... Benjamin emphasizes that in Baudelaire's poem the crowd is not represented; it emerges only through an allusion to the noise of the street in the opening line ... In Whitman there is not even the allusion; it is as though the speaker were alone with the stranger, although I read the poem under the sign of the 'populous city':

Passing stranger! You do not know how longingly I look upon you,
You must be he I was seeking, or she I was seeking, (it comes to me as
                                                                   of a dream,)
I have somewhere surely lived a life of joy with you,
All is recall'd as we flit by each other, fluid, affectionate, chaste, matured,
You grew up with me, were a boy with me or a girl with me,
I ate with you and slept with you, your body has become not yours only
                                                           nor left my body mine only,
You give me the pleasure of your eyes, face, flesh, as we pass, you take of
                                                           my beard, breast, hands, in return,
I am not to speak to you, I am to think of you when I sit alone or wake at
                                                                           night alone,
I am to wait, I do not doubt I am to meet you again,
I am to see to it that I do not lose you.[35]

Whitman imagines an intimacy so great that the speaker and stranger are figured as 'we'. The public space of the street produces the solidarity and exchange that were impossible for the private unrepresentability of the runaway slave. The temporality of Baudelaire's poem differs strongly from Whitman's. Baudelaire's strong 'never' closes a moment of melodramatically rich loss; in contrast Whitman's 'again' prolongs into a shared future the shared past already produced by this encounter. Whitman brings together the acts of reading and city-strolling, the chaos and anonymity of the crowd with the multiplication of copies of one book among all the others ... Neither Whitman nor Baudelaire represents the crowd, but each is implicated in it: they are not protected by the distance of observation; even in passing, an encounter may count.

Through this essay, I have argued against the purism lurking in the critical discourse on *vernacular* and have argued instead for a 'creole' perspective. A creole perspective not only registers more clearly the complex mixtures forming American language and culture; it also links America to a globally tranformative history of colonialism and capitalism, in which the newspaper – emerging in cities as a medium of commercial information and advertisement – became a means of formation for national consciousness and new language practices ...

The global, imperial-colonial process of creolization was part of the economic transformation that brought into existence the daily life of a world metropolis, which Wordsworth in London, Baudelaire in Paris, and Whitman in New York all lived through, and which marked all of their poetry in different ways. Wordsworth turned to the country to counter the city; Baudelaire and Whitman made the city the center of much of their greatest work. Yet their relations to the city still greatly differed. Benjamin's Baudelaire wrote against his age; in Benjamin's terms, his 'experience' challenged the 'information' of the news. Whitman wrote with his age. Whitman lacked the purity of folk-vernacular or of cultivated art-speech, and he made journalism into his experience. Whitman's nation-building culture was not folk but mass, that is to say capitalist, and from that, as we now say hopefully of the world stretching – as Whitman would see it – westward from China to Poland, real democracy may follow. □

(Jonathan Arac, 'Whitman and the Problems of Vernacular')[36]

The close of Arac's essay echoes Whitman's concern with the poetics of democracy. What we have witnessed throughout the critical history of *Leaves of Grass* are the different ways in which ideas of America, and especially democracy, have been deployed through readings of Whitman's poetry. However, the essays in this concluding chapter have been concerned to explore and to deconstruct those points in Whitman's poetry that seem to expose forces at work in American ideology which its cultural apparatuses struggle to conceal. These final three essays have also shared the realisation that the critical history of *Leaves of Grass* is, itself, one of the most powerful of those cultural apparatuses. This exposing of the *interestedness* with which Whitman has been read since the publication of the first edition of *Leaves of Grass* in 1855 is a reminder of the magnificent power of Whitman's poetry, and of just how partial are our attempts to come to terms with it.

NOTES

INTRODUCTION

1 These lines are taken from the 1855 edition of 'Song of Myself', lines 1314–16, and are quoted from Walt Whitman, *The Complete Poems*, ed. Francis Murphy (1975; rpt. London: Penguin, 1986), p. 737.

2 Ralph Waldo Emerson, 'The Poet', in Sherman Paul, ed., *Emerson's Essays* (London: Dent, 1955), p. 224.

3 See Jerome Loving, *Emerson, Whitman, and the American Mind* (Chapel Hill: University of North Carolina Press, 1982) for an account of the intellectual relationship between Emerson and Whitman.

4 See Joel Myerson, *Whitman in His Own Time: A Biographical Chronicle of His Life, Drawn from Recollections, Memoirs, and Interviews by Friends and Associates* (Columbia, S.C.: Omnigraphics, 1991), p. 173; and David S. Reynolds, *Walt Whitman's America: A Cultural Biography* (New York: Vintage Books, 1996), p. 82.

5 Walt Whitman, 'Preface' to the first edition of *Leaves of Grass* (1855). Quoted from Murphy, ed., pp. 741–3.

6 Murphy, ed., p. 762.

7 Roy Harvey Pearce, 'Introduction', in *Walt Whitman: A Collection of Critical Essays*, ed., Roy Harvey Pearce (Englewood Cliffs, NJ: Prentice-Hall, 1962), p. 2.

8 'So Long!', the final poem of the last edition of *Leaves of Grass* prepared during Whitman's lifetime. Murphy, ed., pp. 513–14.

CHAPTER ONE

1 Whitman describes himself – or at least his poetic persona – as 'one of the roughs' in line 499 of the 1855 edition of 'Song of Myself', the poem which opens that first edition of *Leaves of Grass*. His claim that his poetry is 'commensurate with America' is made in an appendix – which takes the form of an open letter addressed to Emerson – to the second edition of *Leaves of Grass*, August 1856.

2 In the letter to Emerson appended to the second edition of *Leaves of Grass*.

3 Letter from Ralph Waldo Emerson to Whitman, 21 July 1855. Taken from Milton Hundus, ed., *Walt Whitman: The Critical Heritage* (London: Routledge and Kegan Paul, 1971), pp. 21–2.

4 Ralph L. Rusk, *The Life of Ralph Waldo Emerson* (New York: Charles Scribner's Sons, 1949), p. 317. See also Joann P. Krieg, *A Whitman Chronology* (Iowa City: University of Iowa Press, 1998), p. 33.

5 Ralph Waldo Emerson, 'The Poet', in *Emerson's Essays*, ed. Sherman Paul (London: Dent, 1955), p. 205.

6 Walt Whitman, unsigned review of *Leaves of Grass*, *United States Review* (1855). This was reprinted in *Leaves of Grass Imprints*, pp. 7–13, a pamphlet of advertisements for, and reviews of, *Leaves of Grass* which was distributed with its third-Boston-edition.

7 Anonymous review, *New York Daily Times* (1856). This review, however, was included in *Leaves of Grass Imprints*, pp. 20–7.

8 Charles A. Dana, 'Notice of *Leaves of Grass*', *New York Daily Tribune* (23 July 1855).

9 See Charles A. Dana, *Recollections of the Civil War* (1898; rpt. Lincoln: University of Nebraska Press, 1996), pp. viii–ix.

10 Charles Eliot Norton, 'Review of *Leaves of Grass*', *Putnam's Monthly* (September 1855).

159

11 See David S. Reynolds, *Walt Whitman's America: A Cultural Biography* (New York: Vintage Books, 1996), pp. 304–5 and 346–7.

12 Charles Eliot Norton in *Putnam's Monthly* (September 1855). Much of this anonymous review in *The Critic* parallels comments in Norton's review. See Norton above, pp. 15–16.

13 In his letter to Whitman, 21 July 1855. See above, pp. 8–9.

14 Anonymous review of *Leaves of Grass*, the *Critic* (London, 1 April 1856).

15 Anonymous review, *Boston Intelligencer* (3 May 1856). This review was reprinted in an Appendix, titled 'The Opinions, 1855–56', to the second edition of *Leaves of Grass*.

16 Edward Everett Hale, (unsigned) review of *Leaves of Grass*, *North American Review*, 82–170 (January 1856), pp. 275–7.

17 Henry David Thoreau, letter to Harrison Blake, 7 December 1856. Published in Thoreau's *Letters to Various Persons* (Boston, 1865), pp. 146–8.

18 *eupeptic*: 'Of or pertaining to "eupepsy" or good digestion; characteristic of, or resulting from, good digestion' (*OED*). Hence, in this context, meaning 'cheerful', and 'optimistic'.

19 This 1855 Preface is discussed above in the 'Introduction', pp. 3–4.

20 *Schopenhauer*: Arthur Schopenhauer (1788–1860). Philosopher born in Gdanacsk. His chief work was *Die Welt als Wille und Vorstellung* [*The World as Will and Idea*] (1819), and his concept of the Will as an indomitable force opposed Enlightenment doctrines. His work influenced Romantic and early modernist writers and artists such as Wagner, Tolstoy, Proust and Mann.

21 John Robertson, *Walt Whitman: Poet and Democrat* (Edinburgh: William Brown, 1884), pp. 5–52.

CHAPTER TWO

1 Ezra Pound, 'A Pact', in *Personae: Collected Shorter Poems of Ezra Pound* (London: Faber & Faber, 1952), p. 98.

2 Edwin Haviland Miller, ed., *Walt Whitman: The Complete Correspondence* (New York: New York University Press, 1961–77), vol. 5, p. 73. See also, Joann P. Krieg, *A Whitman Chronology* (Iowa City: University of Iowa Press, 1998), pp. 158 and 168; J. R. LeMaster and Donald D. Kummings, eds, *Walt Whitman: An Encyclopedia* (New York and London: Garland, 1998), pp. 701–2 and David S. Reynolds, *Walt Whitman's America: A Cultural Biography* (New York: Vintage Books, 1996), pp. 198 and 396–7.

3 These prose passages are taken from 'Democratic Vistas'. 'Democratic Vistas' is reprinted in *The Portable Walt Whitman*, ed. Mark Van Doren, rev. Malcolm Cowley (1945, rev. 1974; rpt. London: Penguin, 1977), pp. 317–82.

4 John Addington Symonds, *Walt Whitman: A Study* (1893; new ed. London: John C. Nimmo, 1896), pp. 1–140.

5 George Santayana, 'The Poetry of Barbarism', in Irving Singer, ed., *Essays in Literary Criticism of George Santayana* (New York: Charles Scribner's Sons, 1956), pp. 149–61. This essay was originally published in George Santayana, *Interpretations of Poetry and Religion* (1900), pp. 174–88.

6 Santayana, 'The Poetry of Barbarism', pp. 53–61.

7 See, for example, his *Guide to Kulchur* (1938) and *ABC of Reading* (1951).

8 *maramis*: Pound's precise meaning here is not clear. 'Maramis' appears in neither the *OED* nor *Webster's* dictionary.

9 This quotation should read: *Patriam quam odi et amo*. Pound's exact source is unknown, though it appears to be Dante, echoing Catullus.

10 Pound's exact source from Petrarch is unknown.

11 Ezra Pound, 'What I feel about Walt Whitman' (1909) reprinted in William Cookson, ed., *Ezra Pound: Selected prose, 1909–1965* (London: Faber and Faber, 1973), pp. 115–16.

12 Lawrence, pp. 162–71. *Consummatum est*: 'It is finished' (Latin), the final words of Jesus on the cross.

13 D. H. Lawrence, *Studies in Classic American Literature* (New York: Thomas Seltzer, 1923), p. 11.
14 Lawrence, pp. 171–6.

CHAPTER THREE

1 F. O. Matthiessen, *American Renaissance: Art and Expression in the Age of Emerson and Whitman* (London and New York: Oxford University Press, 1941), p. vii.
2 Matthiessen, p. ix.
3 Matthiessen, pp. 517–32.
4 Charles Feidelson, *Symbolism and American Literature* (Chicago: University of Chicago Press, 1953), pp. 3–4.
5 *Lycidas:* poetic elegy (1637) by John Milton. *Adonais:* poetic elegy (1821) on the death of John Keats by Percy Bysshe Shelley.
6 Feidelson, pp. 16–27.
7 *Georg Wilhelm Fredrich Hegel* (1770–1831): German philosopher. Hegel developed a dialectical philosophical scheme that emphasised the progress of history and of ideas from thesis to antithesis and thence to a synthesis. He develops an idea of 'Absolute Spirit' which draws on pantheistic ideas of the identity of the universe and God, and argues that the mind of God becomes actual only via the minds of his creatures, who serve as its vehicle. Such idealist metaphysics exerted an enormous influence on nineteenth-century European thought, and profoundly shaped Karl Marx's notion of 'dialectic materialism', the idea that history progresses through class conflicts (thesis and antithesis) towards a revolutionary synthesis. Hegel's works include *The Phenomenology of Mind* (1807) and the *Encyclopedia of the Philosophical Sciences in Outline* (1817).
8 Randall Jarrell, 'Some Lines from Whitman', in *Poetry and the Age* (London: Faber and Faber, 1955), pp. 106–23.

CHAPTER FOUR

1 For an excellent synopsis of 'New Criticism', see Catherine Belsey, *Critical Practice* (London: Methuen, 1980), pp. 15–20.
2 See Cleanth Brooks *The Well Wrought Urn: Studies in the Structure of Poetry* (1949; rev. ed. London: Dobson, 1968). Brooks takes the phrase from John Donne's poem 'The Canonization' (1633), see Herbert J. C. Grierson, ed., *Donne: Poetical Works* (1929; rpt. Oxford: Oxford University Press, 1979), p. 15.
3 Terry Eagleton, *Literary Theory: An Introduction* (Oxford: Basil Blackwell, 1983), p. 47.
4 Belsey, *Critical Practice*, p. 15.
5 An effect noted by Eagleton, *Literary Theory*, p. 46.
6 Eagleton, *Literary Theory*, p. 50.
7 R. W. B. Lewis, *The American Adam: Innocence, Tragedy and Tradition in the Nineteenth Century* (Chicago: The University of Chicago Press, 1955), pp. 28–53.
8 Henry Nash Smith, 'Can "American Studies" Develop a Method?' in *Studies in American Culture: Dominant Ideas and Images,* ed., Joseph J. Kwiat and Mary C. Turpie (Minneapolis: University of Minnesota Press, 1960), pp. 3–15. This essay was originally published in *American Quarterly,* 9 (Summer, 1957), 197–208.
9 Henry Nash Smith, pp. 5 and 15.
10 See Cecil F. Tate, *The Search for a Method in American Studies* (Minneapolis: University of Minnesota Press, 1973), esp. the chapter 'Myth and Holism in American Studies', pp. 9–24.
11 Roy Harvey Pearce, *The Continuity of American Poetry* (Princeton: Princeton University Press, 1961), p. 109.
12 Pearce, pp. 164–74.

CHAPTER FIVE

1 David S. Reynolds, *Beneath the American Renaissance: The Subversive Imagination in the Age of Emerson and Melville* (Cambridge, MA and London: Harvard University Press, 1988), pp. 561–2.

2 David S. Reynolds, *Beneath the American Renaissance*, p. 563.

3 David S. Reynolds, *Beneath the American Renaissance*, p. 563.

4 M. Wynn Thomas, *The Lunar Light of Whitman's Poetry* (Cambridge, MA and London: Harvard University Press, 1987), p. 2.

5 Thomas quotes from Walt Whitman, *Leaves of Grass: A Textual Variorum*, ed. Sculley Bradley, Harold W. Blodgett, Arthur Golden, and William White, 3 vols (New York: New York University Press, 1980), vol. 1, p. 1.

6 [Thomas's note] Whitman, *Leaves of Grass: A Textual Variorum*, vol. 1, p. 25.

7 [Thomas's note] Whitman, *Leaves of Grass: A Textual Variorum*, vol. 1, p. 22.

8 [Thomas's note] Thomas Stone, in *The Dial* (New York: Russell and Russell, 1961), 4: 275.

9 [Thomas's note] Terence Hawkes, *Structuralism and Semiotics* (London: Methuen, 1977), p. 27.

10 [Thomas's note] *The Riverside Edition of Emerson's Complete Works* (London: Routledge, 1883), vol. 2, pp. 85–6.

11 [Thomas's note] Whitman, *Leaves of Grass: A Textual Variorum*, vol. 1, p. 2.

12 [Thomas's note] Walt Whitman, *Prose Works, 1892*, ed. Floyd Stovall, 2 vols (New York: New York University Press, 1963, 1964), vol. 2, p. 445.

13 [Thomas's note] Anthony Beale, ed., *D. H. Lawrence: Selected Literary Criticism* (London: Heinemann, 1961), p. 42.

14 [Thomas's note] Whitman, *Leaves of Grass: A Textual Variorum*, vol. 1, p. 33.

15 [Thomas's note] Whitman, *Leaves of Grass: A Textual Variorum*, vol. 1, pp. 32–3.

16 [Thomas's note] Emerson in *The Dial*, 2, p. 149.

17 [Thomas's note] Edward Pessen, *Jacksonian America* (Homewood, Ill.: Dorsey Press, 1969), p. 34. Whitman's feelings about his money-making society were further complicated by his own family's involvement in business, and his mixed reactions to that, as has been shown by Ivan Marki, *The Trials of the Poet* (New York: Columbia University Press, 1976), pp. 63–4.

18 [Thomas's note] Sean Wilentz, *Chants Democratic: New York City and the Rise of the American Working Class, 1788–1850* (New York and Oxford: Oxford University Press, 1984), pp. 5, 6.

19 [Thomas's note] The difference between these two stages has most usefully been summarized by Raymond Williams in *Culture* (Glasgow: Fontana, 1981).

20 [Thomas's note] See Michael Lebowitz, 'The Jacksonians: Paradox Lost', in B. J. Bernstein, ed., *Towards a New Past* (London: Chatto and Windus, 1970), pp. 65–89.

21 Thomas, pp. 40–71.

22 Ed Folsom, 'Preface', *Whitman's Native Representations* (Cambridge: Cambridge University Press, 1994), p. x.

23 Folsom, 'Preface', p. x.

24 [Folsom's note] Virginia Woolf, 'American Fiction', in *The Movement and Other Essays* (New York: Harcourt, Brace, 1948), p. 113.

25 [Folsom's note] Woolf, p. 116.

26 [Folsom's note] Woolf, p. 123.

27 [Folsom's note] Woolf, pp. 126–7.

28 [Folsom's note] Michael Clark, *Dos Passos' Early Fiction, 1912–1938* (Selinsgrove, PA: Susquehanna University Press, 1987), pp. 18–19.

29 [Folsom's note] Michael Gold, '3 Schools of U. S. Writing', *New Masses*, 4 (September 1928), pp. 13–14.

30 [Folsom's note] Horace Traubel, *With Walt Whitman in Camden*, vol. 4, ed. Sculley Bradley (Philadelphia: University of Pennsylvania Press, 1953), p. 508.

31 [Folsom's note] Clifton Joseph Furness, 'Walt Whitman looks at Boston', *New England Quarterly*, 1 (1928), p. 358.

32 [Folsom's note] Horace Traubel, *With Walt Whitman in Camden*, vol. 4, ed. Sculley Bradley (Philadelphia: University of Pennsylvania Press, 1953), p. 223.

33 [Folsom's note] Cleveland Rogers and John Black, eds, *The Gathering of Forces*, 2 Vols (New York: Putnam, 1920), pp. 201–9.

34 [Folsom's note] Quoted in Warren Goldstein, *Playing for Keeps: A History of Early Baseball* (Ithaca, NY: Cornell University Press, 1989), p. 41.

35 [Folsom's note] Floyd Stovall, ed., *Walt Whitman: Prose Works, 1892*, 2 vols (New York: New York University Press, 1963), pp. 414–15.

36 Folsom quotes, here, from *Leaves of Grass* in the Norton Critical Edition, eds, Sculley Bradley and Harold W. Blodgett (New York: Norton, 1973), p. 32.

37 [Folsom's note] Allen Guttmann, *Sports Spectators* (New York: Columbia University Press, 1986).

38 [Folsom's note] Quoted in Guttmann, p. 112.

39 [Folsom's note] Traubel, p. 142.

40 Laws forbidding secular, public celebrations on a Sunday were known as 'Blue Laws': 'During the colonial period of United States history, the town of New Haven, Conn., passed a series of social regulations that dealt with both public and private behavior. These regulations came to be called blue laws because of the blue paper on which they were originally printed' (*Encyclopedia Britannica*).

41 [Folsom's note] Traubel, vol. 2, p. 52.

42 [Folsom's note] George Gipe, *The Great American Sports Book* (Garden City, NY: Doubleday, 1978), p. 473.

43 [Folsom's note] Traubel, vol. 1, p. 267.

44 [Folsom's note] Traubel, vol. 6, pp. 128–9.

45 Folsom quotes, here, from *Leaves of Grass* in the Norton Critical Edition, eds, Sculley Bradley and Harold W. Blodgett (New York: Norton, 1973), p. 727.

46 [Folsom's note] Traubel, vol. 3, p. 528.

47 Folsom quotes, here, from *Leaves of Grass* in the Norton Critical Edition, eds, Sculley Bradley and Harold W. Blodgett (New York: Norton, 1973), p. 402.

48 [Folsom's note] Traubel, vol. 3, p. 527–8.

49 Folsom, pp. 28–54.

50 [Reynolds' note] Walt Whitman, *Prose Works 1892*, ed. Floyd Stovall (New York: New York University Press, 1963–64), vol. 2, pp. 492–3.

51 [Reynolds' note] Walt Whitman, *Notes and Fragments*, ed. *Richard Maurice Bucke* (Ontario: A. Talbot, n.d.), p. 146.

52 [Reynolds' note] Whitman, *Prose Works*, vol. 2, p. 414.

53 Reynolds quotes here from Walt Whitman, *Leaves of Grass: Comprehensive Reader's Edition*, ed. Harold W. Blodgett and Sculley Bradley (New York: New York University Press, 1965), p. 31.

54 [Reynolds' note] Whitman, *Notes and Fragments*, p. 40.

55 [Reynolds' note] Whitman, *Notes and Fragments*, p. 66.

56 [Reynolds' note] Walt Whitman, *Notebooks and Unpublished Prose Manuscripts*, ed. Edward F. Grier (New York: New York University Press, 1984), vol. 1, p. 413.

57 Reynolds quotes here from Blodgett and Bradley, eds, p. 93.

58 Reynolds quotes here from Blodgett and Bradley, eds, p. 39.

59 David S. Reynolds, 'Whitman and Nineteenth-Century Views of Gender and Sexuality', in Geoffrey M. Still, ed., *Walt Whitman of Mickle Street: A Centennial Collection* (Knoxville: University of Tennessee Press, 1994), pp. 38–45.

CHAPTER SIX

1 See David S. Reynolds, *Walt Whitman's America: A Cultural Biography* (New York: Vintage Books, 1996), pp. 342–3; and J. R. LeMaster and Donald D. Kummings, eds, *Walt Whitman: An Encyclopedia* (New York and London: Garland, 1998), pp. 628–32.

2 See Louis Althusser, 'Ideology and Ideological State Apparatuses', in *Lenin and Philosophy and Other Essays*, tr. Ben Brewster (London: New Left Books, 1971), pp. 121–73.

3 See Althusser, p. 155. Quoted in Fredric Jameson, 'Postmodernism, or the Cultural Logic of Late Capitalism', *New Left Review*, 146 (1984), p. 90.

4 For useful discussions of Althusser's notion of Ideology see Catherine Belsey, *Critical Practice* (London: Methuen, 1980), pp. 56–63 and Terry Eagleton, *Literary Theory: An Introduction* (Oxford: Basil Blackwell, 1983), pp. 171–3.

5 Malcolm Cowley, 'Whitman: The Poet and the Mask' (1948), rpt. in *A Many-Windowed House: Collected Essays on American Writers and American Writing* (Carbondale and Edwardsville: Southern Illinois University Press, 1970), pp. 35–75. This essay was originally published as the introduction to *The Complete Poetry and Prose of Walt Whitman* (New York: Pellegrini and Cudahy, 1948), 2 Vols.

6 Robert K. Martin, *The Homosexual Tradition in American Poetry: An Expanded Edition* (1979; rev. ed. Iowa City: University of Iowa Press, 1998), p. 3. The first edition of this book was originally published, in 1979, by University of Texas Press.

7 [Martin's note] See Richard Slotkin, *Regeneration through Violence: Mythology of the American Frontier 1600–1860* (Middletown, Connecticut, 1973).

8 [Martin's note] The suppression of nonprocreative sex is discussed by Freud in *Civilization and its Discontents* and by Marcuse in *Eros and Civilization*.

9 Martin, pp. 51–89.

10 [Selby's note] It is necessary to make clear that, in line with the usage of Whitman 'America' throughout this [essay] designates 'The United States of America'. It should not, therefore, be confused either with North America (which includes Canada) or with the Continent of America. Such conventional shorthand conveys a sense of the power of America's political presence over and above the mere fact of its geographical presence in the world.

11 [Selby's note] Robert K. Martin, *The Homosexual Tradition in American Poetry* (Austin and London: University of Texas Press, 1979), pp. xvi–xvii.

12 [Selby's note] Walt Whitman, *The Complete Poems*, ed. Francis Murphy (1975; rpt. London: Penguin Books, 1986), p. 155. Subsequent references to Whitman's work in this extract will be to this edition, unless otherwise stated.

13 [Selby's note] Whitman, p. 156.

14 [Selby's note] An interesting parallel to this same-sex embrace as a model for the romantic embrace of American democratic idealism is found in the fourth chapter of Melville's *Moby-Dick*, 'The Counterpane'.

15 [Selby's note] Whitman, p. 150.

16 [Selby's note] Martin Duberman, *About Time: Exploring the Gay Past* (rev. ed. New York: Meridian, 1991), p. 289. The essay (pp. 288–304) from which this quotation is taken is an informative discussion of the history and changing theories of bisexuality. See also Jonathan Dollimore, *Sexual Dissidence. Augustine to Wilde, Freud to Foucault* (Oxford: Clarendon Press, 1991), p. 217, for a discussion of Freud's theory of the 'polymorphous perverse' and its relation to his notion of 'full bisexuality'.

17 [Selby's note] Judith Butler, *Gender Trouble: Feminism and the Subversion of Identity* (London: Routledge and Kegan Paul, 1990), p. 61.

18 [Selby's note] Butler, p. 61. See also Dollimore, p. 255.

19 [Selby's note] David S. Reynolds, *Walt Whitman's America: A Cultural Biography* (New York: Alfred A. Knopf, 1995), p. 199.

20 [Selby's note] Reynolds, pp. 198–9.

21 [Selby's note] Whitman, p. 136.

22 [Selby's note] Whitman, p. 137.

23 [Selby's note] John D'Emilio and Estelle B. Freedman, *Intimate Matters: A History of Sexuality in America* (New York: Harper and Row, 1988), p. 111.

24 [Selby's note] Stephen Heath, *The Sexual Fix* (Basingstoke: Macmillan, 1982), p. 16.

25 [Selby's note] Michel Foucault, *The History of Sexuality. Volume 1: An Introduction*, trans. Robert Hurley (1979; rpt. Harmondsworth: Penguin, 1990), pp. 113–14, esp., details the production of sexuality within capitalism.

26 [Selby's note] 'Song of Myself' (1891–92 version), Section 21, in Whitman, p. 83.

27 [Selby's note] 'Song of Myself' (1891–92 version), Section 24, in Whitman, pp. 86–7. The 1855 version of the poem makes even more explicit the interpenetration of Whitman's poetic and American identities within the sexual and somatic. He writes there: 'Walt Whitman, an American, one of the roughs, a kosmos, / Disorderly, fleshly and sensual… / Through me many long dumb voices, / Voices of the interminable generations of slaves, / Voices of prostitutes and of deformed persons…' etc… See Whitman, 'Appendix 4', pp. 698–9.

28 [Selby's note] See Camille Paglia, *Sex, Art and American Culture: Essays* (Harmondsworth: Viking Penguin, 1992), p. 11.

29 [Selby's note] 'Song of Myself' (1891–92 version), in Whitman, p. 73.

30 [Selby's note] The quotation is from Section 51 of 'Song of Myself' (1891–92 version), in Whitman, p. 123.

31 [Selby's note] 'Song of Myself' (1891–92 version), in Whitman, p. 72.

32 Nick Selby, 'Queer Shoulders to the Wheel': Whitman, Ginsberg and a Bisexual Poetics', in Phoebe Davidson, Jo Eadie, Clare Hemmings, Ann Koloski and Merl Storr, eds, *The Bisexual Imaginary: Representation, Identity and Desire* (London and Washington: Cassell, 1997), pp. 120–40.

CHAPTER SEVEN

1 Jonathan Culler, *On Deconstruction: Theory and Criticism after Structuralism* (London: Routledge & Kegan Paul, 1983), p. 86.

2 Karen Sanchez-Eppler, 'To Stand Between: Walt Whitman's Poetics of Merger and Embodiment', in *Touching Liberty: abolition, feminism, and the politics of the body* (1993; rpt. Berkeley and London: University of California Press, 1997), p. 82.

3 [Sanchez-Eppler's note] *Family Notes and Autobiography: Brooklyn and New York*, vol. 1 of *The Collected Writings of Walt Whitman: Notebooks and Unpublished Prose Manuscripts*, ed. Edward F. Grier (New York: New York University Press, 1984, 67.

4 [Sanchez-Eppler's note] *Walt Whitman's Leaves of Grass: the First (1855) Edition*, ed. Malcolm Cowley (New York: Penguin Classics, 1986) ll. 422–3.

5 [Sanchez-Eppler's note] See Whitman's own description of the Creole Margaret in *Franklin Evans*.

6 [Sanchez-Eppler's note] Fredric Jameson defines mediation as 'the classical dialectical term for the establishment of relationships between, say, the formal analysis of a work of art and its social ground, or between the internal dynamics of the political state and its economic base' *(The Political Unconscious: Narrative as Socially Symbolic Act* [Ithaca, N.Y.: Cornell University Press, 1981], 39; Jameson discusses this concept of mediation on 39–44 and 225–26).

7 Sanchez-Eppler, pp. 50–82.

8 [Grossman's note] F. O. Matthiessen, *From the Heart of Europe* (New York: Oxford University Press, 1948), p. 90.

9 [Grossman's note] For Whitman on abolition, see Whitman's essays in *The Brooklyn Daily Eagle* in 1846 and 1847, reprinted in Cleveland Rodgers and John Black, *The Gathering of Forces* (New York: G. P. Putnam's Sons, 1920), vol. 1, pp. 179–238.

10 [Grossman's note] Emory Holloway, *The Uncollected Poetry and Prose of Walt Whitman* (Garden City, NY: Doubleday, Page & Co., 1921), vol. 2, p. 69.

11 [Grossman's note] See 'Fragment on Free Labor', and 'Address before the Wisconsin State Agricultural Society, Milwaukee, Wisconsin', 30 September 1859 in Roy P. Basler *et al.*, *The Collected Works of Abraham Lincoln* (New Brunswick, NJ: Rutgers University Press, 1954), vol. 3, p. 462 and pp. 471 ff.

12 [Grossman's note] Edward Sapir, *Language: an Introduction to the Study of Speech* (New York: Harcourt Brace, 1949), p. 224; D. H. Lawrence, *Studies in Classical American Literature* (New York: Viking Press, 1964), p. 170 [see Chapter 2, pp. 84–101]; For Cesare Pavese, see Gay Wilson Allen, *The New Walt Whitman Handbook* (New York: New York University Press, 1975), p. 317.

13 [Grossman's note] In 'Democratic Vistas' at p. 981, *Walt Whitman: Complete Poetry and Collected Prose* (New York: Library of America, 1982).

14 [Grossman's note] 'The Eighteenth Presidency' in Clifton Joseph Furness, *Walt Whitman's Workshop* (Cambridge: Harvard university Press, 1928), p. 109.

15 [Grossman's note] Basler, vol. 5, p. 535.

16 [Grossman's note] Basler, vol. 5, p. 537.

17 Allen Grossman, 'The Poetics of Union in Whitman and Lincoln: An Inquiry toward the Relationship of Art and Policy', in Walter Benn Michaels and Donald E. Pease, *The American Renaissance Reconsidered* (Baltimore and London: The Johns Hopkins University Press, 1985), pp. 184–98.

18 Arac quotes here from Jerome Loving, *Walt Whitman's Champion: William Douglas O'Connor* (College Station: Texas A & M University Press, 1978), p. 453; and from Paul Zweig, *Walt Whitman: The Making of the Poet* (New York: Basic, 1984), p. 182.

19 See Kenneth Cmiel, *Democratic Eloquence: The Fight over Popular Speech in Nineteenth-Century America* (Cambridge: Cambridge University Press, 1991). The Matthiessen discussion to which Arac refers is excerpted in Chapter 3 above, pp. 57–61.

20 As his conceptual models, Arac refers here to Paul Gilroy, *The Black Atlantic: Modernity and Double Consciousness* (Cambridge: Cambridge University Press, 1993); and Joseph A. Roach, *Circum-Atlantic Performance* (New York: Columbia University Press, 1996).

21 [Arac's note] Smith, p. 3.

22 [Arac's note] Smith, p. 4.

23 [Arac's note] Smith, p. 4.

24 [Arac's note] Smith, p. 4.

25 [Arac's note] Smith, pp. 8 and 16.

26 Walt Whitman, *Leaves of Grass*, ed. Sculley Bradley and Harold W. Blodgett (New York: Norton, 1973), pp. 37–8.

27 [Arac's note] Smith, p. 7.

28 [Arac's note] Smith, p. 8.

29 [Arac's note] Smith, p. 8.

30 [Arac's note] Houston A. Baker in *Blues, Ideology, and Afro-American Literature* (Chicago: University of Chicago Press, 1984) cites this etymology as first epigraph to the book, which tries to develop what its subtitle calls a 'vernacular theory', and which cites as its second epigraph Whitman from the 1855 preface. As I do in this essay, Baker sees 'vernacular' as inseparable from problems of cultural nationalism, which in his book take the form of redefining what he calls 'AMERICA' (the capitals to indicate that the term is an ideological construct).

31 [Arac's note] Walter Benjamin, 'Central Park', tr. Lloyd Spencer, *New German Critique*, 34 (1985), p. 50.

32 [Arac's note] David Harvey, *Consciousness and the Urban Experience* (Baltimore: The Johns Hopkins University Press, 1985), p. 202.

33 [Arac's note] Roman Jakobson, 'Linguistics and Poetics', in Thomas A. Sebeok, ed., *Style in Language* (Cambridge: Massachusetts Institute of Technology Press, 1960), p. 358.

34 [Arac's note] Karl Marx, *Capital: A Critique of Political Economy*, trans. Samuel Moore and Edward Aveling (New York: International, 1967), vol. 1, p. 132.

35 Walt Whitman, *Leaves of Grass*, ed. *Sculley Bradley and Harold W. Blodgett* (New York: Norton, 1973), p. 127.
36 Jonathan Arac, 'Whitman and the Problems of Vernacular', in Betsy Erkkila and Jay Grossman, eds, *Breaking Bounds: Whitman and American Cultural Studies* (New York and Oxford: Oxford University Press, 1996), pp. 44–58.

BIBLIOGRAPHY

GENERAL WORKS ON/BY WHITMAN

Gay Wilson Allen, 'The Growth of *Leaves of Grass* and the *Prose Works*', *Walt Whitman Handbook* (Chicago, 1946), pp. 104–227.

——, *The New Walt Whitman Handbook* (New York: New York University Press, 1975).

Milton Hundus, ed., *Walt Whitman: The Critical Heritage* (London: Routledge and Kegan Paul, 1971).

Joann P. Krieg, *A Whitman Chronology* (Iowa City: University of Iowa Press, 1998).

J. R. Le Master and Donald D. Kummings, eds, *Walt Whitman: An Encyclopedia* (New York and London: Garland, 1998).

Edwin Haviland Miller, ed., *Walt Whitman: The Complete Correspondence* (New York: New York University Press, 1961–77), 6 Vols.

Joel Myerson, *Whitman in His Own Time: A Biographical Chronicle of His Life, Drawn from Recollections, Memoirs, and Interviews by Friends and Associates* (Columbia, SC: Omnigraphics, 1991).

Roy Harvey Pearce, ed., *Walt Whitman: A Collection of Critical Essays* (Englewood Cliffs, NJ: Prentice-Hall, 1962).

Horace Traubel, *With Walt Whitman in Camden*, ed., Sculley Bradley (Philadelphia: University of Pennsylvania Press, 1953), 4 Vols.

Walt Whitman, *The Gathering of Forces*, ed., Cleveland Rodgers and John Black (New York: G. P. Putnam's Sons, 1920), 2 Vols.

——, *The Uncollected Poetry and Prose of Walt Whitman*, ed., Emory Holloway (Garden City, NY: Doubleday, Page & Co., 1921), 2 Vols.

——, *The Complete Poetry and Prose of Walt Whitman*, ed., Malcolm Cowley (New York: Pellegrini and Cudahy, 1948), 2 Vols.

——, *Prose Works*, 1892, ed., Floyd Stovall (New York: New York University Press, 1963, 1964), 2 Vols.

——, *Leaves of Grass: Comprehensive Reader's Edition*, ed., Harold W. Blodgett and Sculley Bradley (New York: New York University Press, 1965).

——, *Leaves of Grass* [Norton Critical Edition], eds, Sculley Bradley and Harold W. Blodgett (New York: Norton, 1973).

——, *The Portable Walt Whitman*, ed., Mark Van Doren, rev. Malcolm Cowley (1945, rev. 1974; rpt London: Penguin, 1977).

——, *Leaves of Grass: A Textual Variorum*, ed., Scully Bradley, Harold W. Blodgett, Arthur Golden and William White (New York: New York University press, 1980), 3 Vols.

——, *Notebooks and Unpublished Prose Manuscripts*, ed., Edward F. Grier (New York: New York University Press, 1984), 6 Vols.

——, *The Complete Poems*, ed., Francis Murphy (1975; rpt London: Penguin, 1986).

——, *Notes and Fragments*, ed., Richard Maurice Bucke (Ontario: A. Talbot, n.d.).

FIRST REACTIONS

Anonymous review of *Leaves of Grass*, the *Critic* (London, 1 April 1856).

Anonymous review of *Leaves of Grass*, Boston *Intelligencer* (3 May 1856).

Anonymous review of *Leaves of Grass*, *New York Daily Times* (1856).

John Burroughs, *Notes on Walt Whitman, as Poet and Person* (New York: J. S. Redfield, 1971).

Charles A. Dana, 'Notice of *Leaves of Grass*', *New York Daily Tribune* (23 July 1855).

Edward Everett Hale, (unsigned) review of *Leaves of Grass, North American Review*, 82–170 (January 1856), pp. 275–7.

Charles Eliot Norton, 'Review of *Leaves of Grass'*, *Putnam's Monthly* (September, 1855).

William O'Connor, *The Good Gray Poet: A Vindication* (New York: Bruce & Harrington, 1866).

John Robertson, *Walt Whitman: Poet and Democrat* (Edinburgh: William Brown, 1884).

Charles A. Roe, 'Walt Whitman, Schoolmaster: Notes of a Conversation with Charles A. Roe, 1894', ed., Horace Traubel. *Walt Whitman Fellowship Papers*, no. 14 (April 1895).

John Addington Symonds, *Walt Whitman: A Study* (1893; new edn. London: John C. Nimmo, 1896).

Walt Whitman, (unsigned) review of *Leaves of Grass, United States Review* (1855).

WHITMAN IN THE EARLY-TWENTIETH CENTURY

Henry B. Binns, *A Life of Walt Whitman* (London: Methuen, 1905).

Richard Bucke, *Walt Whitman* (Philadelphia: David McKay, 1883).

Edward Carpenter, *Days with Walt Whitman* (New York: Macmillan, 1906).

Jean Catel, *Walt Whitman: La Naissance du Poète* (Paris: Rieder, 1929).

Basil De Selincourt, *Walt Whitman: A Critical Study* (London: M. Secker, 1914).

Clifton Joseph Furness, *Walt Whitman's Workshop* (Cambridge: Harvard University Press, 1928).

Emory Holloway, *Whitman: An Interpretation in Narrative* (New York: Alfred A. Knopf, 1926).

D. H. Lawrence, *Studies in Classic American Literature* (New York: Thomas Seltzer, 1923).

——, *D. H. Lawrence: Selected Literary Criticism*, ed., Anthony Beale (London: Heinemann, 1961).

H. L. Mencken, *The American Language* (1919; rev. New York: Knopf, 1937).

Bliss Perry, *Walt Whitman: His Life and Work* (Boston: Houghton Mifflin & Co., 1906).

Ezra Pound, *Personae: Collected Shorter Poems of Ezra Pound* (London: Faber & Faber, 1952).

——, *Ezra Pound: Selected Prose, 1909–1965*, ed., William Cookson (London: Faber and Faber, 1973).

Cleveland Rogers and John Black, eds, *The Gathering of Forces* (New York: Putnam, 1920), 2 Vols.

George Santayana, *Essays in Literary Criticism of George Santayana*, ed., Irving Singer (New York: Charles Scribner's Sons, 1956).

Frederik Schyberg, *Walt Whitman* [1933], trans. E. Allen (New York, 1951).

WHITMAN IN THE MID-TWENTIETH CENTURY

Gay Wilson Allen, *The Solitary Singer: A Critical Biography of Walt Whitman* (New York: Macmillan, 1955).

Roger Asselineau, *L'Evolution de Walt Whitman Après La Première Edition des Feuilles D'Herbe* (Paris, 1954).

Cleanth Brooks *The Well Wrought Urn: Studies in the Structure of Poetry* (1949; rev. edn. London: Dobson, 1968).

Malcolm Cowley, 'Whitman: The Poet and the Mask' (1948), rpt. in *A Many-Windowed House: Collected Essays on American Writers and American Writing* (Carbondale and Edwardsville: Southern Illinois University Press, 1970), pp. 35–75.

Charles Feidelson, *Symbolism and American Literature* (Chicago: University of Chicago Press, 1953).

Milton Hindus, ed., Leaves of Grass: One Hundred Years After (Stanford: Stanford University Press, 1955).

Randall Jarrell, 'Some Lines from Whitman', in *Poetry and the Age* (London: Faber and Faber, 1955), pp. 106–23.

R. W. B. Lewis, *The American Adam: Innocence, Tragedy and Tradition in the Nineteenth Century* (Chicago: The University of Chicago Press, 1955).

F. O. Matthiessen, *American Renaissance: Art and Expression in the Age of Emerson and Whitman* (London and New York: Oxford University Press, 1941).

——, *From the Heart of Europe* (New York: Oxford University Press, 1948).

James Miller, *A Critical Guide to Leaves of Grass* (Chicago: University of Chicago Press, 1957).

Roy Harvey Pearce, *The Continuity of American Poetry* (Princeton: Princeton University Press, 1961).

Henry Nash Smith, 'Can "American Studies" Develop a Method?' in *Studies in American Culture: Dominant Ideas and Images*, ed., Joseph J. Kwiat and Mary C. Turpie (Minneapolis: University of Minnesota Press, 1960), pp. 3–15.

Cecil F. Tate, *The Search for a Method in American Studies* (Minneapolis: University of Minnesota Press, 1973).

RECENT WHITMAN CRITICISM

Jonathan Arac, 'Whitman and the Problems of Vernacular', in Betsy Erkkila and Jay Grossman, eds, *Breaking Bounds: Whitman and American Cultural Studies* (New York and Oxford: Oxford University Press, 1996), pp. 44–58.

Betsy Erkkila and Jay Grossman, eds, *Breaking Bounds: Whitman and American Cultural Studies* (New York and Oxford: Oxford University Press, 1996).

Ed Folsom, *Whitman's Native Representations* (Cambridge: Cambridge University Press, 1994).

Allen Grossman, 'The Poetics of Union in Whitman and Lincoln: An Inquiry toward the Relationship of Art and Policy,' in Walter Benn Michaels and Donald E. Pease, eds, The *American Renaissance Reconsidered* (Baltimore and London: The Johns Hopkins University Press, 1985), pp. 184–98.

Jerome Loving, *Walt Whitman's Champion: William Douglas O'Connor* (College Station: Texas A & M University Press, 1978).

——, *Emerson, Whitman, and the American Mind* (Chapel Hill: University of North Carolina Press, 1982).

Ivan Marki, *The Trials of the Poet* (New York: Columbia University Press, 1976).

Robert K. Martin, *The Homosexual Tradition in American Poetry: An Expanded Edition* (1979; rev. ed. Iowa City: University of Iowa Press, 1998).

Walter Benn Michaels and Donald E. Pease, eds, *The American Renaissance Reconsidered* (Baltimore and London: The Johns Hopkins University Press, 1985).

David S. Reynolds, *Beneath the American Renaissance: The Subversive Imagination in the Age of Emerson and Melville* (Cambridge, MA and London: Harvard University Press, 1988).

——, 'Whitman and Nineteenth-Century views of Gender and Sexuality', in Geoffrey M. Still, ed., *Walt Whitman of Mickle Street: A Centennial Collection* (Knoxville: University of Tennessee Press, 1994), pp. 38–45.

——, *Walt Whitman's America: A Cultural Biography* (New York: Vintage Books, 1996).

Karen Sanchez-Eppler, 'To Stand Between: Walt Whitman's Poetics of Merger and Embodiment,' in *Touching Liberty: Abolition, Feminism, and the Politics of the Body* (1993; rpt Berkeley and London: University of California Press, 1997), pp. 50–82.

Nick Selby, 'Queer Shoulders to the wheel': Whitman, Ginsberg and a Bisexual Poetics', in Phoebe Davidson, Jo Eadie, Clare Hemmings, Ann Koloski and Merl Storr, eds, *The Bisexual Imaginary: Representation, Identity and Desire* (London and Washington: Cassell, 1997), pp. 120–40.

Geoffrey M. Still, ed., *Walt Whitman of Mickle Street: A Centennial Collection* (Knoxville: University of Tennessee Press, 1994).

M. Wynn Thomas, *The Lunar Light of Whitman's Poetry* (Cambridge, MA and London: Harvard University Press, 1987).

Paul Zweig, *Walt Whitman: The Making of the Poet* (New York: Basic, 1984).

OTHER WORKS CITED

Theodor Adorno, 'On Lyric Poetry and Society' (1957), *Notes to Literature*, Vol. 1, ed., Rolf Tiedmann, trans. Shierry Weber Nicholsen (New York: Columbia University Press, 1991).

Louis Althusser, *Lenin and Philosophy and Other Essays*, tr. Ben Brewster (London: New Left Books, 1971).

Houston A. Baker in *Blues, Ideology, and Afro-American Literature* (Chicago: University of Chicago Press, 1984).

Roy P. Basler et al., *The Collected Works of Abraham Lincoln* (New Brunswick, NJ: Rutgers University Press, 1954), 9 Vols.

Catherine Belsey, *Critical Practice* (London: Methuen, 1980).

Walter Benjamin, 'Central Park,' trans. Lloyd Spencer, *New German Critique*, 34 (1985), p. 50.

Judith Butler, *Gender Trouble: Feminism and the Subversion of Identity* (London: Routledge and Kegan Paul, 1990).

Michael Clark, *Dos Passos' Early Fiction, 1912–1938* (Selinsgrove, PA: Susquehanna University Press, 1987).

Kenneth Cmiel, *Democratic Eloquence: The Fight over Popular Speech in Nineteenth-Century America* (Cambridge: Cambridge University Press, 1991).

Jonathan Culler, *On Deconstruction: Theory and Criticism after Structuralism* (London: Routledge & Kegan Paul, 1983).

Charles A. Dana, *Recollections of the Civil War* (1898; rpt Lincoln: University of Nebraska Press, 1996).

John D'Emilio and Estelle B. Freedman, *Intimate Matters: A History of Sexuality in America* (New York: Harper and Row, 1988).

Jonathan Dollimore, *Sexual Dissidence. Augustine to Wilde, Freud to Foucault* (Oxford: Clarendon Press, 1991).

Martin Duberman, *About Time: Exploring the Gay Past* (Rev. edn New York: Meridian, 1991).

Terry Eagleton, *Literary Theory: An Introduction* (Oxford: Basil Blackwell, 1983).

Ralph Waldo Emerson, *The Riverside Edition of Emerson's Complete Works* (London: Routledge, 1883).

——, *Emerson's Essays*, ed., Sherman Paul (London: Dent, 1955).

Michel Foucault, *The History of Sexuality. Volume 1: An Introduction*, trans. Robert Hurley (1979; rpt Harmondsworth: Penguin, 1990).

Paul Gilroy, *The Black Atlantic: Modernity and Double Consciousness* (Cambridge: Cambridge University Press, 1993).

George Gipe, *The Great American Sports Book* (Garden City, NY: Doubleday, 1978).

Warren Goldstein, *Playing for Keeps: A History of Early Baseball* (Ithaca, NY: Cornell University Press, 1989).

Allen Guttmann, *Sports Spectators* (New York: Columbia University Press, 1986).

David Harvey, *Consciousness and the Urban Experience* (Baltimore: The Johns Hopkins University Press, 1985).

Terence Hawkes, *Structuralism and Semiotics* (London: Methuen, 1977).

Stephen Heath, *The Sexual Fix* (Basingstoke: Macmillan, 1982).

Roman Jakobson, 'Linguistics and Poetics', in Thomas A. Sebeok, ed., *Style in Language* (Cambridge: Massachusetts Institute of Technology Press, 1960).

Fredric Jameson, *The Political Unconscious: Narrative as Socially Symbolic Act* (Ithaca, NY: Cornell University Press, 1981).

——, 'Postmodernism, or The Cultural Logic of Late Capitalism', *New Left Review*, 146 (1984), pp. 53–92.

Michael Lebowitz, 'The Jacksonians: Paradox Lost,' in B. J. Bernstein, ed., *Towards a New Past* (London: Chatto and Windus, 1970), pp. 65–89.

Karl Marx, *Capital: A Critique of Political Economy*, trans. Samuel Moore and Edward Aveling (New York: International, 1967), 3 Vols.

Camille Paglia, *Sex, Art and American Culture: Essays* (Harmondsworth: Viking Penguin, 1992).

Edward Pessen, *Jacksonian America* (Homewood, IL.: Dorsey Press, 1969).

Joseph A. Roach, *Circum-Atlantic Performance* (New York: Columbia University Press, 1996).

Ralph L. Rusk, *The Life of Ralph Waldo Emerson* (New York: Charles Scribner's Sons, 1949).

Edward Sapir, *Language: An Introduction to the Study of Speech* (New York: Harcourt Brace, 1949).

Richard Slotkin, *Regeneration through Violence: Mythology of the American Frontier 1600–1860* (Middletown, Connecticut, 1973).

Albert G. Spalding, *America's National Game* (New York: American Sports, 1911).

Henry David Thoreau, *Letters to Various Persons* (Boston, 1865).

Sean Wilentz, *Chants Democratic: New York City and the Rise of the American Working Class, 1788–1850* (New York and Oxford: Oxford University Press, 1984).

Raymond Williams, *Culture* (Glasgow: Fontana, 1981).

Virginia Woolf, *The Movement and Other Essays* (New York: Harcourt, Brace, 1948).

William Wordsworth, *Poetical Works*, ed., Thomas Hutchinson and Ernest de Selincourt, reprint edn (London: Oxford University Press, 1969).

INDEX

Adamism 80–7
'adhesiveness' 37–8, 121
Althusser, Louis 117
'amativeness' 37–8
America, attitudes to 16–17
American culture and Americanness
 1–4, 13–15, 20, 30, 54, 78–9, 85, 91,
 96, 102–3, 110–12, 139, 155
American literature 5, 15, 28–9, 54–5
An American Primer 57–8
'American Renaissance' 55–7, 95, 147
American Studies 74–5, 84–5, 91,
 147, 152, 156
'The Answerer' 148
Arac, Jonathan 138, 151–8
Asselineau, Roger 116–18

Barnum, Phineas T. 16
baseball 103–8
Baudelaire, Charles 155–8
Beale, Anthony 99
Belsey, Catherine 77
Benjamin, Walter 155–7
bisexuality and bisexual
 politics 131–6
Blackmur, R.P. 77
Boston Globe 107
Boston Intelligencer 19–20
Brook Farm community 14
Brooklyn Daily Eagle 112
Brooks, Cleanth 77
Browning, Robert 38–9
Burns, Robert 60
Burroughs, John 60, 82
Butler, Judith 131

'Calamus' poems 33, 113, 121–2,
 125–31, 157
*Cambridge History of American
 Literature* 29
capitalism 101–2, 134, 158
Carlyle, Thomas 23–4
Carroll, Lewis 73
'Children of Adam' 33, 80, 113
'cleansing rhetoric' 114
Cmiel, Kenneth 152

Coleridge, Samuel Taylor 80
comradeship 33–6, 49, 121
Conway, Moncure 26–7
Cowley, Malcolm 117–24
creolization of language 154–5, 158
The Criterion (journal) 19
The Critic (journal) 16–19
'Crossing Brooklyn Ferry' 83–4
Culler, Jonathan 137

Dana, Charles A. 14
Dante 2, 42–3
D'Emilio, John 134
de Mille, Cecil B. 69
deconstruction of discourse 137
democracy 24, 36–7, 44, 49–50, 53,
 56–7, 61–2, 106, 121–2, 158
Democratic Vistas 121–2, 127
Dickens, Charles 156
Dickinson, Emily 69
Dorian mood 34
Dos Passos, John 104
Doyle, Peter 121
Duberman, Martin 131

Eagleton, Terry 78
ego 86–8
Emerson, Ralph Waldo 2–3, 18–19,
 24, 50–1, 55–60, 67, 72, 81, 85–6,
 89, 91, 98, 101, 104, 116, 119, 138
 letter to Whitman (July
 1855) 8–9, 79
Erskine, John 29

Feidelson, Charles 57, 61–2,
 67–9, 75
Fern, Fanny 16
first-person singular, use of 87
Folsom, Ed 96, 102–10, 138
foreign language words, use of 59
Foucault, Michel 134
Fowler, Orson and Lorenzo 113
Franklin Evans 3
Freedman, Estelle B. 134
Freud, Sigmund 131–2
Furness, J. 150

Gold, Michael 104
Grossman, Allen 138, 147–51
Guttmann, Allen 107

Hale, Edward Everett 20–1
Hardy, Thomas 72
Hawkes, Terence 97
Hawthorne, Nathaniel 2, 50, 55–6, 67
Heath, Stephen 134
Holloway, Emory 120
Homer 21, 73
homosexuality, Whitman's 116–18,
    121–33
Hugo, Victor 155–6
humour in Whitman 24–5

'intentional fallacy' 76
'I Sing the Body Electric' 142–3

Jakobson, Roman 156
Jarrell, Randall 56–7, 68–74

Lawrence, D.H. 5, 28–9, 42–4, 48–54,
    99, 150
Leaves of Grass, publication and
    reception of 1–3, 8–22, 30, 36,
    55–7, 64, 79, 85–8, 93, 116–19,
    136–9, 143, 146–7, 154, 158
    Whitman's preface to
        (1855) 4, 146
Lewis, R.W.B. 74–5, 78–85, 91
Lincoln, Abraham 23–4, 138, 147–51
Lippard, George 111
Longfellow, Henry
    Wadsworth 50, 153

Martin, Robert K. 123–33
Marx, Karl 156
Marx, Leo 152–6
Matthiessen, F.O. 55–62, 68–9, 75,
    78, 95, 124, 139, 147–52 passim
Melville, Herman 2, 50–3, 55–6, 67,
    69, 73, 127
'A Memorandum at a Venture' 111
Mill, J.S. 148
Milton, John 22–3
modernity 42
mysticism 41

Nash Smith, Henry 152
'New Americanist' criticism 147

'New Criticism' 29, 62, 68, 75–8, 91
New York Daily Times 13
New York Daily Tribune 14
Nichol, John 28
North American Review 20–1
Norton, Charles Eliot 15–16, 19
November Boughs 60

optimism in Whitman 25
'Out of the Cradle Endlessly Rocking'
    89–90

Paglia, Camille 135
Paine, Tom 61
'Passage to India' 67
Pavese, Cesare 150
Pearce, Roy Harvey 6, 74–5, 78,
    84–91
Pease, Donald 147
personality, meaning of 32
Pesson, Edward 101
phrenology 112–15, 148
Poe, Edgar Allan 35, 50, 91
postmodernism 137
Pound, Ezra 5, 29–30, 42–3, 54
psychoanalysis 127
Putnam's Monthly 15

Ransom, John Crowe 77
'reconstructive criticism' 94–5
Reynolds, David 94–6, 110–15, 124,
    132, 138
Robertson, John 22–3
romanticism 67, 81, 152
Roosevelt, Theodore 153
Rossetti, W.M. 26–7
Rousseau, Jean-Jacques 41

Sanchez-Eppler, Karen
    138–47, 152
Santayana, George 38–42, 53–4
Sapir, Edward 150
Schopenhauer, A. 25
Selby, Nick 129–38
sexuality 12, 30, 33, 35, 111–17;
    see also homosexuality
Shakespeare, William 57
slavery 50, 138–49, 156
'The Sleepers' 88–9
Smith, Henry Nash 84–5, 91, 152
'So Long?' 6

'Song of Myself'   97–102, 105–6,
    112–14, 119–20, 134, 139–44, 149,
    152–3
Stone, Thomas   97
Stow, Harriet Beecher   156
symbolism in Whitman's poetry   61–4
Symonds, John Addington   30–1,
    37–8, 116

Tate, Allen   77
Tennyson, Alfred   72
Thomas, M. Wynn   95–7, 102–3, 138
Thompson, George   111–12
Thoreau, Henry David   2, 21–2,
    55–6, 61, 79
Traubel, Horace   57, 104–5, 108–10
Trowbridge, John Townsend   3
Twain, Mark   127, 152

United States Review   10

Van Doren, Carl   29
vernacular, use of   152–5, 158
Virgil   125
vocabulary, Whitman's   58–9, 154

'When I Heard at the
    Close of Day'   130
'When Lilacs Last in the Dooryard
    Bloomed'   61, 64–6
Wimsatt, W.K.   76–7
Wolfe, Thomas   69–70
'A Woman Waits for
    Me'   132, 136
Woolf, Virginia   103–4
Wordsworth, William   158